100 DAYS
THAT CHANGED CANADA

CANADA'S
HISTORY

100
DAYS
THAT CHANGED
CANADA

EDITED BY **MARK REID,** *CANADA'S HISTORY* MAGAZINE

FOREWORD BY **CHARLOTTE GRAY**

PREFACE BY **DEBORAH MORRISON**

HarperCollins*PublishersLtd*
A PHYLLIS BRUCE BOOK

HarperCollins Publishers Ltd
2 Bloor Street East, 20th Floor
Toronto, Ontario, Canada
M4W 1A8

www.harpercollins.ca

Library and Archives Canada Cataloguing in Publication
information is available upon request

ISBN 978-1-44340-564-5

Copy-editing and proofreading: Camilla Blakeley, Phil Koch,
Nelle Oosterom, Beverley Tallon, and Janice Weaver

www.canadashistory.ca

Printed and bound in China
P+ 9 8 7 6 5 4 3 2 1

Contents

LIST OF DAYS

CHARLOTTE GRAY

I love exploring photo albums. I treasure my own family albums, in which are glued pictures of long-dead relatives and of my three sons (now adults) as small boys, and I am enthralled by leather-bound scrapbooks that I find in archives when researching my books. Everything about such collections intrigues me—the dusty smell of the old volumes, the unexpected images that challenge my memories, the reminders that today's world is the result of all those yesterdays.

In photographs, you come face to face with the past. A young woman's excitement in 1946 as she arrives as a war bride in Canada or the anger of demonstrators at Toronto's G20 protests in 2010 is almost palpable. Photographs offer vivid evidence of events that made our history change direction, and of emotions that have driven Canadians to great accomplishments or personal triumphs. They remind us of the breadth of the Canadian experience. What would

Canada be like today if there had been no transcontinental railway, no Tim Hortons, no Quebec nationalism, no Giller Prize?

The history of Canada has always been too complex, too multilayered to shoehorn into one national narrative. Historians of previous generations tried their best to do so, in textbooks that told the story of national elites who passed laws, built railroads, policed the West, and ran the country. Portraits of the bewhiskered heroes of this narrative, with British or French names, still line the walls of our legislatures. But there is so much more to the story, and there are other groups demanding and deserving their place in our history.

As you make your way through the days we have chosen for this album, you will see the rough outline of a larger and more interesting picture emerge. You will see the dominance of those bewhiskered patriarchs toppled as new groups claimed their place in the mainstream—women, francophones, First Nations, northerners, immigrants. That's what makes this collection of essays such a thrilling way to explore our collective past. My family albums recall for me different chapters in my own life; *100 Days That Changed Canada* reminds me of the dozens of stories that flow alongside one another, or blend together, or meet in a mighty roar of whitewater in our national history.

In 1867 Canada was a poor and sparsely populated land dependent on agricultural exports. Steeped in the ideology of imperialism, it was one smear of pink within the larger British Empire. Today we live in one of the wealthiest countries in the world, which boasts a robust economy fuelled by scientific and business achievements. This is not always a sunny tale of unalloyed progress:

during these years, our politics have become more antagonistic and our society is perhaps more fractured. But there is a strong sense of national identity (think of the coast-to-coast euphoria produced by the 2010 Vancouver Olympics!) and a confidence in our country's stability. In *100 Days That Changed Canada*, we show you some of the people and events that have made us the way we are.

Marianne Helm

DEBORAH MORRISON

We've all experienced moments when something suddenly causes a fundamental shift in our thinking. It could be the moment you fall in love; the moment the company you work for makes a new acquisition; or, as in Egypt in early 2011, the moment you believe that protest will lead to revolution. Canadian writer Malcolm Gladwell calls these moments "tipping points." They come upon us unexpectedly, and it's only with the opportunity to look back on what happened that we begin to understand how and why they were able to cause significant change.

Gladwell suggests that tipping points require two things: an idea and a means to communicate it. With each generation, the rate of change has risen exponentially. Ideas can come from anywhere, and today's technologies allow them to spread widely and rapidly. Change is no longer simply constant—it's compelling. As individuals and as a society, we can no longer simply embrace change. We need to anticipate it, and in some respects, drive it.

The idea behind this book is a good example. In 2008, Mark Reid was inspired to create a feature story for *The Beaver* (now called *Canada's History*) magazine using photographs as an innovative approach to talking about key moments in our history. The magazine article sparked an exhibition at Library and Archives Canada, and then a publishing partnership with HarperCollins Canada. *100 Photos That Changed Canada* became the best-selling history book in Canada for 2009, giving us the confidence to present you with this newest one.

Canada's History Society strives to create these types of tipping points all the time. We began in 1920 with our flagship magazine, *The Beaver*, which today, published as *Canada's History*, is the second-oldest consumer magazine in the country. We've developed children's programming with *Kayak: Canada's History Magazine for Kids*, the Kayak Kids' Illustrated Story Challenge, and Heritage Fairs. The Governor General's Awards for Excellence in Teaching History have precipitated a number of initiatives to share lesson plans and teaching strategies, as well as to create curriculum-linked resources using the contents of our magazines. Through Canada's History Awards we've developed partnerships with other leading history organizations. Most recently, we've launched CanadasHistory.ca, a dynamic new web portal where all sectors of the history community converge. Canadians can now retrieve and comment on news and events in the field of history, academic research, genealogy advice, and travel tips.

Although celebrating our stories remains at the core of what we do, the role that Canada's History plays has shifted from magazine publisher to community service provider. Canada's History has become what Malcolm Gladwell described as the "connector" with the past, creating the entry points for all Canadians to see themselves in our national story.

A project like *100 Days That Changed Canada* provides us with a hundred tipping points, and a hundred stories about those moments. We hope it will spark an interest to share your own story, or to discover others. Together we can create thousands more. The dialogue continues online at CanadasHistory.ca. We hope to see you there!

Marianne Helm

INTRODUCTION

MARK REID

In the early spring of 1977, an eighteen-year-old Vancouver man received the worst news he could have expected.

Handsome and athletic, Terry Fox had plenty going for him. He came from a tight-knit family and was taking courses toward a kinesiology degree at Simon Fraser University. He had recently visited a doctor to complain of soreness in his leg. It was a nagging pain that just wouldn't go away—more frustrating than anything, as it hampered him when he played sports. Terry thought it was probably nothing. But on March 2, 1977, the doctor told him that he was actually suffering from osteosarcoma—cancer of the bone.

On any given day, dozens of Canadians across the country will receive similar life-altering diagnoses. For most, it will forever change their lives. But change the country? Not likely.

Today, of course, we can look back at that moment in 1977 and call it a turning point not only for Terry but also for the nation. There were others in

Terry's life, such as April 12, 1980, the day he dipped his artificial leg in the Atlantic off Newfoundland and began his Marathon of Hope. For *100 Days That Changed Canada*, we chose to highlight a darker moment from Terry's journey—September 1, 1980—the date he announced that his cancer had returned, and that he would have to halt his run.

As you can see, the story of Canada—our story—is rich with momentous events, some proud, some shameful, others joyous or sad. Only when they are viewed together do we get a complete image of who we are as a nation, and of where we are going.

The challenge in creating *100 Days That Changed Canada* comes not in finding milestones but in choosing only a hundred among the countless events that have collectively shaped our country. For instance, consider Sir John A. Macdonald's national dream of building a railway across Canada. What moment would you highlight? The date the first spike was hammered or the last? Would it be Macdonald's return to power in 1878—five years after the Pacific Scandal drove him from office—which enabled him to revive his railway plan? We chose July 24, 1886, a moment of personal triumph for our first prime minister. It's the day he and his wife, Agnes, completed their train journey across Canada on the railway he had fought so long to build.

As you thumb through *100 Days That Changed Canada*, you'll discover moments that make you smile or bring you to tears. Some will be unfamiliar, others instantly recognizable and relevant. You'll read the accompanying essays and learn why these diverse moments matter.

Whether they're major milestones such as sending Canadian troops to Afghanistan, cultural moments like Joni Mitchell's first significant public performance, at Mariposa, or golden moments from the Vancouver 2010 Winter Games, each of these hundred days is part of the mosaic that makes up the Canadian experience. Ultimately, *100 Days That Changed Canada* is about connection—uniting Canadians with their past, and all of us with each other.

100 DAYS
THAT CHANGED CANADA

PART ONE

BUILDING A NATION
1867–1929

Her Most Gracious Majesty did ordain, declare, and command, that on and after the 1st day of July 1867, the Provinces of Canada [Ontario and Quebec], Nova Scotia and New Brunswick should form and be one Dominion under the name of Canada.

—ROYAL PROCLAMATION OF QUEEN VICTORIA, 1867

There were celebrations in Kingston and festivities in Montreal. As Confederation was proclaimed on July 1, 1867, the *Globe* newspaper predicted great things for the fledgling nation: "We firmly believe, that from this day, Canada enters on a new and happier career, and that a time of great prosperity and advancement is before us."

It was a bold forecast, based as much on optimism as on evidence, but it spoke to the exuberance of the times. We were no longer merely a collection of British colonies, but a country—or rather, a dominion.

But amid all the popping of champagne and tossing of streamers, unrest was already afoot. Nova Scotia had been dragged into the union, and many there wanted out. The day after Confederation, one newspaper, the *Morning Chronicle*, went so far as to mock the celebrants who had marched through Halifax. "About six hundred people—as many as have occasionally attended a decent funeral in the city—were all that could be scraped up to join in this great display," the newspaper sneered. "Six hundred out of a population of more than thirty thousand. . . ."

It was a moment of mixed emotions. What was Canada, anyway? What did a fisherman in Pictou have in common with a lawyer in Montreal or a Toronto merchant, other than a shared desire not to become an American? In truth, the marriage of Quebec, Ontario, New Brunswick, and Nova Scotia was one of necessity. Big decisions faced the former British colonies. What was to become of the vast hinterland to the northwest? For centuries, it had been the fiefdom of the Hudson's Bay Company, occupied by voyageurs and First Nations. If the eastern provinces didn't present a united front, the entire territory might end up in the clutches of the United States. The Fathers of Confederation knew they had unfinished business; already, trouble was brewing at the Red River Colony, in modern-day Winnipeg.

Then there was British Columbia, far away on the Pacific coast. Most Canadians thought it should be part of the dominion. But British Columbians wouldn't even consider joining Canada unless it built a transnational rail line. Could a railway be driven through such unforgiving extremes of terrain? And if so, who would pay for it? The nation's to-do list seemed insurmountable.

On July 1, 1867, Canadians signalled their willingness to join the family of nations. We weren't yet completely independent from Britain. Key decisions, such as whether Canadians would go to war, were still not ours to make. But working together, we were determined to stand on our own. A new century beckoned. Whether it would belong to Canada was up to us.

—Mark Reid

1

The Fathers of Confederation, Quebec City, 1864.
Copy of 1883 painting by Robert Harris.
Artist: Rex Woods.

United Nation

July 1, 1867—Canadians ring in Confederation.

CHRISTOPHER MOORE

At midnight, bonfires blazed and cathedral bells chimed. At dawn, artillery salutes thundered. All day long and into the evening, Canadians gathered in the streets, parks, and public squares of the new nation. Victorian Canadians loved festivals, and their celebration of Canada's first-ever public holiday was lavish.

It had been a long time coming. There had been lengthy negotiations, vigorous debate, and many setbacks. Finally, Queen Victoria signed the British North America Act into law in March 1867. All was to come into effect in high summer: Monday, July 1, 1867.

Confederation was a bold innovation. For the first time, former colonials were peacefully taking up their right to govern themselves. The new nation would have parliamentary democracy on the British model, and its governments would be accountable to representative legislatures elected by one of the widest franchises the world had seen (even though women and some men could not yet vote). The new federal structure promised the sharing of power between a national government and provinces empowered to run local matters and sustain local cultures.

Not everyone celebrated. Some had wanted a referendum or election first. Some Quebecers feared the new nation was part of an old plot to assimilate and crush them. Prince Edward Island and Newfoundland had declined the opportunity to be founding provinces. "Died! Last night at twelve o'clock, the free and enlightened province of Nova Scotia . . . at the hands of some of her ungrateful sons," declared a Halifax headline. Still, even where doubts were strongest, there were large crowds and enthusiastic celebrations.

In Canada's new capital, there was business to transact. Ottawa was a small, raw town in 1867, but when George Brown, one of the makers of Confederation, first saw Ottawa's imposing new Parliament Buildings, he said, "A hundred years hence people will fancy the men of these days were giants." Inside the building, the new nation's governor general took the oath of office that morning. He then swore in the first prime minister and cabinet. Even as most Canadians enjoyed their holiday, the cabinet settled down to work that afternoon.

The Constitution of 1867 was the first ever made in Canada for Canada by Canadians, a plan "not suggested by others or imposed on us, but one the work of ourselves," said D'Arcy McGee, the great orator of Confederation. McGee foresaw Canada's boundaries reaching out east, west, and north, to "the blue rim of ocean." The people of what had been four small colonies now had the opportunity to expand across the continent and take their place among the nations of the world. The object of the Canadians, said London's *Economist* in admiration, "is to form a nation." This was cause for celebration.

From Lunenburg to Sarnia, the people came out for elaborate parades. There were marching bands, bright files of soldiers, and lavishly decorated floats. Triumphal arches soared over the street corners. Canadians roasted oxen, rode in hot-air balloons, and launched boat excursions. They organized sports matches and track meets. They enjoyed picnics and musical performances. And fireworks! That night the skies of every town blazed with colourful explosions.

In Canada, July 1 has been pretty much like that ever since.

The Real Deal

November 19, 1869—Canada purchases Rupert's Land.

JOE MARTIN

On November 19, 1869, the Hudson's Bay Company transferred Rupert's Land to the new Dominion of Canada. This was not only the largest real estate deal in Canadian history, but one of the largest in the history of the world, involving an area three times the size of the Louisiana Purchase in the United States.

Prior to the transfer, the young dominion hugged the Great Lakes and the St. Lawrence River, and included present-day New Brunswick and Nova Scotia. Out of Rupert's Land would come all of modern-day Manitoba and most of Saskatchewan, southern Alberta, and northern Ontario and Quebec, as well as southern Nunavut. Canada gained almost 6 million square kilometres, increasing its area sixfold and making it one of the largest geographic entities in the world. In return, the HBC received £300,000 (nearly $1.5 million) and 2.8 million hectares of arable land, plus another twenty thousand hectares around its trading posts.

Even more important, the bold acquisition of Rupert's Land ensured that the empty northwest would not become part of the United States of America. Advocates of America's manifest destiny had the territory in their crosshairs, already having acquired all of Oregon, which was formerly part of British North America; Texas in the south, formerly part of Mexico; and Alaska in the northwest, formerly part of Russia.

From today's vantage point, the decision to acquire Rupert's Land may seem obvious. But it was not so obvious at the time, especially given the cost: in the fiscal year of the acquisition, Canada's total budgetary expenditures were only $16 million.

The initial fallout from the acquisition was unfortunate—the Red River Rebellion of 1869–1870. But in the late 1890s, settlers started to pour into the Prairies for land "fit for the plow." They came from eastern Canada, the United Kingdom, the United States, and Europe.

The growth in the West brought optimism, but also tension, to the national stage. Many in eastern Canada saw the new Prairie provinces as colonies of the founding provinces, in that they did not have control of their own lands, forests, and minerals until 1930. This was far different from the treatment given to the four original provinces, plus Prince Edward Island and British Columbia, and unlike the United States, where the American territories had a formula for statehood. Unquestionably, the long-term benefits to Canada of the purchase have been immense. Without it, Prime Minister Sir John A. Macdonald would not have been able to announce his National Policy in 1878: two of the three key provisions required Rupert's Land—namely, the construction of a railway to the Pacific and the settlement of the West.

Canada certainly benefits from the forests, minerals, and hydro power of the former Rupert's Land territories in northern Ontario, Quebec, and southern Nunavut. However, the greatest benefits are derived from ownership of the present-day Prairie provinces. Home to nearly 20 percent of Canada's population and an abundance of natural resources—including oil and gas, potash and other minerals, grain, and livestock— the Prairies today produce more than 20 percent of Canada's gross domestic product and have become the fastest-growing region of the country.

2

After the sale of Rupert's Land,
the Hudson's Bay Company refocused
its efforts on retail and land sales.
Photographer: Anonymous.

3

The Indian Act dominated the lives of Aboriginals like Thomas Moore, shown here before and after entering residential school in Saskatchewan circa 1896.
Photographer: Anonymous.

Vanishing Act

April 12, 1876—The Indian Act binds First Nations.

TINA LOO

Even though he wasn't yet born when it became the law of the land, Thomas Moore was a child of Canada's first Indian Act. Sent to a Regina residential school in 1896, the boy—his transformation captured in a before-and-after series of photos—represented what generations of legislators had dreamed of. Civilization and assimilation had been the aims of Indian policy in British North America before Canada was a country. But with the passage of the 1876 Act, they—like young Thomas—shape-shifted: instead of remaining long-term aspirations they became immediate objectives.

The Act came into force on April 12, 1876, at a time the government was resettling the Prairie West, negotiating the numbered treaties. The new dominion would grow by pushing indigenous peoples aside. But having done that in central and eastern Canada, the government recognized it also had to integrate them into the nation. The 1876 Act pointed the way. While it didn't establish the residential schools that remade Thomas Moore, the Act did something more fundamental. It consolidated the existing laws relating to Indian administration into a single piece of legislation that did nothing less than set out the framework for how indigenous peoples would fit into the political, economic, and social structure of Canada. It literally defined who could be an "Indian," and spelled out ways that status could be stripped; later amendments would ban key cultural practices, such as the potlatch.

The starting point for the Act was the idea that Indians were not yet equipped to function in Canadian society because they lacked the education, morals, and discipline that defined peoples and cultures as "civilized." Left to their own devices, Indians could be exploited by the unscrupulous and might also corrupt the morals of white society. Given their "primitive" nature, Indians had to be protected and made morally literate, somewhere out of harm's way, on land reserved by the Crown for that purpose.

Indeed, the Act was as concerned with Indian lands as it was with Indians, devoting half its sections to delineating how reserves were to be managed and protected from encroachment. Land got the attention it did because legislators considered it the key to civilizing and assimilating Indians. When they could prove they were civilized, Indians were granted provisional title to their reserve lands in the form of a "location ticket." The bar was so high that most Canadians would have been tripped up by its requirements: according to the Act, the civilized were literate, free of debt, and of high moral character. Even so, location-ticket holders were made to pass one more test before being granted ownership outright. If they improved their land and used it productively within three years, they not only got title but also became "enfranchised." They stopped being Indians in law and became Canadians, and the lands they held ceased to be part of the reserve.

A magic trick of the first order, the 1876 Act made Indians and Indian lands disappear. As with other sleights of hand, the key to this one rested in convincing the audience there was something there—a coin, a rubber ball—in the first place. The power of Ottawa's legislative wizards lay more in making us see Indians as people who had to vanish than in turning them into Canadians.

Signed, Sealed, Delivered

September 22, 1877—Treaty No. 7 clears way for a railway to the West.

GARRETT WILSON

A rail connection to central Canada was the 1870 promise that induced British Columbia to join Prime Minister Sir John A. Macdonald's Confederation. It meant that Ottawa had to secure full title to the more than two thousand kilometres of route that lay between Lake Superior and the Rocky Mountains, land inhabited by several disparate bands of Indians. Treaties would have to be negotiated.

By 1876 six treaties had been signed, stating that those Indian inhabitants did "cede, release, surrender, and yield up to Her Majesty the Queen" all the arable lands west of Lake Superior, up to and including the Cypress Hills. Remaining was the territory west to the Rocky Mountains, today's southern Alberta, home of the then Blackfeet (later Blackfoot) Confederacy, made up of the Blackfoot, Blood, and Piegan bands and their Sarcee allies.

Ottawa had been somewhat casual in securing the treaties and, although warned not to take the Blackfeet for granted, did not make arrangements to meet with them until September 1877. By then intervening events in the United States had made negotiating a treaty with the warlike members of the confederacy a matter of critical urgency. After grievously defeating the U.S. 7th Cavalry at Little Big Horn in June 1876, several thousand American Sioux fled into Canada. Their leader, Sitting Bull, was known to have met with Crowfoot, the chief of the Blackfoot, and to have proposed an alliance against all white people.

For the Blackfeet treaty negotiations, Ottawa gave itself a powerful card by appointing as one of its treaty commissioners James Macleod, commissioner of the North West Mounted Police, who served with David Laird, lieutenant-governor of the North-West Territories. Three years earlier, in 1874, Macleod, then assistant commissioner, had been the senior officer of the NWMP when the force arrived in the West and ended the American whisky trade that had debauched and impoverished the Blackfeet. Macleod had acquired from the Blackfeet not only their gratitude but also their confidence and trust.

On the appointed day—Monday, September 17, 1877—a large assembly of Indians began to gather at Blackfoot Crossing on the Bow River, a hundred kilometres east of Calgary. The Blackfoot and the neighbouring Stoney peoples arrived first, followed a day or two later by the Piegan and the Sarcee. When the Blood tribe came in with their head chief, Red Crow, some five thousand Indians and fifteen thousand horses filled the valley along the Bow.

Government officials explained the treaty's terms to the Indians, who then considered the terms in their councils. On Friday afternoon, Crowfoot rose, spoke warmly of the NWMP and Macleod, and declared, "I will sign." Red Crow concurred: "I entirely trust Macleod. I will sign with Crowfoot." The next day, September 22, 1877, Crowfoot and Red Crow stepped forward and placed their marks on Treaty No. 7, followed by forty-nine chiefs and councillors.

The Pacific railway route from Lake Superior to the Rocky Mountains was now secure—but life for the Treaty No. 7 bands would never be the same. Not even two years later the buffalo failed and the proud and independent peoples who had signed the treaty found themselves wards of the Ottawa government, dependent for the meagre rations that barely kept them from starvation while they struggled to transform themselves from nomadic hunters into sedentary farmers.

From left, Three Bulls, Sitting on an Eagle Tail Feathers, Crowfoot, Red Crow—all signatories of Treaty No. 7—in 1884.
Photographer: Anonymous.

4

Bison bones stacked and ready for shipment in Saskatchewan circa 1890.

Photographer: Richard Henry Trueman.

5

Senseless Slaughter

June 26, 1879—Canada awakens to the decimation of the bison.

NELLE OOSTEROM

In the early 1800s about 60 million bison thundered across the Prairies, ensuring plentiful food, shelter, and clothing for the First Nations of the Plains. By the end of the century, almost all that was left was piles upon piles of bleached bones. The North American buffalo was on the edge of extinction. And the indigenous peoples of the Prairies were starving.

The terrible slaughter still pricks at our twenty-first-century conscience, a symbol of wanton wildlife destruction. From a nineteenth-century settlement perspective, the buffalo were in the way of progress. They got in the way of the newly built railroads, leading "sportsmen" to shoot at herds from moving trains for fun, leaving the untouched carcasses to rot on the ground. They got in the way of settlers bringing in herds of tractable cattle and sheep. Wild buffalo tramping over cow pastures did not fit the picture of a frontier brought to heel with fences and private land ownership.

And they got in the way of efforts to "civilize" the Natives. "The civilization of the Indian is impossible while the buffalo remains upon the plains," declared the American secretary of the interior, Columbus Delano, in 1873. The U.S. Army adopted a deliberate policy of bison extermination aimed at forcing Aboriginal people to settle on reservations. The Sioux and other nations rose up, leading to the killing of George Armstrong Custer and his troops at Little Bighorn in 1876, which prompted Sitting Bull and thousands of his followers to seek refuge in Canada.

While the Canadian government did not have a policy of bison extermination, overhunting was rife and the outcome was the same. By 1879, famine stalked thousands of Native people in the North-West Territories.

Fearing an uprising by desperate tribes who might sabotage his cross-continent railway-building project, Prime Minister Sir John A. Macdonald sent the newly appointed indian commissioner, Edgar Dewdney, west to fix the problem. Dewdney's orders were to distribute relief, convincing those Natives who had not already done so to settle on reserves and support themselves through agriculture. He was also to persuade Sitting Bull and his followers to return to the United States.

Dewdney arrived at the North West Mounted Police post of Fort Walsh in the Cypress Hills on June 26, 1879. Thousands of hungry tribespeople had gathered. Some had resorted to eating dogs and gophers. In his report to Ottawa, Dewdney concluded that the disappearance of the buffalo meant the government would have to provide for the Indians for a long time.

By 1889, the number of buffalo in North America had shrunk to about a thousand. The early 1900s saw the Canadian government finally act to protect the few remaining beasts by purchasing bison from a Montana rancher's private herd and later, in 1922, establishing Wood Buffalo National Park in northern Alberta and the southern Northwest Territories as a refuge for the animals. Today, free-roaming herds exist in several Canadian and American parks. And the population of bison raised on farms for meat numbers about 200,000 in Canada alone.

The bison also lives on as a symbol, most poignantly when a rare white calf is born. Sacred to the Plains First Nations, a white bison is a sign of hope and renewal.

Messiah or Madman?

November 16, 1885—Louis Riel is executed.

JACQUES LACOURSIÈRE

On November 16, 1885, in Regina, Louis Riel was hanged for high treason, polarizing the nation.

He was executed for leading a rebellion—many would argue, a resistance—against the Canadian government, which had legal jurisdiction over the North-West Territories. The troubles had begun in the early 1880s, at a time of high tension among the Indians, the Métis, and the federal government in Ottawa.

In 1884 Métis delegates went to Montana to meet Louis Riel, who was working there while in exile. They asked him to join them and lead an uprising against the "oppressive" Canadian government. Riel, who had established a provisional government for Manitoba in 1870, accepted the offer.

At the time, Riel was having more and more "messianic visions," and some thought he had become mentally ill. That would not stop him from effectively leading the insurgency, which made its move on March 18, 1885. There were several battles with members of the North West Mounted Police, with Riel's forces aided by French Canadian militiamen, Indians, and Métis.

The final battle took place in Batoche, in modern-day Saskatchewan, from May 9 to May 12, 1885. A defeated Riel surrendered to General Frederick D. Middleton on May 15. Shortly thereafter, the famous prisoner was transferred to Regina. His arrest brought cries of joy in Ontario. One Toronto newspaper wrote, "Strangle Riel with the French flag! That is the only use that rag can have in this country." This was a triumph for Ontario Orangemen, who had never forgotten the 1870 execution of one of their own—Thomas Scott—in Winnipeg for plotting against the provisional government there.

Riel's trial began in Regina on July 20. He was part of a group of seventy-three prisoners, all accused of various crimes related to the uprising. Riel would be tried by a jury of six—all anglophones. Riel's lawyer wanted him to plead insanity, but he refused. On August 1 the jury deliberated for only one hour. Afterward, Judge Hugh Richardson passed this sentence: "That on the upcoming 18th of September, you are to be taken to the appointed place of your execution, there to be hanged by the neck until dead, and may God have mercy upon your soul."

History has shown that Riel's hanging did not occur until November. Why was it delayed? A wave of unrest first swept through the province of Quebec and then made its way to French-speaking New England. The big question was whether Louis Riel was sane. The sentence was appealed, but the appeal was dismissed by the British Privy Council. Delays in the execution of the sentence were granted on a few occasions. Some Quebec newspapers asked for clemency, while the English-language dailies demanded that the death sentence be upheld.

Following the hanging on November 16, Quebecers were quick to react with anger. Arguably, this was the first separatist crisis since Confederation.

Today, Riel's role is still debated. In Manitoba he's considered the father of that province, honoured by a statue erected at the provincial legislature. In Quebec he's considered by some to be a martyr for the French-language cause in Canada.

6

Louis Riel, circa 1879.
Photographer: A. J. Owen.

7

Sir John A. Macdonald and his wife, Agnes, near Mission, B.C., during their 1886 train trip.
Photographer: Oliver B. Buell.

Dream Come True

July 24, 1886—Canada's first prime minister surveys the nation he united.

CONRAD BLACK

Prime Minister Sir John A. Macdonald and his wife, Agnes, left Ottawa on July 10, 1886, for a transcontinental rail trip that lasted a leisurely fifty days. The train travelled at about sixty-five kilometres per hour during the day and stopped for most of the night to assure the prime minister and Lady Macdonald's sleep.

As they started into the Rockies, the Macdonalds jauntily occupied comfortable chairs placed on the great cowcatcher at the very front of the engine. With no smoke or steam, but the wind bracingly in their faces, they sat for hours and admired the spectacular gorges, rivers, and cliffs, appreciating both the glories of the panorama and the astounding engineering achievement of connecting these vast geographic zones that the train's chief passenger, more than anyone else, had welded into a country. They even took their places there at night, admiring the stars, the loom of the mountains in the moonlit darkness, with the roar of the locomotive at their back and the engine's lamp piercing the way ahead.

Macdonald had often said, including at several whistle stops along this route, that his vision did not end at the Pacific shore but extended across the Pacific to the Far East.

On July 24, 1886, the Macdonalds embarked on the *Princess Louise* from Port Moody, near Vancouver, for Victoria, to holiday at Government House. Earlier on the trip, Macdonald had met with the Blackfoot Indians and their eminent chief, Crowfoot, who had rallied this important tribe in personal loyalty to Macdonald in the daunting days of the North-West Rebellion, just eighteen months before. At the time, the managers of the underfinanced Canadian Pacific had been forced to pay the company's dividend and payroll personally. Canada had greatly gained in stature in that short time, would no longer be shaken by Métis uprisings or the fluid adherences of Indian tribes, and had a solidly profitable national railway.

The railway was both one of the engineering feats of the modern world—in the same category as the greatest American railways and the Suez Canal—and the linchpin of a new nation. As the United States bound up its wounds after a terrible and costly civil war—and as the final steps were being taken toward the unification of Germany, the Meiji restoration of the Japanese empire, the re-establishment of republican rule in France, and the emergence of a united Italy—another nation was launched, largely by this man and in the ark of this railway. Sir John A. Macdonald was as responsible for the Dominion of Canada as Abraham Lincoln was for the victory of the American union, or Otto von Bismarck and Count Cavour for the unifications of Germany and of Italy.

Of course, Canada's Confederation was less significant at the time than these grand changes in the world's great powers. But taking communities strung together along the American border, calling them a country, and binding them with a railway, proclaiming two official languages where official policy had been for one to assimilate the other—this too was a project of ambition and grandeur that would eventually influence the world.

As the *Princess Louise* approached Victoria Harbour in the evening of July 24, no one can know—but we may imagine—Macdonald's sense of accomplishment on that day.

Super Natural

June 23, 1887—Banff becomes Canada's first national park.

KEN McGOOGAN

Try to imagine a Canada with no national parks. Instead of strolling along an empty beach in Pacific Rim National Park, watching the whitecaps roll in, you could be shunting along a crowded boardwalk beneath a grotesque amusement park. Instead of hiking a rugged trail in Banff National Park, heading for the spectacular Valley of the Ten Peaks, you could be driving a suburban roadway in an alternative Banff— a polluted Canadian Rockies city with a population of 2 million. Oh, and those red sand beaches of Prince Edward Island National Park? They were expropriated long ago and turned into a bustling shopping centre named after Lucy Maud Montgomery.

Fortunately, this parallel-universe Canada remains imaginary. In reality, Canadians possess an array of national parks that help define who we are. That is thanks to decisions taken in the 1880s, when the Canadian Pacific Railway was still being built. In 1883 three men working in the Rockies for the CPR chanced upon a cave containing a natural hot springs at the foot of Sulphur Mountain. These three—brothers Tom and William McCardell and their partner, Frank McCabe— were not the first to discover what are now called the Cave and Basin hot springs, but they were the first to claim ownership.

For centuries, First Nations had viewed the hot springs as sacred, as a place that could cure illness and maintain health. And in 1859, while exploring with the Palliser expedition, geologist James Hector had stumbled across the warm, sulphurous waters. But no one owned them.

The three CPR men sensed an opportunity. They knew that the railway would soon bring tourists, so they buttressed their claim by building a fence around the cave and constructing a crude cabin. But then a well-placed Nova Scotian MP, a lawyer named D. B. Woodworth, tricked the CPR men into assigning their land rights to him. Woodworth purchased a jerry-built hotel with a view to moving it onto the site.

The ensuing legal wrangle caught the eye of that savvy politician Sir John A. Macdonald, then serving his final term as prime minister. In November 1885, Macdonald put an end to the ruckus by creating the Banff Hot Springs Reserve, protecting ten square miles (twenty-six square kilometres) around the cave from development. Less than two years later, on June 23, 1887, he went one crucial step further. He passed the Rocky Mountains Park Act, expanding the protected area to 260 square miles (673 square kilometres) and designating it Canada's first national park. Decades later, in 1930, the federal government would pass the National Parks Act, renaming the original protected area Banff National Park and expanding it to almost ten times its size. Most important, it set up a nationwide parks system.

Today, Canada has forty-two spectacular national parks, at least one in each province and territory, all set aside by law for the "benefit, education, and enjoyment" of the people of Canada. Did Macdonald anticipate this evolution? Not likely. Yet if he had not passed the Rocky Mountains Park Act, the national parks system might never have come into existence. That makes June 23, 1887, a Canadian date to remember.

8

Horseback riding near Mount Lefroy in Banff National Park, circa 1930.

A sourdough pans for gold during the Klondike gold rush, circa 1898.
Photographer: Leonard Delano.

9

All That Glitters

August 16, 1896—Klondike strike sparks gold fever.

CHARLOTTE GRAY

As the late summer sun slid across a wide blue northern sky that day, four people struggled through the tangled underbrush and cranberry bushes of the Yukon wilderness. The gold digger whose name has come down through history was George Carmack, a Californian miner, but three other people from the local Tagish Nation were part of the discovery. Alongside Shaaw Tláa (Carmack's wife, whom he called Kate) were her brother Keish, known as Skookum Jim, and her nephew Káa Goox, nicknamed Tagish Charlie.

One of them caught the glint of gold in a creek bed and casually began to pan for gold in the trickling tributary of the Klondike River. Perhaps there would be a few flakes of "colour," or if they were really lucky a couple of nuggets. Instead, the first pan yielded an incredible quarter of an ounce of gold, and Carmack and his Tagish relatives could see that gold lay between layers of schist rock like a thick slice of cheese in a sandwich. They scrambled off to stake their claim on the creek that would soon be called Bonanza. It was August 16, 1896, and the last great gold rush in North American history had begun.

Ever since that August day, the Yukon gold rush has been firmly embedded in both Canadian history and the Canadian imagination. Yet it was not a glorious get-rich-quick adventure. It did not yield as much gold as gold rushes elsewhere, and few of the prospectors who stampeded toward the midnight sun made their fortunes. Only forty thousand of the hundred thousand who set off for the gold fields completed the brutal journey; only three hundred of the twenty thousand miners who worked claims made more than $300,000 in today's currency. Of these successful miners, only fifty managed to leave the Yukon with their wealth. The big money winners were Seattle outfitters and the owners (many of them Americans) of Dawson City's saloons, brothels, and gambling tables.

Moreover, the Klondike gold rush destroyed the way of life of many First Nations in the Yukon, including Carmack's Tagish relatives. Dysentery and other diseases ravaged their communities. Relations between the region's original peoples and the newcomers quickly soured in the race for resources. The Han people had camped on the mud flat at the confluence of the Klondike and Yukon rivers for generations, but their traditional fishing grounds were destroyed as the raucous, rough-and-tumble boomtown of Dawson City was hastily hammered together. They were forced to move downstream to a new settlement, and in the century ahead they watched their language and culture erode and saw their children shipped off to residential schools.

Nonetheless, the gold rush has come to symbolize aspects of Canada that shape its economy and haunt the national psyche. It sustains our unspoken assumption that continued prosperity is guaranteed by a treasure chest of mineral wealth, hidden in our vast landscape behind mountain ranges and under layers of ice. And the gold rush drew attention to the robust grandeur of the Far North that continues to inspire adventurers and artists of all types, from Lawren Harris to Margaret Atwood, Glenn Gould to Mordecai Richler.

Making the Mounties

June 22, 1897—The NWMP steals the limelight at the Diamond Jubilee.

MARK REID

The 2010 Winter Games in Vancouver offered up plenty of memorable moments, perhaps none as unforgettable as the wacky closing ceremony featuring a cast of Canadian icons. There were clogging lumberjacks, floating moose, jaunty voyageurs, and even a giant beaver. And everywhere during the extravaganza, there were Mounties: real ones, carrying the Olympic flag; dancing ones, sporting red serge miniskirts; and inflatable ones—three storeys high!—standing at attention during the comic send-up of all things Canadian.

Most of us got the joke. We know the world defines us by clichés, and none is more ubiquitous than the noble Mountie. With Stetsons firmly set, these fearless lawmen stride through the pages of our history, freeing the West of whisky peddlers, bringing law and order to the North, and always—always—getting their man. From Superintendent Sam Steele to Dudley Do-Right of *The Rocky and Bullwinkle Show*, the larger-than-life legend of the RCMP is known around the world. But few realize that it began across the pond, during the Diamond Jubilee of Queen Victoria.

In 1897 Victoria was celebrating sixty years on the throne, and dominion governments everywhere sent delegations to join in the festivities. The highlight of the event was a parade through London on June 22, 1897, featuring fighting men from across the Empire. Soldiers from eleven dominions, including Australia, New Zealand, and India, were represented. But it was the Canadians who drew the loudest applause. The centre of attention was a rearguard of thirty North West Mounted Police officers, resplendent in their red serge and Stetsons. Selected specifically for their physique and their height—most were around six feet tall—these men were unlike any the crowds had seen before. *These* were the men who had tamed the West:

ruggedly handsome Mounties with sweeping moustaches, striped pants, and knee-high leather boots.

"It was an extraordinary journey from the western prairies to the streets of London, the first time that the mounted police had appeared in uniform outside of Western Canada," Library and Archives Canada archivist Glenn Wright writes in the virtual exhibition *"Without Fear, Favour or Affection": The Men of the North West Mounted Police*. Wright notes, "The prime minister was impressed, as were the public and the press. . . . By June 1897 . . . the red-coated Mountie . . . was now the toast of the Empire, having become the embodiment of strength and virtue, and a living symbol of Canada itself."

One thing has changed since the Diamond Jubilee. It's often said of the Mounties that they always get their man. Well, in 1974 they finally got their women. That's the year the RCMP accepted its first cohort of female recruits.

10

Mounties in London, England, for Queen Victoria's Diamond Jubilee in 1897.
Photographer: Anonymous.

Canadian troops from 2nd Battalion, Royal Canadian Regiment, in South Africa, 1900.
Photographer: Anonymous.

11

King and Country

November 29, 1899—Canadian troops head to South Africa.

TIM COOK

The Canadians climbing this kopje look like British soldiers. With their pith helmets and khaki uniforms, the 2nd Battalion, Royal Canadian Regiment, could easily have been mistaken as British soldiers. They were not. This was Canada's first official expeditionary force, and it was fighting in support of the British Empire in the South African War of 1899–1902.

The thousand soldiers of the RCR would be joined by another 7,300 men and a handful of nurses. They would serve throughout the four-year war and face a resilient enemy. Boer farmers proved adept and skilled, but Canadians also faced cruel weather, rampant disease, and shockingly rugged and difficult terrain.

Few had predicted these problems in October 1899, when Canada had agreed to send an overseas force in support of Britain. As a dominion, Canada had historically been protected by Britain against its traditional enemy, the United States. But now Canada was called upon to support the Empire. The patriotic and imperialistic responded with vigour. Others, including a majority of French Canadians and recent immigrants, wondered why Canadians should travel halfway around the world to fight against farmers. Prime Minister Sir Wilfrid Laurier was caught in the middle. When the strain almost brought down his government, he agreed to allow a volunteer force to serve—separate from imperial units and distinguished with the maple leaf.

The first troops departed Canada on November 29, 1899, sent on their way by throngs of cheering Canadians. At the Battle of Paardeberg, in February 1900, Canadians fought with British troops to defeat a large Boer army. It was the first significant victory in the war, and many believed that the Boers would surrender. Laurier was so proud that he proclaimed, "A new power has arisen in the West."

But the Boers refused to surrender and instead turned to guerrilla war. Running the enemy to ground required grim tactics and new troops. Mounted patrols were sent off looking for the canny Boers. Sympathetic farms were burned. Boer women and children were put into concentration camps, where thousands died of disease. Canadian mounted troops were involved in these operations. They proved to be proficient soldiers, although some of the British believed them undisciplined, more willing to brawl than to accept orders. The Canadians (along with Australians) played up this unsoldierly reputation, and they often took on the look of tough western cowboys.

The war ended in 1902 and most Canadians returned home, although some tried to make a go of farming in South Africa or of serving in a constabulary police force. Some 270 lay buried in cemeteries.

The cheering and welcome-home parties smothered the smouldering anger of Canadians who had sought to keep the country from being dragged into an imperial war. In Canada's willingness to send an expeditionary force, the dominion had made that important leap from defending its own territory to contributing actively to the defence of the British Empire. Over the next fifty years, these expeditionary forces—fighting in the Great War of 1914–1918 and in the Second World War of 1939–1945—would lead to dramatic changes in Canada and in how others viewed it.

The conflicts in which they engaged would also cost more than 110,000 lives.

Wired Less

December 12, 1901—Marconi receives first transatlantic wireless message.

CHRISTOPHER MOORE

"Can you hear anything, Mr. Kemp?" Guglielmo Marconi said to his assistant in a bare room in the Cabot Tower above St. John's, Newfoundland, as they took turns jamming a single earpiece against their straining ears. In 1901 wireless telegraphy was new and hotly competitive, and Marconi knew the importance of spectacular results. He had decided to stun the world with the first transatlantic wireless telegraph transmission.

Electromagnetic waves fascinated both theoretical physicists and tinkering inventors in the late nineteenth century. In 1888 the German physicist Heinrich Hertz demonstrated that radio waves could be sent and received wirelessly. He saw no practical application, but inventors around the world mimicked his results and pondered what the waves might transmit. Electrical power? Death rays? Information?

The ambitious and brilliant young Italian Guglielmo Marconi combined a solid grasp of the science, a sure hand in technical applications, and a head for business. By 1895, just twenty, he had made a wireless signal ring a bell across a room in the family home at Pontecchio, Italy. Soon he was sending Morse code signals across valleys and hills—wireless telegraphy. Marconi could see the commercial possibilities of his technology. He sought backing for his new Wireless Telegraph & Signal Company in Britain and the United States. Returning from the United States to Britain in 1899, he rigged up an onboard transmitter and announced his ship's arrival from a hundred kilometres offshore. Funding poured in to Marconi's company, but he knew competitors were scrambling to improve on his technology and seize the lead.

In 1901 Marconi had a big transmitting station built at Poldhu Cove in Cornwall, but he did not dare wait for something similar to be built in North America. He arrived in St. John's on December 6, 1901, with only an array of wires, kites, and balloons to form his receiving antenna. It proved just enough. The island's government gave him the use of the Cabot Tower on Signal Hill. Surging winds carried off his balloons, so he turned to kites on a 180-metre line. Six days after his arrival, just after noon on Thursday, December 12, 1901, both Marconi and Kemp heard in their earphones the signal they had asked wireless operators at Poldhu to send out. It was simply dot-dot-dot repeated, the letter S in Morse code.

"I knew that the day on which I should be able to send full messages without wires or cables across the Atlantic was not far distant," said Marconi. He was gone from St. John's before the end of December, and the Signal Hill message, never repeated, was little more than a test. Indeed, doubts have never entirely faded as to how Marconi's wildly bucking kite-borne antenna could actually have received the signal he reported. But within a year his permanent wireless telegraph station at Glace Bay, Nova Scotia, was in regular communication with Poldhu Cove. Within five years, many ships were equipped with radio equipment, often bearing the Marconi brand, and Canadian Reginald Fessenden had achieved the first voice and music transmissions—wireless telephony.

The world's airwaves have never been silent since, except once. When Guglielmo Marconi died in 1937, radio transmitters in Canada and around the world observed two minutes of silence in his honour.

12

Guglielmo Marconi and assistant George Kemp
receive the first transatlantic wireless signal in 1901.
Photographer: Anonymous.

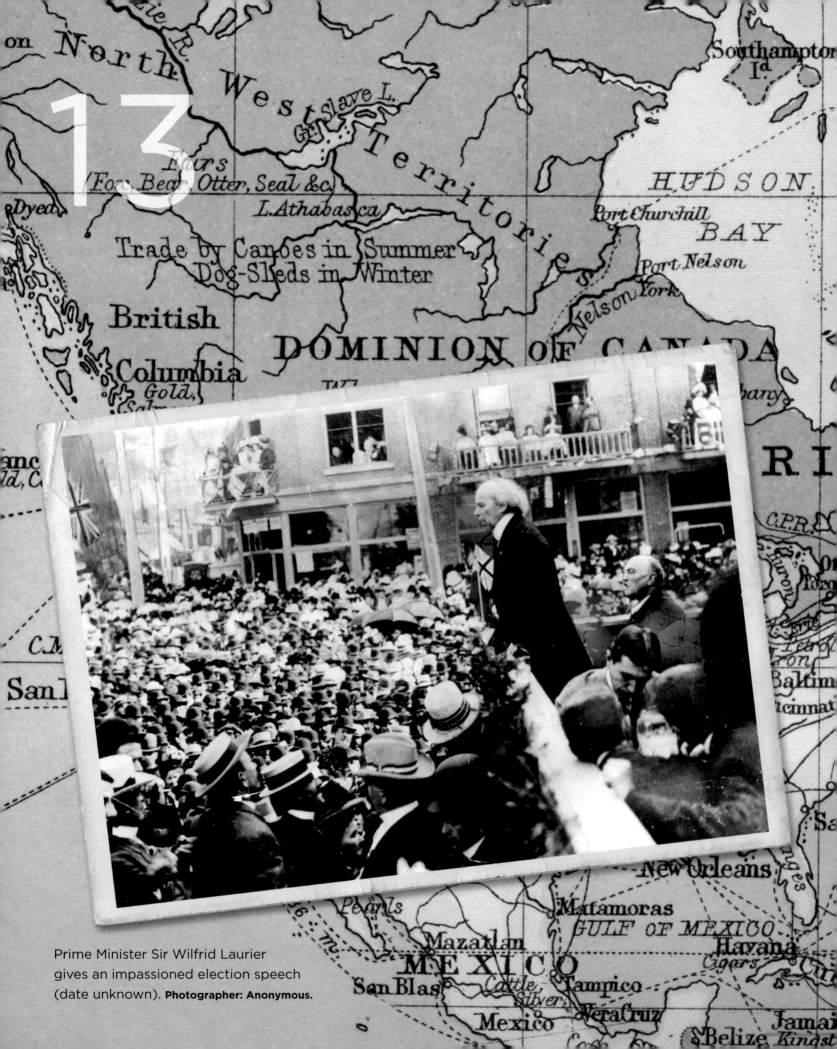

13

Prime Minister Sir Wilfrid Laurier gives an impassioned election speech (date unknown). **Photographer: Anonymous.**

Canada's Century

January 18, 1904—Laurier declares the twentieth century will belong to Canada.

CHARLOTTE GRAY

When the silver-haired, silver-tongued orator Sir Wilfrid Laurier rose to address the Canadian Club of Ottawa in 1904, Canada was still a ragtag collection of seven provinces and two territories, with a total population of less than 6 million. Saskatchewan and Alberta would not become full provinces until the following year, and it would be a further forty-five years before Newfoundland flew the Canadian flag.

The capital itself, where the country's seventh post-Confederation leader was speaking, was still hideously raw and provincial by international standards: most roads were unpaved, and piles of sawdust and lumber lined the banks of the Ottawa River. The country had no distinctive flag of its own, no official anthem, no common mythology, and no widely recognized literary, musical, or artistic culture.

Yet Laurier, Liberal prime minister of Canada since 1896, sensed the giddy optimism in the air. The country was growing by leaps and bounds: immigrants poured into the West, and the economy was booming thanks to Massey-Harris harvesters, new mining technology, a rapidly expanding web of railways, and the development of hardy, high-yield grains like Red Fife wheat. Laurier himself symbolized the country's emerging sophistication. Urbane and gracious, the first French Canadian to hold the top office since Confederation, he had nimbly navigated through challenging issues that threatened national unity. He had been knighted in London at Queen Victoria's Diamond Jubilee, and was the type of politician Canada would come to know well—a middle-of-the-road pragmatist who used patronage and personal alliances to keep his government afloat and implement his policies.

During the speech to the Canadian Club, Sir Wilfrid uttered a remark that has subsequently been reshaped into a well-loved, often-repeated aphorism: "The twentieth century belongs to Canada." A contemporary account of the evening suggests that his wording was slightly different: "Canada has been modest in its history, although its history is heroic in many ways. But its history, in my estimation, is only commencing. . . . The nineteenth century was the century of the United States. I think we can claim that it is Canada that shall fill the twentieth century."

In later speeches, the prime minister made it clear that he was talking primarily about population growth. No matter. On this and every other occasion that Laurier played with the notion of Canada's future greatness, his audience cheered wildly. All those frock-coated gentlemen (the Canadian Club did not permit women members) wanted the twentieth century to land in their laps. And it seemed as if it might. During the first decade of the twentieth century, Canada had the world's fastest-growing economy. Its vast landscape and northern regions promised untold resources and untapped potential.

Was the prophecy accurate? Immigration came to a grinding halt when war broke out in 1914, and by 2011 Canada's population was 34.5 million, not the 80 million that the *Montreal Daily Star* had predicted in 1911. Laurier did not anticipate the devastating wars and economic slowdowns of the twentieth century. But he did capture the sense that the dominion's fortunes could only improve—and he was right. By the end of the last century, Canada was among the dozen wealthiest countries per capita in the world.

Day of Rest

March 16, 1907—Lord's Day Act gives workers a break.

BEVERLEY TALLON

Workers in early Canada often endured deplorable conditions, engaging in gruelling labour for up to twelve hours a day, often seven days per week. Employed in unsanitary environments for low wages, they faced ever-present danger. Neither young children nor the elderly were spared. In 1881, for instance, coal mine general manager Richard H. Brown noted the latest death in the deeps at Sydney Mines, Nova Scotia: "Boy Bob Burchell was killed in the pit at 3 p.m. by trying to get on a trip of tubs and falling between them." For exhausted and overworked labourers, such accidents were all too common. But with a large labour pool from which employers could draw, workers did not dare complain. Thus, many considered it a great victory when the Lord's Day Act was passed in 1907.

Leading the charge for a shorter work week was the Presbyterian reverend John G. Shearer of Toronto, who founded the Moral and Social Reform Council of Canada. Religious groups believed it was immoral not to observe the Sabbath. Labour groups felt their members were being worked to death. Facing pressure from all sides, Prime Minister Sir Wilfrid Laurier's Liberal government introduced the Lord's Day Act, which Parliament passed on March 16, 1907. It prohibited sporting events, entertainment, and almost all commerce on Sundays, while leaving room for provincial governments to make certain exceptions as warranted.

For many Canadians, the law was a welcome relief. It gave the devoutly religious time to worship, and then later to enjoy a hearty Sunday dinner—prepared the day before, of course. And for more secular Canadians, the Lord's Day Act meant free time could be spent enjoying picnics or strolling in parks with loved ones.

Not everyone was pleased. Some critics called the Act elitist. Why could cars run on Sunday but not trains or streetcars? Others called it discriminatory. The Lord's Day Act was based on scripture, but many new immigrants weren't Christians. Sometimes, local authorities used the Act to harass non-Christian minorities. Then there was the unpractical side of the law. For farmers and other rural workers dependent on the weather, not working on Sundays could mean losing their crops.

The Lord's Day Act paved the way for other social benefits we now take for granted, such as the eight-hour workday, pensions, strict child-labour laws, and the right to a living wage. But the inequalities in the law eventually led to challenges. In 1962 a pair of Hamilton, Ontario, businessmen were charged under the Act for opening their bowling alley on Sundays. Owners Walter Robertson and Fred Rosetanni argued that the Act violated the freedom of religion guaranteed by the Canadian Bill of Rights. They lost. Twenty years later, the Big M Drug Mart in Calgary was charged for opening on Sundays. The case went to the Supreme Court of Canada, which ruled on April 24, 1985, in favour of the defendants on the grounds that the Act violated the 1982 Canadian Charter of Rights and Freedoms.

Today, all Canadian provinces allow Sunday shopping to some extent, and little thought is given to buying what you want when you want. Convenience is king, and a day free of commercialism is a thing of the past.

The Lord's Day Act gave families like this one a well-deserved break.

Photographer: Anonymous.

14

15

Canadians' love of Anne Shirley was renewed by the 1980s television series *Anne of Green Gables*, starring Megan Follows.
Photographer: Anonymous.

Page-turner

June 20, 1908—Canadians embrace Anne of Green Gables.

ELIZABETH WATERSTON

On June 20, 1908, Lucy Maud Montgomery received her first copy of the just-published *Anne of Green Gables*. Within months, fan letters began arriving in Prince Edward Island from all over the English-speaking world—from famous people like Mark Twain to ordinary readers who just wanted to say, "I love Anne! This book has changed my life!"

The first change Anne brought to Canada was a burst of tourism. Hundreds of readers wanted to see "Anne's Island." Crossing the border into Canada, they shifted the emphasis on mosquitoes and snow expressed by early travellers into a twentieth-century awareness of charms brought into focus through Anne's imaginative eyes: red-sand beaches, pretty gardens, haunted woods, autumn splendour. The first British edition in 1908 and the next European edition, from Sweden in 1909, brought thousands more travellers. Late in a long list, the first Japanese edition in 1952 would bring planeloads of new Anne addicts to Canada.

For Canadian women, the book came at a crucial moment. In 1908 militant suffragists, both British and American, bitterly protested the lack of opportunities for girls in education, politics, arts, and business. In Canada, Nellie McClung launched a lifetime career of feisty feminist politics with her own 1908 bestseller, *Sowing Seeds in Danny*, about an indomitable girl fighting inequity. L. M. Montgomery struck a gentler blow. In her witty tale, a girl sent "by mistake" in place of a boy proves bright and creative, and eventually becomes happily accepted and supported by her family and her community.

Anne of Green Gables wrought changes in its readers, and in Canada, that were deeper and more complex than the welcome influx of tourists or the gentle shift in attitudes toward women's rights. Six generations of readers have identified with this homely, unwelcome child. We have suffered alongside her as others underestimate her, bully her, exclude her from their friendships, or make fun of her appearance. We emerge with Anne into self-esteem; we find our own style and defend our own language.

In particular, Anne's confidence has bolstered Canadian authors, both male and female. The poet/dramatist James Reaney recalled "Cinderella days" when *Anne of Green Gables* maintained his faith in words as the best response to a hostile environment. Like earlier women writers, Margaret Atwood, Alice Munro, and Jane Urquhart still acknowledge the power of this book to stimulate and confirm their own ambitions. Since 1908 *Anne of Green Gables* has embodied Canadian peculiarities: faith in our own way of talking and acting; acceptance of our particular place in the international scheme of things; and relish of ironic humour.

Books have wrought major changes in modern views of nature, of politics, of human personality. Does *Anne of Green Gables* deserve a place on the shelf of world changers like *On the Origin of Species* or *Das Kapital*? We Canadians, in spite of our famous modesty (which Anne never shared), say half-laughingly, "Yes!"

Arctic Ambition

July 1, 1909—Canada claims the Northwest Passage.

KEN McGOOGAN

The Far North is changing. Where once great barriers of ice prevented ships from navigating a labyrinth of islands, today the Northwest Passage provides clear sailing for weeks on end. Soon, that passage will offer even oil tankers an Atlantic–Pacific route seven thousand kilometres shorter than any other, saving time, fuel, and transit fees.

That is why Arctic sovereignty matters. If the passage is an international strait, as many Europeans and Americans contend, then potentially hazardous tankers will be able to sail through with impunity. If it is considered Canadian internal waters, this country can pass laws to protect our northern environment and citizens. Canada's sovereignty claim is built on twin pillars. First is the long occupation of the Arctic Archipelago by the Inuit. Second, for those demanding a documented trail, we have the mapping, or "discovery," of the Arctic by British explorers, which began in the 1500s with Martin Frobisher and continued through the 1800s.

In 1880, as Russia and other nations became increasingly active in the North, Britain ceded its Arctic territories to Canada. But the Canadian government did not begin to confirm its jurisdiction until 1906, when it sent Joseph-Elzéar Bernier on three voyages to assert sovereignty over the Arctic Archipelago. Sailing on the *Arctic*, Bernier gathered records left by early explorers, built cairns and markers, and raised the Canadian flag throughout the Arctic. By the time he was done, he had formally annexed more than two dozen islands, including Baffin, Bylot, Beechey, and Ellesmere.

At each location, after choosing a high point visible from the water, Bernier built a rock cairn to cover and protect a metal box. Each box contained a proclamation asserting that on such-and-such a date, "the Canadian Government Steamer *Arctic* landed on this island, and planted the Canadian flag and took possession of this island and all islands adjacent to it in the name of the Dominion of Canada."

Bernier's most significant gesture came on July 1, 1909. To celebrate Canada's forty-second birthday he placed a plaque at Winter Harbour on Melville Island in the Northwest Passage, first reached from the Atlantic by William Edward Parry in 1819. On this occasion, Bernier claimed not just the surrounding islands but "all the British territory in the northern waters of the continent of America and the Arctic Ocean," reaching as far north as the North Pole. On a massive boulder called Parry's Rock, Bernier affixed a bronze plaque asserting this claim. "All our flags were flying," he wrote later, "and the day itself was all that could be desired. At dinner we drank a toast to the Dominion and the prime minister of Canada; then all assembled around Parry's Rock to witness the unveiling of a tablet placed at the rock, commemorating the annexing of the whole of the Arctic Archipelago."

The word *archipelago*, from the Greek for Aegean Sea, had already evolved to mean "any sea studded with islands"—a definition encompassing the waters around those islands. Bernier took photos to mark this historic occasion. Today, the photos constitute documentary evidence of a sovereign claim that runs unbroken from the 1500s. The meaning of July 1, 1909, is unmistakable: the Northwest Passage belongs to Canada.

16

Joseph-Elzéar Bernier claims the Arctic on
July 1, 1909, at Winter Harbour on Melville Island.
Photographer: Anonymous.

17

Smirle Lawson carries the ball for the University of Toronto in 1908. He starred in the 1909 Grey Cup.
Photographer: Anonymous.

Getting Our Kicks

December 4, 1909—The first Grey Cup game is played.

RICHARD W. POUND

Agovernor general of Canada in tune with the public's interest in sport would almost certainly have been willing to present a trophy to celebrate a dominion championship in ice hockey. But in 1909 Governor General Albert Henry George Grey, 4th Earl, was beaten to the punch by Sir H. Montagu Allan, who donated the Allan Cup to be awarded to the nation's top amateur hockey team.

Despite this setback, Grey was persuaded by Philip Dansken Ross, editor and owner of the *Ottawa Evening Journal*, to donate and lend his name to a trophy to recognize the winner of the senior amateur rugby football championship of Canada. On a cold and blustery day at Toronto's Rosedale Field, on December 4, 1909, a sparse crowd of 3,800 spectators watched the University of Toronto Varsity Blues defeat the Toronto Parkdale Canoe Club 26–6 in the inaugural match for what has become known as the Grey Cup. The match was better organized than Grey's staff, who forgot to have the forty-eight-dollar trophy made in time for the occasion, with the result that the cup was presented to the winners some three months later.

The Grey Cup, originally intended for amateur competition, has now become the trophy awarded to the champions of the Canadian Football League, composed solely of professional players. Canada's geography is highlighted by the fact that the championship game is a fiercely partisan East–West contest. And while the United States also plays football, Canada's separate identity is celebrated by devotion to "our" version of the game, with twelve players, a larger field, a required quota of Canadian players, and the increased incentive for risky and productive offences coming from only three downs.

In addition to a week-long celebration in the host city and tens of thousands of spectators in the stands, the annual Grey Cup game provides the nation's largest televised sports spectacle, with the 2009 and 2010 games each attracting well over 6 million viewers. Its importance is well recognized by Canadian politicians, who attend to be seen and who welcome the publicity that comes from presenting the cup to the winning team on national television.

Despite its current success, the Canadian Football League has had its share of problems. Major teams have withdrawn, including Montreal and Ottawa. Expansion into the United States, where it was stifled by the overwhelming presence of the American game, proved disastrous. The all-Canadian version of the league is much better suited to the national psyche. Smaller communities unable to attract major league teams in other sports can still identify with, cheer on, and aspire to Canadian football franchises. While covered stadiums now remove some of the seasonal weather risks with which Canadians are all too familiar, the Grey Cup games have had their share of adventures. The 1950 championship was dubbed the Mud Bowl, and the 1962 title match, known as the Fog Bowl, had to be continued the following day.

Little noticed at the time, December 4, 1909, also marked the founding of what would grow to be another Canadian icon, the Montreal Canadiens hockey franchise.

Bucking Stereotypes

September 2, 1912—Albertans lassoed by the first Calgary Stampede.

COLETTE DERWORIZ

For ten days every July, a transformation takes place in Calgary. Practically overnight, hay bales and wooden fences are plunked in front of office towers. Business suits and freshly polished shoes are shelved for cowboy hats and big, shiny belt buckles. Long days at the office turn into sun-drenched afternoons at the rodeo, followed by late-night drinks in a makeshift saloon.

The scene is steeped in tradition, and it started with the vision of Guy Weadick—a well-known cowboy and entertainer who performed in travelling Wild West shows in the early 1900s. On September 2, 1912, he realized his dream of celebrating the authentic culture of the Old West with the first Frontier Days and Cowboy Championship Contest, held in Calgary. Pat Burns, George Lane, A. E. Cross, and A. J. Maclean—rich cattle barons who were known as the Big Four—provided the money. Weadick returned in 1919 to create a second event, aptly named the Victory Stampede in honour of the end of the First World War.

By 1923 the two events had melded into the Calgary Exhibition and Stampede. Since then, the Stampede has been an annual event, complete with bull riding, downtown street fairs, and chuckwagon races. The show is famous worldwide and over the years has attracted many celebrities, from American politician Robert Kennedy and singer Bing Crosby to hockey hero Gordie Howe. Thanks to the "Greatest Outdoor Show on Earth," Calgary quickly became entrenched as Cowtown in the minds of most Canadians.

Although the annual salute to Western culture lasts less than two weeks, it's an image that has come to define Calgary on the world stage. The downside is that despite its rapid growth, including an influx of immigrants, the city has long struggled to escape the stereotype of a white bread, redneck town.

Modern Calgary is not simply about cowboys and rodeo. It's grown into a sophisticated, confident city—and in the fall of 2010, the rest of the country finally stood up and took notice of its new diversity. When Calgarians elected their new mayor, the winner was Naheed Nenshi—a thirty-eight-year-old Harvard-educated university professor and first-generation Canadian. The son of Tanzanian parents, he is the first visible-minority mayor of Calgary, and also the first Muslim to lead a major Canadian city. Poised and smart, Nenshi immediately took the opportunity to explain the new Calgary to anyone who would listen. He described it as a city where "any kid, regardless of their ethnicity, their income or what neighbourhood they live in, saw [his election] and went, wow, in this great country and in this great city I can be anything."

Yet Nenshi also embraced—even touted—the significance of the Calgary Stampede, which he called a "remarkably inclusive" event. He said the Stampede fosters a strong sense of community among all Calgarians, while providing the city with an opportunity to show the rest of the world that it doesn't take itself too seriously.

"I own several cowboy hats, and I think I look pretty good in them for ten days of the year," he quipped on CTV's *Power Play* in the days following his election. "But in reality, this is a reflection of what Calgary has always been."

18

Cowboys compete in the wild horse race during the 1952 Calgary Stampede.
Photographer: Harry Befus, Calgary Herald.

Nellie McClung, right, meets British suffragist Emmeline Pankhurst in Edmonton in 1916.
Photographer: McDermid Studio, Edmonton.

19

Nice Women Don't Vote

January 28, 1914—Suffragists hold mock Parliament to demand the vote.

NELLE OOSTEROM

When it comes to fighting for human rights, patiently confronting your opponent with reasonable arguments most often fails. When all civilized avenues have been exhausted, when it seems all that's left is to hit the streets and start shouting, that's when it's time to call in the clowns.

If you can't make 'em listen, make 'em laugh.

If only all rightful causes could be won in the madcap way Nellie McClung and her gang of suffragists managed to gain the vote for women in Manitoba in the early twentieth century. While suffragists in Britain at that time are remembered for setting fires, going on hunger strikes, and getting thrown in prison, their counterparts in Canada staged a clever bit of theatre.

The "Women's Parliament" of January 28, 1914, was put on by McClung, a teacher and best-selling novelist with a wicked sense of humour and a penchant for showy hats. McClung's delegation had tried, and failed, to make a dent in Manitoba premier Rodmond Roblin's staunch opposition to women's voting rights. He famously told McClung that "nice" women did not want the franchise.

He wasn't just being piggish. Like many politicians of that era, Roblin must have weighed the cost. Women would surely, in that temperance-heavy time, vote for the prohibition of alcohol. The government's lucrative liquor tax revenue would drain away.

Newspapers dismissed McClung as a pesky mosquito. But she was not the type to get slapped down; she came roaring back with a powerful sting—satire. She would stage a mock Parliament in which the roles of men and women were reversed. "Women's Parliaments" had been presented in Canada before—Winnipeg staged one in 1893, as did Toronto in 1896 and Vancouver in 1910—but none got the same kind of traction as McClung's production.

On opening night, Winnipeg's Walker Theatre was packed. Among the audience were some Opposition members of the provincial legislature. The curtain opened on a scene of the premier—played by McClung—and her all-female assembly receiving a wheelbarrow full of petitions from men asking if they could please have the vote. Premier McClung rose to speak and politely shot them down: "There is no use giving men votes. They wouldn't use them. They would let them spoil and go to waste. Then again, some men would vote too much."

The audience erupted in gales of laughter. It wasn't so much her words that brought down the house that night; it was the way McClung so cleverly mimicked Premier Roblin's arrogant mannerisms and patronizing patterns of speech. The newspapers loved it; they wrote glowing reviews and sympathetic editorials.

For the premier, McClung's public mockery marked the beginning of a downward slide in his government's popularity. He got caught up in a corruption scandal involving construction of the Manitoba legislature and was booted out of office in 1915. One of the new Liberal government's first orders of business—on January 28, 1916, exactly two years after the mock Parliament—was to extend voting rights to women. Manitoba became the first province in the country to do so.

Canada Dry

April 1, 1918—The federal government invokes prohibition.

JOEL RALPH

Dressed in their perfect white Sunday dresses, the young women of the Hillhurst Presbyterian Sunday School gathered on Kensington Street in Calgary. It was 1916, and the determined troupe was protesting the continued access to alcohol and the many social ills it caused. Decorating their wagon were two shields of justice, one bearing the words "Vote Dry," and the other "Hope." Hope for a kinder society where alcohol, and the tax it imposed on future generations through neglect, violence, and wasted spending, would be gone forever.

It was a scene repeated time and time again at the turn of the twentieth century in Canada. Since the arrival of the first Europeans, a solution to the social ills of alcohol had eluded everyone. That didn't stop governments from trying. In 1864 municipalities in the Province of Canada (modern-day Quebec and Ontario) were granted the right to ban booze. In 1878 the fledgling Dominion of Canada passed the Canada Temperance Act, which extended the same right to cities, towns, and villages across the country. In 1898 there was even a national referendum on prohibition. The anti-alcohol forces won by a slim margin, but Quebecers overwhelmingly rejected the notion of going dry. Prime Minister Sir Wilfrid Laurier—like any crafty Canadian politician—ignored the results because he feared losing votes in Quebec.

Throughout the early 1900s, prohibition remained a hot potato. Politicians bickered, deflecting responsibility to other levels of government. Ultimately, it was decided that provinces would be responsible for dispensing and selling liquor, while the federal government would have jurisdiction over its manufacture and importation.

All the while, women's groups and social gospel leaders held hundreds of events and parades to rail against the evils of alcohol. By the First World War, the government of Prime Minister Sir Robert Borden was feeling the pressure. And so, in the final year of the conflict, on April 1, 1918, Borden's Conservative government outlawed the importation of alcohol into any province where prohibition had been enacted. The effect was a general prohibition that made alcohol almost impossible to obtain—legally, at least.

For social justice advocates, it was a clear victory. But across Canada the results were less than satisfactory. Beneath the veil of prohibition, the traffic in illegal alcohol blossomed. Without the constraints of government taxes and tariffs, liquor was cheap and available without much determined searching. It also became evident that banning booze was not the panacea for society's moral morass. Alcohol use was as much a symptom of social ills as it was a cause.

It became clear to most Canadians that the experiment in prohibition was doomed. After the end of the First World War, Quebec quickly voted to end prohibition. This was followed by the establishment of government-controlled liquor boards across western Canada. Other provinces followed suit by legalizing alcohol sales and consumption. The exception was Prince Edward Island, which hung on until 1948.

Perhaps the most significant change to come out of Canada's dalliance with prohibition was governments' addiction to the revenues generated by taxes on alcohol. No government was willing to prohibit that.

20

Members of Hillhurst Presbyterian Sunday School
parade for prohibition in Calgary, circa 1916.
Photographer: Anonymous.

A Canadian soldier helps two wounded Germans
during the Battle of Passchendaele in 1917.
Photographer: Anonymous.

21

Battle Scars

November 11, 1918—The Great War ends.

TIM COOK

Combat veteran Will Bird, who had served throughout much of the Great War with a Nova Scotia Highland battalion, recounted his experiences on the last day of the war, November 11, 1918. Exhausted and hardened by ceaseless battle, his unit was hunkered down in shallow trenches, awaiting orders for the next attack. From the rear rode a British officer, high on his horse, a perfect target for enemy snipers. The cringing soldiers, mired in the muck, looked at him with concern, wondering if they would have to bury him and his horse together. But he leaned down to Bird and his mates and informed them that the war was over. The poor bloody infantry, as they called themselves, were too shocked to respond, but one cheeky Cockney soldier asked, not so innocently, "Oo's won, sir?"

That futile question seemed to sum up the Great War. Victory on the Western Front was so costly in terms of lives expended that few could distinguish victory from defeat. Allied politicians and propagandists would overplay the victory, but the 10 million dead, millions more maimed, and destruction of empires and the old order left many wondering at the cost. No wonder few cheered in the trenches on November 11.

The war's full effects on Canada would not reveal themselves for years. But the scars were plain to see. With a population of just 8 million, the country had put over 600,000 in uniform. A shocking 60,000 were killed. They were a lost generation. The financial cost of war had nearly beggared the country and would take a generation to pay off, even with the introduction of income tax. The government had intervened in the lives of Canadians in an unprecedented manner, imposing rationing and daylight saving time. Yet nothing was so traumatic as the introduction in late 1917 of conscription, which forced young men to fight against their will.

The decision pitted English against French, farmers against city folk, and labour against owners. The country had begun to unravel at the seams.

Despite the shock and loss, the war had created Canadian heroes and martyrs. Billy Bishop and his comrades ruled the skies. The Canadian Corps on the ground, led by Canadian-born Sir Arthur Currie in the last year and a half of the war, earned a fearsome reputation as elite shock troops. They had delivered victory after victory at Vimy, Hill 70, Passchendaele, and during the Hundred Days campaign. The corps' success and sacrifice had allowed Canada to step out onto the world stage.

Prime Minister Sir Robert Borden had traded heavily on the corps' success and the home front's sacrifice, and he pushed the British to renegotiate constitutional status for the dominions. Canada received international recognition at the Treaty of Versailles, which marked the end of the war, with its own signature on the document, separate from Britain's. Canada also received a position in the League of Nations.

More intangibly, but perhaps more importantly, Canadians saw themselves as something different. The nation had stepped up and made terrible sacrifices. It had held its own. It had earned the right to guide its own destiny. There were many legacies from the Great War, and perhaps one certainty: however the war was viewed—as a senseless slaughter or as a war of independence—Canada was forever changed.

Bloody Saturday

June 21, 1919—Mounties charge into crowds during the Winnipeg Strike.

NOLAN REILLY

Bright sunshine welcomed the thousands of working men and women gathering at Winnipeg's city hall on this fateful Saturday morning. It was June 21, 1919, and the crowd was there to witness the Great War Veterans' Association's silent parade in support of imprisoned strike leaders.

It had been six weeks since a general strike had paralyzed the city. The atmosphere on the streets was filled with anticipation but little anxiety. Children even accompanied their parents to view the march. But the events that would unfold over the next few hours at the corner of Portage and Main proved to be a dark moment in Canada's history. When it was over, two men would be dead of gunshot wounds at the hands of police, and many more citizens would be injured after Royal North West Mounted Police—reinforced by hundreds of untrained special police and militia—attacked the crowds and sent them fleeing back to the safety of their working-class neighbourhoods.

"Bloody Saturday," and the general strike of which it was part, affected Canadians for years to come. In its aftermath, strike leaders were tried and convicted in a juridical process of questionable legitimacy. Equally disturbing for the future was the federal government's adoption of legislation to deport strike leaders before bringing them to trial. This Act to Amend the Immigration Act passed with remarkable haste through the House of Commons and the Senate, and for the first time provided for the deportation of British citizens back to England. The government ultimately decided not to use its new powers against British subjects for fear of a backlash, but other nationals would be deported for years to come with little review. The 1914 War Measures Act—still in place in 1919—also provided legal justification for suspending civil liberties during the Winnipeg strike; it would be used again in peace time by the Trudeau government in 1970 during the FLQ crisis. And new legislation curtailing civil liberties since the 9/11 attacks in 2001—enacted with little informed public debate—further circumscribed the rights of Canadians.

Another disturbing outcome of Bloody Saturday was the willingness of government to use coercion—via the police or the military—against its own citizens. The federal government also expanded its national security services, which then used the "Red scare" of the Winnipeg Strike to delegitimize all but the mainstream political ideologies. Many Canadians would suffer the consequences of such practices well beyond the Second World War.

Workers, on the other hand, won few immediate gains from the confrontation in Winnipeg. Hundreds lost their jobs and many more returned to anti-union shops with deplorable working conditions. But the idea of industrial unionism was now entrenched. After the Second World War, when workers did win significant advances, they built all-inclusive industrial unions, like those found in the auto sector. The memory of Bloody Saturday and the government's hostile attitude to labour led workers to opt for direct representation in government. They formed new, labour-oriented social democratic, socialist, and communist political parties, some of which continue to influence the direction of Canadian politics to this day.

While the union recognition, higher wages, and better working and living conditions that workers sought in 1919 did not come until later, the historical antecedents of these victories are found in Bloody Saturday and other labour confrontations following the First World War.

Police on horseback charge down Main Street on Bloody Saturday during the Winnipeg Strike of 1919.
Photographer: Lewis Benjamin Foote.

22

23

Dr. Frederick Banting, right, and Dr. Charles Best experimented with dogs to produce insulin.
Photographer: Anonymous.

Beating Diabetes

March 22, 1922—Canadians learn of the discovery of insulin.

MICHAEL BLISS

It was only a preliminary report, with the dry title "Pancreatic Extracts in the Treatment of Diabetes," but journalists knew there was a sensational story behind the article in the *Canadian Medical Association Journal* issue mailed to subscribers on March 22, 1922.

"Toronto Doctors on Track of Diabetes Cure" was the headline in that day's *Toronto Star*. "Have They Robbed Diabetes of Its Terror?" asked a caption for pictures of four researchers at the University of Toronto involved in an epic scientific adventure. The team of Frederick Banting, Charles Best, John J. R. Macleod, and James Bertram Collip had managed to produce extracts from animal pancreases that, when injected into human beings with diabetes, erased symptoms of the disease.

"We have a therapeutic measure of unquestionable value," they quietly but triumphantly stated. In their next paper they named their substance "insulin."

At the time, they had treated only seven humans on the diabetes ward of Toronto General Hospital, following many months of work with dogs. But the positive results were so startling—especially on the first case, fourteen-year-old "L.T." (Leonard Thompson)—that the researchers were under tremendous pressure to rush their findings into print. They were under immense pressure to do everything, especially to produce more insulin so they could treat more patients.

What the world did not know was that the research team had buckled under the strain. In January, on the very night of the first successful trial of insulin on the teenager, Banting and Collip had come to blows about credit for the breakthrough, beginning one of the bitterest disputes in the history of medical discovery. A few weeks later Collip, who had first discovered how to make insulin pure enough to use on humans, lost the knack of making any effective batches of the miracle extract. All through March there was no insulin available in Toronto, and the members of the discovery group were barely civil to one another as they worked day and night to rediscover the substance. Banting later wrote that he drank himself to sleep every night that month with alcohol he stole from the lab.

Fortunately—and with more than a little help from the American drug firm Eli Lilly and Company—the Toronto scientists were able to work through their problems. By the summer of 1922, they were achieving astonishing results, restoring emaciated, dying, and sometimes comatose diabetic children to life with insulin. In little more than another year, Banting and Macleod were awarded Canada's first Nobel Prize (they shared the money with Best and Collip).

The four discoverers of insulin never liked one another; more often than not they had behaved like rival hockey players. But their achievement revolutionized the treatment of diabetes and demonstrated to the world, and to future generations, the power of medical research to improve the human condition. As one of the little patients first treated in Toronto exclaimed to her mother, the coming of insulin was "unspeakably wonderful."

He Shoots . . . He Scores!

March 22, 1923—Foster Hewitt calls his first hockey game.

RICHARD W. POUND

The unacknowledged national religion in Canada is ice hockey. No sport seems able to generate national passion on a scale that approaches it. No sporting heroes compare with Canada's hockey greats. If Canada had won only two medals during the 2010 Olympic Winter Games in Vancouver, but they were the two gold medals in hockey, most Canadians would have thought, on the whole, that they were successful Games.

Hockey was not always a national phenomenon, though, despite its popularity across the country. If you were a spectator, you could feel the passion, but if not . . . Newspapers and still photography did not have the emotional power to spread the religion. They were static media and always reached their audiences after the fact. Even great sportswriters could only try to recreate the excitement of a lightning-fast and physical contest. Radio suffered from the same deficiency, as announcers described scores of games already finished and provided commentary that may have informed but certainly did not excite listeners.

All of this changed dramatically in 1923. The *Toronto Daily Star* decided to start its own radio station, CFCA. Meanwhile, a young University of Toronto student, Foster William Hewitt, had left university and a part-time job with a company that manufactured radios to become a sports reporter. When the opportunity arose to broadcast amateur hockey games play by play, Hewitt jumped at the chance.

Little did he know that his first broadcast on CFCA would lead to a career calling NHL games—or that his broadcasts would enhance the emotional involvement of Canadians in their national sport. Early concern on the part of team owners that radio broadcasts might reduce seat sales proved to be wildly misplaced.

Hewitt's fame grew when, in 1952, *Hockey Night in Canada* began airing on televisions across the country. Hewitt was behind the microphone for the historic first English television broadcast, on November 1, 1952, and he remained the voice of *Hockey Night in Canada* for four decades. His weekly Saturday night broadcasts—from his self-designed gondola in Maple Leaf Gardens—began with the formula "Hello, Canada, and hockey fans in the United States and Newfoundland." This was shortened in 1949, when Newfoundland joined Canada.

Like most successful sports broadcasters, Hewitt had a distinctive voice and expressions, the most famous of which was "He shoots . . . He scores!" Hewitt was also a shameless Toronto Maple Leafs fan; during one broadcast, in describing a rush by the opposing team, he blurted out a variation on his normal formula: "He shoots . . . Oh shit, he scored."

Hewitt retired from television in 1963 and returned to broadcasting on radio. However, in 1972 he was urged out of retirement to broadcast the Summit Series between Canada and the Soviet Union. Hockey fans of that generation, who will always remember where they were when the final goal was scored, will acknowledge that there was no one better suited than Foster Hewitt to make the timeless call: "Henderson has scored for Canada!"

24

Foster Hewitt, who coined "He shoots . . . He scores," calls a hockey game in the 1940s.

Photographer: Michael Burns.

Unemployed men eat at a Montreal soup kitchen in 1931.
Photographer: Anonymous.

25

Downturn

October 29, 1929—Canada suffers through the Great Depression.

JOE MARTIN

On October 29, 1929, the Montreal Stock Exchange, then the leading Canadian exchange, crashed, setting spectacular records. Sixty-two stocks plummeted to new lows. The Toronto *Globe* called it a "tidal wave of liquidation . . . which sent prices crashing downward in the greatest collapse ever witnessed in Canada." Meanwhile, in Ottawa, Prime Minister William Lyon Mackenzie King was assuring the nation that "economic conditions were never better."

While the stock market crash was more important than acknowledged by the prime minister, Canada's per capita gross domestic product had begun declining a year earlier and continued to do so until 1933. Full recovery was not achieved until 1940. Over that time the Great Depression became, by far, the worst economic period in Canadian history. This country suffered more in terms of depth and severity than any other developed nation.

Few Canadians were untouched. Hard-working individuals who had been employed all their working years suddenly found themselves out of work and forced into the ignominy of applying for relief. Many who were fortunate enough to keep their jobs did so at much lower wages. All industries were hit. Agriculture, especially wheat farming on the Prairies, was devastated, declining by nearly 75 percent; manufacturing dropped by more than half. The result was disaster for automakers as people started hanging on to their cars rather than trading them in every two or three years.

Politically, Canada entered a new era. While Nazism and Fascism did not take root, communism did enjoy niche popularity. The hard-hit Prairies turned to socialism in the form of the CCF and Social Credit, while Quebecers found solace in the Union Nationale. Canadians looked more to the federal government for assistance than to private charities or even local and provincial governments. The fact was that their treasuries were bare as well. Many local governments were put into trusteeship. Some provinces renegotiated interest payments on their debt, and Alberta actually defaulted.

Throughout the 1930s the federal government ran a deficit as revenues declined and expenditures increased. Unemployment and farm relief quickly accounted for over 20 percent of the total budget. The Bank of Canada was created, originally as a financial adviser to government, but in the longer term as a decider of monetary policy. Based on the recommendations of the Rowell-Sirois Commission, unemployment insurance—a forerunner of many other social programs—was introduced, as well as equalization payments among the provinces. In trade policy both the United States and Canada realized the folly of protectionism and began the move to freer trade on a global basis.

This was the major long-term change resulting from the Great Depression: the intrusion of government into everyday life to a level that would have startled John Maynard Keynes. But one thing does not change—collective amnesia. As a consequence, each new downturn is compared to the Great Depression, even though none has been even close in terms of severity or length. Indeed, a 2011 Statistics Canada report confirmed that the so-called Great Recession of 2008–2009 was "less severe than the two previous ones, which started in 1990 and 1981."

PART TWO

FINDING OUR WAY

1930–1963

People must know the past to understand the present and to face the future.

—NELLIE McCLUNG, 1935

As Canada entered the 1930s, it still bore the battle scars of the First World War. We had wrung nationhood from the bloody muck of Vimy, Passchendaele, and Arras. But a people can't lose an entire generation of its young men and remain whole.

The promise of a postwar jobs bonanza had proven false. Now, as the Great Depression mired economies throughout the world, despair muted optimism and we became increasingly turned in on ourselves.

We built cenotaphs and memorials throughout the country to exalt our noble dead. We didn't realize that the "war to end all wars" was just a prelude. In 1939 Canada joined England and France in the battle against Germany. It was our first independent declaration of war. That Canadians even had a choice in the matter was a direct result of sacrifices we made in the First World War.

During the Second World War, Canadian troops fought in Hong Kong and in Italy, on the beaches of Normandy, and in the flooded polders of Holland. The Battle of the Atlantic was won primarily because of the dogged perseverance of Canadian navy and merchant navy crews. The air war was fuelled by Canada's role as the main training centre for Allied air crews.

With thousands of men away fighting, women headed to the fields and factories to produce the goods and armaments necessary to defeat the Axis powers, and saved every scrap at home as they adjusted to rationing.

When war finally ended in 1945, we were all a bit shell-shocked. Millions had died worldwide, and many cities had been pulverized. Out of these horrors came a new sense of moral and social responsibility. We began to repeal the bigoted laws that prevented non-Europeans from migrating to Canada. We also began to strengthen the fabric of our fragile social safety net. We didn't know it at the time, but Canada was taking its first tentative steps toward becoming a modern, multicultural nation.

The postwar period was a challenging time for women. After tasting economic freedom, they were expected to return to their old lives and traditional roles in society. Most did, but many with regret; the struggle for equality with men would be continued by future generations.

By the 1950s the economy was revving, but Canadian culture seemed stuck in second gear. To the rest of the world, we were Americans with funny accents. Hooked on U.S. radio, television, and movies, Canada increasingly seemed like a satellite nation orbiting planet America. Something had to be done to protect and promote our artists, writers, and musicians.

At the same time, we launched a series of megaprojects—such as the Trans-Canada Highway, the St. Lawrence Seaway, and the TransCanada Pipeline—intended to bind us tighter as a country.

With the 1960s on the horizon, our centennial was fast approaching. Many expected it would be Canada's turn to shine.

—Mark Reid

26

PABLUM

NET WEIGHT 1 LB.

PRE-COOKED

MEAD JOHNSON & CO.

Packed with nutrients, Pablum became a staple for children following its invention in 1930.

Photographer: Lucien Aigner.

Oh, Baby!

September 12, 1930—Toronto scientists invent Pablum.

CHARLOTTE GRAY

In the 1920s one in six Canadian children never reached a fifth birthday. Major causes of this appalling mortality rate were that babies either were not getting enough to eat or were eating food that was contaminated or lacked the calories and nutrients they needed. In many households, youngsters were fed cereal and biscuits from which all the bran and germ had been removed because whole grain cereal was difficult for a baby to digest. The overprocessed mush lacked minerals such as iron, copper, and calcium, as well as the essential vitamins A, B1, B2, D, and E.

At Toronto's Hospital for Sick Children, known as SickKids, a team of scientists decided to focus all its efforts on producing the perfect infant food. The team was led by Dr. Frederick Tisdall—appointed director of the hospital's Nutritional Research Laboratories in 1929—and Dr. Theodore Drake. They began to experiment with different mixtures, and tested them on groups of children in the hospital and in orphanages. They were looking for a product that contained the essential vitamins and nutrients, did not cause constipation or diarrhea, would keep indefinitely, and could be mixed with milk and spoon-fed to babies.

The breakthrough came in 1930, when Tisdall announced that his team had successfully produced a flaky grey powder, consisting of wheatmeal, oatmeal, cornmeal, wheat germ, bone meal, brewer's yeast, and alfalfa. The mixture had been ground up and then thoroughly dried at a high temperature for thirty minutes. This process, noted Tisdall, "reduces the moisture and destroys the insect eggs which are present in all grains." He named his invention—perfected on September 12, 1930—Pablum, from *pabulum*, Latin for "food."

Tisdall was an entrepreneurial publicity genius as well as a scientist, and he was determined to bring Pablum to a mass market. He persuaded SickKids to take out a patent and then grant the U.S. pharmaceutical company Mead Johnson the exclusive right to manufacture and market this new miracle baby food for twenty-five years. In return, the hospital received a royalty on every box sold.

The pharmaceutical company made a killing, but the payoff for SickKids—and Canadian families—was considerable. Pablum royalties financed a research bonanza at the Toronto hospital, turning it into the internationally respected research institution that we know today.

Most gratifying for the SickKids team was the steady drop in child mortality figures across North America. The reduction in children's deaths became startlingly evident with the end of the Second World War, when the boys came marching home and the birth rate jumped. By 1959 three babies were being born for every two born twenty years earlier, and thanks to Pablum almost all of them saw their fifth birthday. Together with an increase in immigration, this baby boom meant that the population of Canada exploded—from 10 million when Tisdall invented Pablum to 18 million in 1960. The name of the cereal soon became synonymous with the way we characterize the fifties today: colourless, tasteless, and bland. But Pablum helped make Canada one of the healthiest countries in the world.

Unmasked

April 19, 1938—Grey Owl's hoax is exposed.

TINA LOO

"'Grey Owl' Was Not a Red Indian—He Was a Sussex Man!" shouted the *Evening Argus* in Brighton, England, on April 19, 1938. Six days after his death from pneumonia, the newspaper had confirmed the rumours swirling around the identity of the world's most famous conservationist: Grey Owl was a fraud.

But then something remarkable happened. There were no yelps of betrayal or shouts of condemnation, no cynical editorials that delighted in cutting the celebrated down to size. Instead, the *Winnipeg Tribune* led its exposé with the headline "Fun to Be Fooled," taking pleasure in "the suggestion that the national leg has been well and truly pulled." As Archie Belaney (his true identity), Grey Owl wouldn't have been effective in spreading the gospel of conservation, the newspaper argued. The fact was people didn't listen to "simple truths except when uttered by exotic personalities." Others agreed. The blue-eyed Indian from Hastings, England, might have been a fake, but his ideas rang true.

The reaction spoke in part to the times. In a world darkened by the Great Depression and the looming shadow of war, Grey Owl was a beacon of hope. People were drawn to his message about living in harmony with nature and diverted by the antics of his rodent retainers. Just as he had once guided tourists on wilderness canoe trips through northern Ontario, Grey Owl led his readers to a new world, one in which people approached nature with humility rather than arrogance. "Remember that you belong to nature," he said, "not it to you."

It was a simple message, and effective. His second book, *Pilgrims of the Wild*, sold five thousand copies a month following its publication in 1935. His children's story, *The Adventures of Sajo and Her Beaver People*, sold equally well and helped him draw audiences of over a half a million people on one extended tour. At the peak of his influence, Grey Owl earned $30,000 a year—an incredible sum given the economic times.

The world needed Grey Owl. That was why those who knew his true identity while he was alive chose not to unmask him, and it was why few criticized him after his death. There were no awkward questions about his drinking, the women he'd married—five, and not always serially—or the children he'd abandoned. Just as Belaney had escaped the unhappiness of his childhood by playing Indian, so too did the Canadian, American, and British public play along with him, escaping the disquieting times they lived in.

The revelations about his identity didn't end that need. If anything, it was intensified: all 100,000 copies of *The Green Leaf: A Tribute to Grey Owl* disappeared within two days of its release, and over the years his writings have seen multiple printings. Belaney conjured up Grey Owl because he worried that his message would only be as effective as the messenger. Little did he know that the words he had Grey Owl speak would have a life of their own, long after his illusion had been shattered.

Grey Owl feeds a baby beaver at Prince Albert National Park, circa 1936.
Photographer: Anonymous.

27

John Grierson, left, chairman of the Wartime Information Board, and Ralph Foster, NFB head of graphics, in 1944.

Photographer: Ronny Jaques

Moving Pictures

May 2, 1939—The National Film Board is born.

JIM BURANT

Canadians of a certain generation no doubt remember that first time—perhaps a drowsy spring day as they daydreamed at their school desks—when their teacher lowered the blinds, fumbled with the looping of a reel into a projector, and then flicked the switch to start a film. Maybe it was *Neighbours*, Norman McLaren's extraordinary take on how conflicts arise, or perhaps it was about current events—the Canada Carries On series or *Royal Journey*, about Princess Elizabeth's 1951 Canadian tour. If it was a film being shown to students about Canada, it was invariably a National Film Board production.

In many ways NFB productions are the cinematic ties that bind us as a nation. The National Film Act was passed on May 2, 1939, creating what was soon to be known as the National Film Board of Canada. Its mission was "to make and distribute films across the country that were designed to help Canadians everywhere in Canada understand the problems and way of life of Canadians in other parts of the country."

For seventy years, the NFB has fulfilled this mission with huge success, having by 2010 generated more than thirteen thousand productions in a wide range of formats, from live-action full-length movies to animated shorts, in multiple languages, and for both domestic and foreign audiences. In the process, it has garnered no fewer than five thousand major awards, including twelve Academy Awards; has pioneered the development of cinematic technologies, including pixillation and IMAX; and has nurtured younger Canadian filmmakers. Its Studio D, founded in 1974, provided opportunities to women filmmakers to develop in what had been a largely male-dominated field. The NFB has also encouraged filmmakers from disadvantaged, Aboriginal, and minority communities.

In the process the NFB has also changed from an almost propagandist organization during the Second World War into one that has openly criticized the faults and failings of Canadians and has initiated national debates about Canadian society. During the Quiet Revolution and the rise of separatism, some of its films were censored or banned; and veterans and politicians alike were vehement in their outrage over such productions as *Billy Bishop Goes to War* and *The Valour and the Horror*. In examining poverty, sexuality, injustice, and racism, the NFB has often made Canadians uncomfortable about themselves and their attitudes, and on more than one occasion has come close to being dismantled completely.

Perhaps we don't all think about the value of the NFB this way. Our memories revolve instead around the humour (and the anti–Maple Leafs message) of *The Hockey Sweater* and the animated misadventures of *The Cat Came Back*. We remember the experience of *Labyrinth* at Expo 67 and recall the melancholy, searing exploration of small-town Quebec in *Mon Oncle Antoine*. The NFB has left no part of the Canadian experience unexplored—a tremendous achievement for what is, after all, a government agency.

No Safe Port

June 9, 1939—Canada turns away ship carrying Jewish refugees.

IRVING ABELLA

On May 15, 1939, 907 desperate Jews were pushed onto a luxury liner, the *St. Louis*, in Hamburg, Germany. They had been robbed of all their possessions, hounded out of their homes and occupations, and now thrown out of their country by Nazi officials. All they had left was the entrance visa to Cuba each carried on board.

They considered themselves fortunate; they were getting out of a country that had declared war on its Jews. When they arrived in Havana, however, their luck ran out. The Cuban government refused to allow them to disembark. Negotiations with the government failed, and even a threat of mass suicide left officials unmoved. The *St. Louis* was ordered out of Cuban waters. International refugee organizations launched a frantic search for a haven for the ship's passengers. Within two days all the countries of Latin America said no. The United States did not even bother to reply to pleas from the ship's captain; it simply sent out a gunboat to shadow the *St. Louis* and prevent it from getting too close to American shores.

Only Canada remained. It was the refugees' last hope for rescue. Unfortunately, in the 1930s Canada had closed its doors to the hunted Jews of Europe. It had the worst record of any Western democracy in allowing in Jewish refugees fleeing the Third Reich. Nevertheless, some Canadians hoped the tragic plight of the *St. Louis* would strike a spark of humanity and generosity among the closed-minded bureaucrats and politicians who controlled the country's immigration policy.

On June 7, 1939, a prominent group of Canadians sent a telegram to Prime Minister William Lyon Mackenzie King imploring him to allow the *St. Louis* to dock in Canada. King was not moved. The *St. Louis*, he said, was "not a Canadian problem." His director of immigration was even more blunt. "No country," said Frederick Blair, "can open its doors wide enough to take in the hundreds of thousands of Jewish people who want to leave Europe. The line must be drawn somewhere." The passengers' last flickering hopes extinguished, on June 9 the *St. Louis* headed back to Europe, where many on board would die in the ovens and gas chambers of the Third Reich.

This incident has become the symbol of Canada's rejectionist policy during the 1930s and 1940s. It was a different Canada then—a country permeated with racism, xenophobia, and anti-Semitism. But following the end of the war and the arrival of millions of immigrants, a new Canada emerged—generous, open, humane, and diverse. And perhaps the shameful turning away of the *St. Louis* played a role in that transformation. In 1980, when Canada decided to accept thousands of boat people escaping the horrors of Vietnam, the minister of immigration stated that the lesson of the *St. Louis* inspired him to aggressively push his cabinet colleagues to open Canada's gates.

Today there is a memorial to the passengers of the *St. Louis* at Pier 21 in Halifax—ironically, the spot the boat would have docked had it been allowed to land. The monument was dedicated seventy-one years later by a Canadian government determined to make amends, and to remind coming generations of Canadians how far this country has come since those dark days.

29

Passengers of the *St. Louis* are denied
entry into Canada in 1939.
Photographer: Anonymous.

30

Norman Bethune operates on a patient in China, circa 1938–1939.
Photographer: Anonymous.

Medicine Man

November 12, 1939—Norman Bethune dies in China.

ADRIENNE CLARKSON

The day that Norman Bethune died—November 12, 1939, in a wretched northern Chinese village—changed the Canadian psyche forever. His death created in our collective unconscious the knowledge that one person could deeply influence the currents of history.

Born in Gravenhurst, Ontario, Bethune was lauded a month after his death by none other than Mao Zedong, leader of the most successful communist revolution in the world. The Chinese leader called him "a man of moral integrity and above vulgar interests," "a man who is a value to the people" and an example of "absolute selflessness." With Bethune's death, he passed not simply into celebrity or fame but into the blazing glory of one man affecting humanity through his actions.

Bethune served as a stretcher-bearer in the First World War, and then trained as a doctor upon his return to Canada. In 1936 he volunteered in the Spanish Civil War, where he invented the world's first mobile blood transfusion unit. In 1938 he offered his services to the Chinese communist forces who were trying to repel a Japanese invasion. Bethune gave what he could of himself—his inventiveness, his technical skills, his beliefs. While in China he cared not only for the Eighth Route Army of Mao but also for some of the 13 million people among whom he travelled in northwestern China.

Despite his now-mythic status, we should remember that Bethune had human longings and needs, dreaming of friends and good times, of coffee, of rare roast beef, apple pie, and ice cream—what he called in letters home "mirages of heavenly food." During his time in China's war-wracked countryside, he wondered if books were still being written and music being played, what clean sheets on a soft bed felt like, and whether "women still loved to be loved."

When surgical gloves ran out, he operated without them. While exploring a wound with bare hands, Bethune cut himself on a shard of bone. It took less than two weeks for septicemia to spread through his system. He died of blood poisoning.

But he would not have changed what he did for anything in the world. He had written to friends, "I am tired, but I don't think I've been so happy for a long time. I am content. I am doing what I want to do." About the Chinese he said, "I love these people and they love me." How many people can go to the end of their lives—especially such a tumultuous, successful, contradictory, and short life—and say the same? To all that is cautious, comfortable, and prudent in the Canadian character, Bethune can seem an affront. But I prefer to think of him as a challenge—a national challenge to live up to the highest ideals, to adapt to new ways of thinking, and always to keep moving, physically and spiritually.

That he is remembered now by a billion and a half Chinese, as well as by Canadians, shows that we have come to realize the astonishing vitality of his international understanding, his profound demonstration of compassion, and his defiant need to change the world to a better place.

Women Warriors

July 2, 1941—Canadian women join the fight.

NELLE OOSTEROM

For many Canadians during the Second World War, the sight of a female soldier was just about as much of a shock as the war itself. What had civilization come to, with uniformed women taking on male roles—driving trucks, operating radios, rescuing people from the rubble of bombed-out buildings? Even if she was just filling in as a clerk, a woman in the military, other than as a nurse, was an affront to the natural order of things by her mere presence.

It didn't seem to matter that across the pond, women in the beleaguered mother country had from the outset of the war been thrown into manly roles. Even Princess Elizabeth did her part as a Jeep mechanic for the British Army's Auxiliary Territorial Service.

It's not that Canadian women were reluctant to serve. The outbreak of war in September 1939 prompted dozens of unofficial women's corps to spring up across the country. On their own time and expense, women got into shape and learned Morse code, first aid, map reading, arms drills, and other skills. Joan Kennedy, the organizer of the British Columbia Women's Service Corps, lobbied hard to get these eager volunteers into the military.

Meanwhile, thousands of women were by necessity taking over the civilian jobs of men at factories, farms, and offices. Yet the military establishment seemed unconvinced of their fitness for service.

What finally did convince them was desperation—there simply weren't enough men to fill all the jobs in Canada's rapidly expanding armed services. Thus it was that the Canadian Women's Auxiliary Air Force was formed on July 2, 1941, followed quickly by the Canadian Women's Army Corps on August 13, 1941, and the Women's Royal Canadian Naval Service on July 31, 1942.

These early services often caused administrative headaches until they were fully integrated into the regular armed forces. However, the women proved their worth, earning the respect and admiration of their male colleagues. The services were modelled on the regular armed forces, and members were given rank and status. Combat was not an option. CWAC servicewomen, for instance, could train in one of fifty-five *non-combat* roles. Their collar badges proudly bore the robust image of Athena, Greek goddess of war and wisdom. Joan Kennedy became a lieutenant colonel.

Yet traditional attitudes died hard. In 1943 the number of female army recruits dropped sharply. Alarmed, Ottawa hired a polling firm to find out why. Turned out many Canadians viewed female soldiers as "loose women" with low moral standards. Pictures of them smoking cigarettes probably didn't help.

By war's end, about fifty thousand women had served in the Canadian military. The women's divisions were all disbanded in 1946—time for them to go home and do their part for the baby boom.

Their experiences had transformed them, paving the way for a new generation of women to take their place, not only in the military but in every sector of society. As Vancouver-born Rosemond Mildred Greer of the naval service observed, "I have always thought it was the beginning of Women's Lib. . . . We had all changed."

Canadian Women's Army Corps members on a break from a firefighting drill in London, England, in 1943.
Photographer: Captain Frank Royal.

31

32

A Japanese Canadian family relocated to an
internment camp in interior B.C., circa 1942.
Photographer: Anonymous.

Disgraceful Deed

February 26, 1942—People of "Japanese race" are expelled from coastal B.C.

DESMOND MORTON

People of many races developed Canada, but many Canadians long refused to consider that all were equal. In British Columbia, for instance, Asian immigrants were as hard working and law abiding as their neighbours, and given a chance, just as successful. And yet white British Columbians in the early twentieth century feared and resented them. They forgot that in 1914, a Japanese battleship had protected their coast from a German battle squadron. At the time, Japanese Canadians joined Canada's army—but they had to travel to Alberta to enlist. No B.C. unit would accept them.

In 1941 approximately twenty-two thousand people of Japanese origin lived in British Columbia. All but six thousand were Canadian-born or naturalized. On December 7 of that year, Japan attacked Pearl Harbor, a U.S. naval base in Hawaii. Fearing a Japanese invasion, Ottawa ordered the seizure of all Japanese-owned fishing boats and created a hundred-mile-wide protected zone along the coast. Next, Ottawa expelled six thousand non-Canadian Japanese subjects from the zone, forcing them to forfeit any property they could not carry.

That was not enough for most British Columbians. Editors, politicians, and citizens raised a chorus of outrage. The University of British Columbia expelled Japanese Canadian students. Ian Mackenzie, a B.C. federal minister, warned of race riots. Meanwhile, news media bulged with reports of Japanese military successes across the Pacific. Finally, Ottawa moved. On February 26, 1942, an order-in-council created the B.C. Security Commission (BCSC) to expel all people of the "Japanese race" from the protected zone.

It took almost a year to remove them.

Where could up to twenty-two thousand men, women, and children of all ages be put? The BCSC decided to reopen the shabby ghost towns of the Interior that had been abandoned by gold seekers almost a century before. In the meantime, thousands of Japanese Canadians were crammed into the stinking cow barns at Vancouver's Hastings Park. Their homes, farms, and business—even their cars—were left to fall to bits and be vandalized until they could be sold off at deeply depreciated value.

When the war ended in August 1945, no one in Canada wanted the Japanese. Alberta had accepted thousands to harvest its sugar beets, but only on the condition that none would stay. Some Japanese Canadians had gone east to work and study. Provincial ministers there announced that they were not welcome to stay. Ottawa's response? It would force Japanese Canadians to move to starving, war-devastated Japan. Civil libertarians and a handful of friends of the Japanese carried protests to the Canadian Supreme Court and even to the Empire's highest court, but their appeals failed. Vengeful racism trumped human rights.

Gradually, Canadian opinion shifted against a policy that looked more and more like what the Nazis had done to minority races in Europe. When Canada adopted its own citizenship in 1947, critics pointed to the injustice done to naturalized and Canadian-born Japanese Canadians. Forced expulsions ended later that year. Japanese Canadians regained their rights and even gained the right to vote. In 1983 the new Charter of Rights and Freedoms promised all Canadians the protection Japanese Canadians had lacked in 1942. On September 22, 1988, Ottawa formally apologized and offered $21,000 per person in compensation to the surviving among those who had lost everything to racism and panic.

D-Day

June 6, 1944—Canadian soldiers storm Juno Beach.

JOEL RALPH

Nearly seventy years later, D-Day still resonates with Canadians as the most significant battle of the Second World War. The stoic images of Canadian soldiers hunkered down in landing craft, awaiting the fateful moment they would step onto the sands of Normandy, have become etched in our memory of the Good War.

The victory at Normandy on June 6, 1944, has taken an iconic place in books, film, and television. One of the greatest and most anticipated military operations of the war, the amphibious assault—involving more than 156,000 men, supported by more than 11,500 aircraft and 6,900 ships—allowed the Allies to finally secure a foothold in Europe. Canadian heroics at Juno Beach have come to dominate how we remember the Second World War, much in the same way that the Battle of Vimy Ridge has eclipsed other achievements of the First World War. Yet Canadian troops fighting in other theatres at the time had mixed feelings about the operation.

While boosted by the victory, some soldiers found it hard not to feel that D-Day had stolen all the limelight. In Italy, for instance, Canadians saw heavy action during six months of battle, culminating in the capture of Rome. This was largely forgotten when the Allies landed at Normandy two days later. For the rest of the Italian campaign, Canadians would sing the bitterly sarcastic ballad of the "D-Day Dodgers": "When we return we hope you'll say, 'You did your little bit, though far away. All of the D-Day Dodgers, way out there in Italy.'"

Other events of the Second World War—the disasters at Dieppe and Hong Kong; the ambiguity of the bomber campaign against German cities; the unheralded role Canadians played clearing the channel ports, fighting through the hellfire of the Scheldt estuary in Holland; and even the three months of heavy fighting that followed D-Day in Normandy—have all been overshadowed by a single day of fighting that claimed 340 of Canada's almost 45,000 war dead.

Why does D-Day resonate so strongly? It was the ultimate turning point—the pivotal day in the story of a war fought to stamp out Nazism and the evil it represented. With the Soviets advancing steadily in Eastern Europe, success on D-Day meant a secure and democratic Europe was still possible. Given the stark contrasts of success and failure, democracy versus a future of oppression, the Normandy invasion has become the archetype of the "just and true" battle. It proved to the Allied nations that their collective military strength and material wealth could defend democracy anywhere it was threatened.

It's also the story of sacrifice in the face of overwhelming danger. Scenes of soldiers stepping out of their landing craft, only to fall in a storm of bullets or drown in chest-deep water under the weight of their own backpacks, have become seared in our collective memory. Driven, unselfish, and unstoppable: it's how we want to remember our soldiers rather than the bloody killing that preceded or followed this critical day. And in a century scarred by senseless bloodshed, we hold up D-Day as a moment of crystal clarity, a moment of right and wrong, when life or death and victory or defeat hung in the balance.

33

Infantrymen of the Royal Winnipeg Rifles cross the English Channel on D-Day.
Photographer: Anonymous.

Tommy Douglas gives a speech in 1965.
His CCF election victory in Saskatchewan
in 1944 surprised many.
Photographer: Boris Spremo.

34

Left Turn

June 15, 1944—Socialists sweep to power in Saskatchewan.

MARGARET CONRAD

On June 15, 1944, the Co-operative Commonwealth Federation, known as the CCF, swept into office in Saskatchewan. The election launched the first socialist government in North America, and it made some people nervous.

Canada's prime minister, William Lyon Mackenzie King, was one of them. In his diary he admitted that he was not surprised by the outcome of the election. Saskatchewan and other provinces with Liberal administrations, he noted, had been slow to grasp the depth of reform sentiment nurtured by the Great Depression and wartime hardships. King was more astute than most premiers. On the day of the Saskatchewan election, his cabinet had put the finishing touches on its plans for family allowances and generous benefits for veterans. Even the Conservative Party had shed its right-wing image in 1942, adopting the name "Progressive Conservative" and choosing John Bracken, the Liberal-Progressive premier of Manitoba, as its leader. Times were changing.

In electing a socialist government, Saskatchewan voters had nothing to lose. The dust bowl of the 1930s and the collapse of the wheat economy had brought the province to its knees and turned people to new political parties. Among them was the upstart CCF, whose manifesto, adopted at the party's first national convention in Regina in 1933, demanded a "full programme of socialized planning, which will lead to the establishment in Canada of the Co-operative Commonwealth."

While the CCF's platform offered a compelling vision to the electorate, the party's major asset was its leader. Tommy Douglas brought social gospel socialism to Saskatchewan, a pragmatic approach to social reform that won widespread approval. Born in Scotland in 1904 and raised a Baptist in a working-class family,

he moved with his family to Winnipeg in 1910. He witnessed the 1919 general strike, entered the printing trades, and then studied theology at Brandon College. Called to a pulpit at Weyburn, Saskatchewan, he was soon involved in politics and won a seat for the CCF in the 1935 federal election. A compelling orator, he was admired even by his political enemies, who were many. For most of his political career he was on the watch list of the RCMP.

Saskatchewan was not alone in seeking a more equitable society as the Second World War came to an end, but the little province that could led the way. During its first sixteen months, the overworked cabinet introduced 192 bills, transforming social welfare, labour relations, education, human rights, and public services. The achievements were all the more impressive because they were accompanied by balanced budgets, a tribute to a highly efficient civil service that blossomed in the context of comprehensive state planning.

Saskatchewan's CCF government had an impact well beyond the voters who kept it in office for two decades. In 1947 the province pioneered universal, state-sponsored hospital insurance and, in 1962, introduced universal medical care. With proof of concept in place, Ottawa introduced similar legislation. Even the CCF defeat in 1964 had an impact outside the province. As its former civil servants, known fondly as the "Saskatchewan mafia," fanned across the country, they helped Premier Louis Robichaud in New Brunswick to modernize his province and found plenty to do in Ottawa, where state planning for a better society was now a fact of political life.

Crisis Averted

November 22, 1944—Mackenzie King opts for conscription.

J.L. GRANATSTEIN

Canada's soldiers suffered heavy casualties in the second half of 1944 in Normandy, clearing the Scheldt estuary, and breaking the Gothic Line in northern Italy. Infantry units operated at half strength or less, their platoons frequently reduced to a dozen soldiers instead of the normal thirty. And, the soldiers grumbled, there were thousands of "zombies," or home defence conscripts, safe in Canada.

For Prime Minister William Lyon Mackenzie King this was a huge political problem. The war seemed to be almost over, and Canada had avoided imposing conscription for overseas service. Now, his defence minister, Colonel J. Layton Ralston, wanted to send the home defence men overseas to reinforce the front lines. The Quebec ministers and the French-language press bitterly, stubbornly resisted any such move. King certainly didn't want a repeat of the conscription crisis of 1917–1918, which saw rioting in the streets of Quebec. But Ralston, just back from an overseas visit, insisted that the men had to be sent now.

What could King do to avoid a great rift in the nation with victory almost assured? Moving with speed and brutality, he fired Ralston on November 1, astonishing his cabinet and the country, and named General Andrew McNaughton in his place. Ralston had just a year earlier forced McNaughton out of command of the First Canadian Army. The general had his revenge, and as an anti-conscriptionist, he seemed the ideal man to find volunteers for the front.

The difficulty was that only the home defence conscripts were trained and available. McNaughton made his appeals, telling the soldiers that their countrymen at the front needed them. A few stepped forward, but many argued that if the government had to reinforce the army overseas, all it needed to do was tell them to go. Order us. Stop begging.

McNaughton soon began to realize that he could not find the men, and by now his generals, especially on the West Coast, were telling him so. Some were even violating orders and speaking to the newspapers. King's cabinet was on the verge of splitting apart under the strain. Then, on November 22, McNaughton called on King with news that hit like a blow to the stomach: "The headquarters staff here had all advised him that the voluntary system would not get the men." Always a confident man, McNaughton was shaken to his core.

But King saw his moment. He recalled that in June 1942, he had told Parliament that his government would act if conscription became necessary. "Not necessarily conscription, but conscription if necessary," he had stated. "Now whatever the causes," he said in his diary, "whatever the errors, conscription was necessary and the Minister of National Defence said it was."

The prime minister had turned 180 degrees, and although one Quebec minister resigned, King persuaded the rest of his cabinet to stay together and to order sixteen thousand conscripts overseas. French Canada raged, but all in Quebec could grudgingly acknowledge that King had fought against conscription as long as he could. Bobbing and weaving, King survived, Canada remained relatively united, and the war overseas soon ended victoriously. In June, King's government even won re-election. Conscription had been effectively managed.

35

Students of the Université de Montréal
protest against conscription in 1939.
Photographer: Anonymous.

Toronto residents flood Bay Street to celebrate VE Day in 1945.
Photographer: John H. Boyd.

36

VE Day

May 8, 1945—Canadians celebrate victory in Europe.

TIM COOK

Across the country Canadians flooded the streets on May 8, 1945, when it was announced that the war in Europe was over. In Halifax there was a riot worthy of a Stanley Cup victory. The celebrations everywhere were wild, with booze imbibed, kisses given freely, and six years of tension released in the party to end all parties. Hitler was dead and his planned Thousand Year Reich lay in ruins after thirteen murderous years. Canadians had bled for the victory but had emerged a powerful middle power. The country had a hard-hitting army and air force, and the fourth-largest navy in the world. Canadians had stood shoulder to shoulder with Americans, Britons, and other Allies. We had earned our laurels.

Back in the summer of 1939, as war loomed, most Canadians had prayed that peace would prevail in Europe. The prayers went unanswered. When Germany invaded Poland in September 1939 and France and Britain went to war, Canada had to decide if it would fight. No one wanted another conflict, especially after the slaughter of the Great War. And even if Canada wanted to stand by Britain, how could it? The nation was crippled financially by the Great Depression and unable to field any modern military forces. But Britain was threatened, and Hitler and his odious henchmen had to be stopped. And so the nation limped into the Second World War.

The Canadian war effort was led by the unwarlike William Lyon Mackenzie King. While the prime minister paled in comparison to British prime minister Winston Churchill and American president Franklin Roosevelt, he led the country forward, doing his best to balance political interests at home with the demands of waging war overseas. He faced many challenges, the most pressing being the constant calls for conscription.

During the Great War, the issue had divided the country along linguistic lines and also set region against region. Canada could not avoid a repeat of the crisis in the Second World War, but thanks to King's adept stickhandling, conscription, which eventually could not be avoided, was less divisive and damaging to unity this time round.

One of Canada's greatest contributions was to the air war. The dominion became the "aerodrome of democracy"—so labelled by Roosevelt—training more than 130,000 aircrew in the British Commonwealth Air Training Plan. The enormous program brought young men from across the Commonwealth to Canada, where they were trained to fly and to crew fighters and bombers, and then sent them to fight the Axis powers in the skies over Europe or other theatres of war.

Canadians fought on the oceans, in the air, and in multiple land campaigns. On the home front they raised millions by buying Victory Bonds, women entered the workforce, and industries produced thousands of ships, fighter planes, tanks, and trucks.

VE Day was not the end of the Second World War. There was still Japan to be defeated. By the time the conflict ended, Canada had suffered at least 45,000 dead and almost 55,000 wounded. Canada had helped win the war, but at a high cost. We also won the peace. Veterans came back and built up the country. Canada emerged from the Second World War as an acknowledged power with a strong voice on the world stage. Amid the sadness and loss, there was much to celebrate.

The Baby Bonus

July 1, 1945—Canadian women receive a family allowance.

DESMOND MORTON

In 1911 the census asked Canadians how much they earned. If poverty meant earning too little to pay for necessities—food, clothing, shelter, and fuel—then most Canadians were poor. They were still poor when asked the same question in 1921, 1931, and 1941. Canada's infant death rate was the worst of all the predominantly white dominions. In 1951, however, most families claimed enough income to support themselves. By 1961 only 15 percent of Canadians could still be called poor.

What happened? During the labour shortages of 1939–1945, mass firings and layoffs were rare. Unions forced up wage levels, even for the unorganized. In post-war Canada, unemployment was usually short-lived until the late 1950s. The biggest factor was a federal family allowance of five to eight dollars, paid for each child under sixteen. Social scientists had long argued that big families turned a living wage into starvation pay. Feminists had claimed that poverty would vanish once mothers had an income. First issued on July 1, 1945, family allowances helped turn most Canadians into the affluent people we now see in the mirror. Except in Quebec, the allowance went directly to mothers to meet the cost of children's shoes, clothing, and food.

Attacking poverty was not new. Britain and democratic socialist governments in Europe had tackled it between the world wars. During the Depression, Canadian academics debated how poverty could be beaten, but they usually concluded that hard times made change impossible. War in 1939 hardly helped. Ottawa needed billions in tax dollars to keep a million servicemen and -women in uniform and half as many again working to supply them. Who could worry about the poor?

Still, the Dirty Thirties left many Canadians bitterly aware of poverty, the privileges of the rich, and the invasiveness of welfare policies that permitted social workers to explore any beneficiary's private life. On August 4, 1943, Ontario voters made the socialist Co-operative Commonwealth Federation their official opposition. In British Columbia, it was already the alternative. That year, a national poll put the CCF ahead of the governing Liberals. In June 1944 the CCF won power in Saskatchewan. Ottawa awoke with a start. Voters must be appeased.

McGill social scientist Leonard Marsh had persuaded many Canadians that poverty was linked to family size. But why would a boss pay more to a worker with six children than a worker with only two? Marsh advocated a government-sponsored allowance for each school-age child. Others disagreed. Charlotte Whitton, Canada's best-known social worker, raged that "baby bonuses" wasted tax dollars unless social workers could pick deserving beneficiaries. Though a 1919 Australian study had dismissed her notion, she insisted that only by forcing employers to pay more would poverty end.

Marsh persuaded the ruling Liberals. Dr. Herbert Bruce, a Conservative MP, sneered that Marsh's plan was really a bribe to Roman Catholics and Quebecers with big families. In the end, all parties backed the Family Allowance Act in 1944. In June 1945 the Liberals were narrowly re-elected. Family Allowance cheques were mailed on July 1, 1945, to a million Canadian families on behalf of 3 million children. The cost was about $200 million a year—what Ottawa had typically spent on its war effort every two weeks.

The baby bonus especially helped large families—
like the Nagles of Toronto, shown circa 1938.

Photographer: Anonymous.

38

British war bride Elizabeth Rae and her daughter, Anne, en route to Canada in 1946.
Photographer: Arthur Cole.

For Love

February 9, 1946—Canada welcomes the war brides.

BEVERLEY TALLON

My mother always insisted that she was *not* a war bride. Although she fell in love with a tall, good-looking Canadian soldier during the Second World War, she didn't marry him until 1947, after she had already moved to Canada. By definition, though, the war brides of the Second World War are the young women—an estimated forty-eight thousand in total—who arrived in Canada from 1942 to 1948 and married Canadian servicemen. Most of them were from Great Britain, with a few thousand from the Netherlands, France, Belgium, Germany, Italy, Denmark, and other countries.

They came over on converted ocean liners like the grandly named *Queen Mary*, the *Aquitania*, and the *Letitia*. The first designated war-bride ship was the RMS *Mauretania*, which left Liverpool, England, on February 5, 1946, and arrived in Canada four days later. Most war brides docked at Pier 21 in Halifax, and many took long train rides across this vast country to their new homes. Many endured seasickness and homesickness and were travelling with young children—some 21,950 "war babies."

For many, the journey was a happy one: they made new friends en route and enjoyed previously rationed food. "There was delicious white bread instead of the horrible grey stuff we had during the war, and fresh fruit too!" said one war bride. Most received a joyous welcome from their husbands and their new families. But for some war brides things were not as they had envisioned, and as the government only paid travel fares one way, they could not always afford to get back home.

Most brides chose to stay, and although they found things difficult at times, Canada became their home. Some found themselves living in rural areas, with outhouses and no running water or electricity. But the frigid winters, the bug-ridden summers, the social stigma of being a war bride all paled when compared to the love these women felt for the men for whom they had waited.

I've always thought my mother—and the many others who gave up their friends, family, and country—was very brave. I don't know if many of us could do that. Times were different then. During the war years, life was characterized by both immediacy and uncertainty. Would these women ever see their loved ones again? Would the world as they knew it remain the same? It was against this backdrop of living on the edge, and this need for connection, that the grand love story of the war brides was written.

A good friend of my mother's was a war bride. I once asked her why she gave up everything she knew in England to come here. Obviously, she loved the Canadian soldier she had married in 1946; she remained married to him until his death, fifty-seven years later. But was love enough? "We were young and in love—wartime put things in a different perspective. And," she added, "it was a great adventure."

Colour Blind

April 18, 1946—Jackie Robinson breaks the colour barrier.

PETER MANSBRIDGE

The most significant game in Canadian baseball history wasn't even played in Canada. It was played in Jersey City, New Jersey. Fifty thousand people were in the stadium, built to hold just twenty-five thousand. And they were all there to see one man, Jack Roosevelt Robinson, the first black man in professional baseball.

He was a member of the Montreal Royals of the International League, assigned to the team by the parent organization, the Brooklyn Dodgers. It was a daring experiment by Branch Rickey, the Dodgers' president and general manager: signing a black man to a baseball contract outside the Negro leagues, expecting white men to play with him, and expecting white fans to tolerate him. A lot of smart people thought the experiment was doomed. The Royals' manager—the *Royals'* manager—asked Rickey if he believed blacks were actually human.

It was no accident that Rickey sent Robinson to Canada. He knew there was much less prejudice against blacks here than in the United States. As Rachel Robinson, Jackie's wife, remembered, "In so many ways it was the perfect place for Jackie to get his start. We never had a threatening or unpleasant experience there." This certainly wasn't true in other International League cities. In places like Syracuse, Buffalo, and Baltimore, just a few hundred kilometres away, Robinson would become the target of almost unimaginable insult and abuse. Fans sometimes stormed the field to protest his presence.

In the days leading to the first game, everyone understood the stakes. No athlete had ever faced more scrutiny. But Robinson responded with a game for the ages. A home run. Three singles. Two stolen bases. Four runs batted in. Four runs scored. Most of the crowd cheered him. Montreal won easily, 14–1. Robinson later reflected that his first game was crucial. "We all sensed that history was in the making, that the long ban against Negro players was about to come crashing down, setting up reverberations that would echo across a continent, and perhaps around the world."

It's clear that baseball history changed that day. And Robinson's acceptance in the great American pastime became an important milestone in the fight for black equality in the United States as a whole. But how did Canada change on that cold spring day on April 18, 1946? It began with the uniform Robinson was wearing. It had one word across the front—Montreal. It was a bold statement that told the world, and told us too, that we were different. Canada was a place where a black man could be accepted into the community and treated with decency and dignity.

It was really the beginning of change, the possibility of change, that erupted that day. Many Canadians no doubt enjoyed the praise coming from enlightened parts of the United States about how our society was more accepting, more tolerant, more human. And no doubt some Canadians saw for the first time that this open attitude was the right attitude. But change doesn't happen all at once. Just a few months after Jackie Robinson's debut Viola Desmond, a black woman in Nova Scotia, was thrown out of a movie theatre and arrested for insisting on her right to sit on the main floor of the theatre, not in the balcony.

DODGERS
CLUB HOUSE

KEEP OUT

39

Jackie Robinson enters the Brooklyn Dodgers'
clubhouse for the first time, circa 1947.
Photographer: C. W. Greene.

40

Chinese refugees arrive in Vancouver in the 1960s.
Photographer: Anonymous.

Equal Measure

May 14, 1947—The Chinese Exclusion Act is axed.

CHRISTOPHER MOORE

"All human beings are born free and equal in dignity and rights," begins the Universal Declaration of Human Rights, conceived in 1945 in response to the horrors of the recent world war and the Holocaust. In November 1946, a group of Canadians inspired by this new vision of human equality came together to advocate for rights causes in Canada. As their first step, they formed the Committee for the Repeal of the Chinese Immigration Act.

The CRCIA's target was a law the Parliament of Canada had enacted in 1923, more often called the Chinese Exclusion Act. From 1885 until 1923 Chinese people could enter Canada by paying an expensive head tax—and each year a few had managed to pay this humiliating price of entry. The 1923 Act that replaced the head tax was blunt: "No person of Chinese origin or descent . . . shall be permitted to enter or land in Canada." The 1923 Act had been very effective in keeping almost all Chinese people out of Canada, even those seeking to join families already here. But how could Canada endorse the Universal Declaration, or criticize other countries' human rights failures, when it enforced a law that judged people solely by their ethnic origin? The Act was becoming a shame and an embarrassment to Canada. In alliance with Chinese Canadian organizations, the CRCIA demanded its abolition.

The CRCIA attracted a broad membership and opened branches across the country. Members included leaders of major religious denominations, editors of leading publications, labour leaders, lawyers, and scholars. S. K. Ngai, a prominent Toronto surgeon, and Kew Dock Yip, the first Chinese Canadian to become a lawyer, were committee members, as were Kew's old law school classmate Irving Himel, of the new Association for Civil Liberties, and the crusading journalist Margaret Gould. They soon found that many Canadians supported the new ideal of human rights and equality before the law. The committee, one of the first Canadian human rights groups of the postwar era, had caught the tide of public opinion.

Prime Minister William Lyon Mackenzie King was still concerned about public opinion in British Columbia, where fears of being "overrun" by Asiatic masses had always been strong. Nevertheless he agreed the exclusion of Chinese from Canada had been a mistake. On May 1, 1947, King told Parliament that the Chinese Immigration Act would be repealed. Just two weeks later, on May 14, the formal exclusion of all Chinese people from Canada was ended. In less than six months, the CRCIA had seen its goal achieved.

Was this a great triumph for human rights? Not entirely. In the next twenty years, Canada continued to pick which countries it preferred as sources of immigrants, and fewer than 2,500 Chinese reached Canada annually. Only in the 1960s did Canada abandon discriminatory preferences and launch the great multicultural immigration that has transformed the country in recent decades. But ending Chinese exclusion was not a failure either. Canada would never again preserve such explicitly racist legislation on its books. Canadian activists for civil liberties and human rights had learned that with organization and dedication, they could achieve real victories.

Crossing the Line

May 6, 1949—The Riot Act is invoked during the Asbestos strike.

JACQUES LACOURSIÈRE

In 1948 asbestos mining was a key industry in Quebec, employing more than five thousand people. Many were represented by the National Federation of Mining Industry Employees, a subsidiary of the Canadian and Catholic Confederation of Labour, which is now the Confédération des syndicats nationaux.

In mid-January 1949, negotiations for a new contract broke off. The Johns-Manville company, which was operating one of the mines near the town of Asbestos, Quebec, rejected the two thousand workers' demands for a wage increase of fifteen cents an hour. The workers had also asked for an increase of five cents per hour for night work, two weeks of paid vacation per year, paid leave for Catholic holidays, and other benefits. The company offered them only a 5 percent increase, and nothing more.

On Sunday, February 13, the decision to go on strike was made. Johns-Manville hired scabs to keep the mines open. Calling it an illegal strike, the company demanded that the workers return to work so negotiations could resume. The Quebec labour minister threatened to withdraw the union's certification if the strike went on.

The first confrontation took place on February 18, when the determined strikers showed up at the company's offices to collect their paycheques. Company officials responded by calling the municipal police. Moreover, a judge granted their injunction against picketing. Quebec's attorney general and premier, Maurice Duplessis, quickly ordered more than a hundred provincial police officers to be sent to Asbestos to protect the company's property and staff. On February 21, Asbestos city council protested against the presence of provincial police.

Violence quickly escalated. A dynamite explosion destroyed a section of the company's railroad track in the neighbouring town of Danville. The Royal Canadian Mounted Police were brought in to investigate. As the strike continued, some strikers began to experience financial distress. A few members of the Catholic clergy organized a donation drive in their parishes: in addition to money, trucks carrying food and clothes were sent to Asbestos.

The Asbestos strike had symbolic significance. It was debated in the House of Commons. There were articles about it in the foreign press. Duplessis sent police reinforcements, which led to acts of police brutality and increasing arrests.

On May 6 a judge read the Riot Act: gatherings of two or more people were strictly forbidden. The company threatened to close down the mine if the workers pursued their wage demands. The conflict dragged on. There was pressure on both company officials and union leaders. Even the archbishop of the diocese of Quebec, Maurice Roy, intervened.

The strike finally ended on July 1, 1949. The faith that average Quebecers had held in their provincial government was shaken badly. Looking back, many today view the Asbestos strike as an early sign of what would later be called the Quiet Revolution.

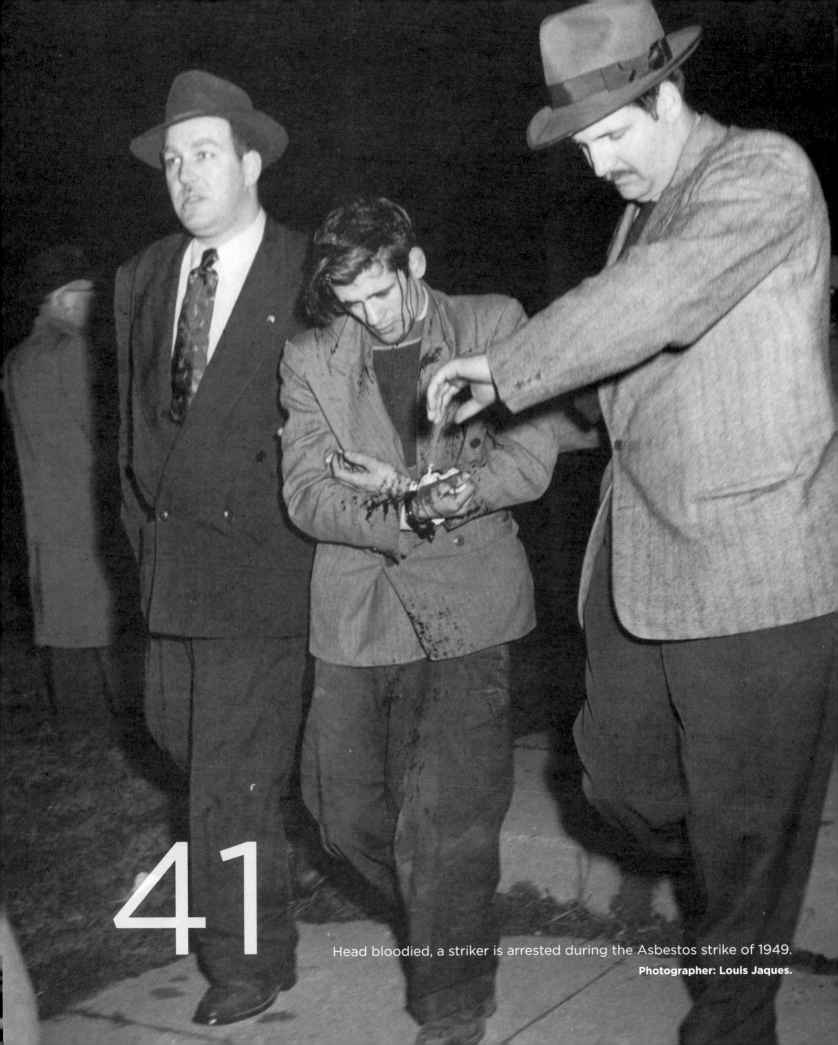

41

Head bloodied, a striker is arrested during the Asbestos strike of 1949.

Photographer: Louis Jaques.

42

A police officer on patrol during the
Winnipeg flood of 1950.
Photographer: Anonymous.

Duff's Ditch

April 15, 1950—After the great flood, Winnipeg digs in.

JOE MARTIN

The city of Winnipeg is situated at the bottom of an ancient glacial lake. Much of the lake floor is almost perfectly level. As a consequence, the modern Red River Valley is very flat.

On April 15, 1950, the Red River overflowed its banks, creating a flood of historic proportions. Dikes gave way and much of the city, as well as 410,000 acres of southern Manitoba farmland, was submerged, resulting in millions of dollars in damage. The flooding forced as many as 100,000 people to flee their homes. It remained the largest evacuation in Canadian history until the Mississauga train derailment in 1979.

In spite of a heavy snow in the winter of 1949 and heavy rains in the spring of 1950, the city was ill prepared for the huge swell of water. By mid-May nearly 20 percent of Winnipeg was under water. Thousands of volunteers worked day and night to build dikes and fill and stack sandbags. Meanwhile, Canadians everywhere pledged gifts of money, manpower, and material. All party leaders in the House of Commons promised financial assistance. And Winnipeg survived.

In the flood's wake there was some discussion of permanent federal legislation to deal with national emergencies, but no immediate action was taken. In 1958 Duff Roblin became premier of Manitoba, and he made it his goal to build a floodway around Winnipeg to divert excess river water. But there was an enormous cost attached: $63 million (nearly $500 million in current dollars) would be required to construct the floodway, a holding dam, and a diversion channel on the Assiniboine River.

By late 1961 the cost-sharing formula was finalized, and work began in 1962. It was a gigantic undertaking—the largest excavation project in Canadian history. At forty-seven kilometres long, nine metres deep, and sixty metres wide, the Winnipeg floodway necessitated moving more earth than for the Canadian section of the St. Lawrence Seaway and slightly more than for the Suez Canal. The Manitoba government paid its share out of current revenues to avoid incurring interest.

Not everyone backed the project. Critics in both the legislature and the provincial business community called it "Roblin's Folly" and compared its utility to that of the Egyptian pyramids. But they were wrong. Since its completion in 1968, the floodway has been used many times to keep Winnipeg high and dry, including during the 1997 "flood of the century," which exceeded the 1950 flood by 50 percent and rendered thirty-five thousand unprotected Americans homeless in North Dakota.

Over time, Roblin's Folly has become affectionately known as Duff's Ditch. At a 1998 conference on natural disasters, the Winnipeg floodway was cited as a cost-effective means of mitigating damages. It has been designated a National Historic Site and called an outstanding example of Canadian engineering and technology, as well as a symbol of humankind's struggle to find accommodation with nature.

A note of poignant interest: on the day that Roblin died—May 30, 2010—the floodway gates once more had to be opened to accommodate flood waters. Duff's Ditch had saved the day again.

Canada's Renaissance

June 1, 1951—The Massey Commission tables its report on Canadian culture.

PHIL KOCH

Postwar Canada felt a sense of accomplishment and even the stirrings of a new national identity with greater independence from Britain. After helping the country survive the Depression, and following the successful war effort, the federal government was ready to enter new areas such as social security—but it was hesitant to be seen as interfering with provincial responsibilities like education and culture.

A number of factors combined to overcome that reticence. It was clear that the country's cultural scene needed help: many Canadian artists were forced to go abroad to earn a living, and only a handful of novels were published each year. At the same time, U.S. mass media and commercial entertainments were seen as threatening our own culture and sovereignty, particularly for English-speaking Canadians. More pressing for the government, universities faced a dire financial situation, while there were many questions concerning broadcasting regulation and new technologies such as television. Canada also had obligations related to UNESCO and the cosmopolitan cultural exchanges that were expected to counter the newest totalitarian threat, communism.

In April 1949, Prime Minister Louis St. Laurent put all this and more in the hands of the five-member Royal Commission on National Development in the Arts, Letters and Sciences, more commonly known as the Massey Commission, after its chairman Vincent Massey. The commission travelled the country, holding 114 public hearings, receiving 462 formal submissions, and hearing from more than 1,200 witnesses before tabling its weighty report in the House of Commons on June 1, 1951. While there is disagreement regarding its ultimate benefit, there is almost universal recognition that the report had a major impact. It has been described

as "comprehensive," "effective," and "compelling," and it was certainly broad in scope. Its 146 recommendations included more federal support for the National Film Board, a new national library and museums, the preservation of historic monuments, the promotion of Canadian culture abroad, and much more.

The government responded quickly in the areas of broadcasting policy, including support for the CBC, and aid to universities. But other major recommendations were enacted more slowly. The commission's most recognized achievement is the establishment in 1957 of what became the Canada Council for the Arts.

Outside the Quebec government of Maurice Duplessis, there were few complaints about federal intrusions into areas of provincial jurisdiction. The fact that funding came in the form of arm's-length grants not only eased provincial concerns, it also suited a particular vision of culture—as producing both national identity and informed, responsible citizens—that in the Cold War era was opposed to totalitarian propagandizing and state control of culture.

On the report's fiftieth anniversary in 2001, two opposing assessments appeared only a month apart. Peter Herndorff claimed that, "without question, Vincent Massey and his colleagues provided the cultural framework that led to the emergence of several generations of gifted, innovative, and fiercely independent Canadian artists," while Robert Fulford argued that the report "framed support of the arts in essentially political terms, and we have been burdened by those terms ever since."

Despite its broad reach, the Massey Commission's report in fact rejected political interference in favour of stable support for outstanding Canadian work in media, scholarship, and the arts.

43

Celia Franca of the National Ballet in 1956. The Massey Report urged
Canadians to support arts groups.

Photographer: Ken Bell.

44

Len Johnson, left, and Jim Dalrymple marooned atop a car in North York.
Photographer: Anonymous.

Toronto the Devastated

October 15, 1954—Hurricane Hazel hammers Ontario's capital.

JAMES GIFFORD

The forecast for Toronto on Friday, October 15, 1954, read "rain tonight," and many in the city were rocked to sleep that evening by the howling winds that tore at the eaves and the heavy rain that pounded on their windows. But others, finding themselves stranded by rising floodwaters, will never forget the night that Hazel came to town.

Hurricane Hazel was an unlikely weather event for Toronto, a city that sees little extreme weather. After tearing north through the eastern United States, the storm shot over Lake Ontario, with Toronto directly in its path. The winds had calmed from hurricane strength, but the rain overwhelmed waterways across the city, more than twenty centimetres in only twenty-four hours, causing the worst flooding in two hundred years. Ken Gibbs, who delivered furniture for Eaton's, was stranded. "I saw the creek at Islington Avenue and Dundas Street overflow into a used car lot and lift the automobiles like little blocks of wood and send them crashing into each other." The Humber River, which snakes through the west end, was fuelled by water surging south from an overrun earthen dam in Woodbridge. Houses were torn from their foundations. A stretch of Raymore Drive in Weston, along the Humber, was wiped away when a swing bridge tore loose and funnelled the river right into the tidy row of bungalows. Dave Phillips, on his way home from a date, watched in horror. "The homes were literally lifted off their foundations and swept away. You could hear the people screaming. Many of them were standing on their roofs. In many cases the screaming just stopped; the homes just disintegrated, and that was the end of it."

The *Toronto Telegram* photo opposite shows two teens, Len Johnson and Jim Dalrymple, straddling a 1954 Ford Fordor sedan. Their expressions reflect the feelings of many young people; that they were undertaking a grand adventure. Some Boy Scouts had spent Friday night polishing apples for the next day's Apple Day while the wind howled outside. In the days after, they found themselves conscripted to search for bodies.

For the families of the eighty-one people who lost their lives, the storm was a catastrophe. More than four thousand people lost their homes, and many were forced to live in trailers well into the following year. A Royal Commission estimated the immediate damage from the storm to be in excess of $25 million (up to $100 million when considering the long-term impact)—more than $1 billion in today's dollars.

Some good came in Hazel's wake. The city and the province of Ontario formed the Metropolitan Toronto and Region Conservation Authority to assess the damage and to make recommendations for avoiding future disasters. The MTRCA expropriated land along major waterways, where people had lived for over a century, cleared off the houses, and built dams and reservoirs. The site of so much carnage has now become 26,000 acres of lush parkland. Despite the tremendous loss of life and property, Toronto can thank the storm for making the city a better place to live, a city that is much more prepared for the next storm of the century.

Keeping the Peace

November 7, 1956—Canada helps invent peacekeeping.

BOB RAE

Canada's rise as a middle power and influential diplomatic player is best symbolized by a historic vote at the UN General Assembly on November 7, 1956. On that day the United Nations decided to create an emergency force to supervise the withdrawal of Israeli, British, and French troops from Egyptian territory, and to ensure a ceasefire agreement that would last for eleven years. UNEF, as the force was called, soon became known as "the blue berets"—soldiers working under the flag not of their own country but of the United Nations. Peacekeeping was born.

The Canadian front and centre on this day in New York was Lester Pearson, Canada's secretary of state for external affairs. His personal contribution received due recognition when he was awarded the Nobel Peace Prize the following December, the first and only Canadian to be honoured in this way.

Gamal Abdel Nasser's decision as Egyptian president to nationalize the Suez Canal electrified his people with its boldness. British prime minister Anthony Eden considered it an echo of Hitler's steady grab for territory in the 1930s and a direct threat to British interests. The French saw these parallels as well. The country was also concerned about what this nationalism would mean to neighbouring Algeria and other colonies. Israel, a fledgling country whose very existence Nasser saw as an affront to Arab pride and sovereignty, was alarmed for its own reasons. At a series of secret meetings, long denied but now well confirmed, Israel and the two European powers agreed to engineer an attack by Israel on Egypt, to which the British and French would respond by sending in troops to "protect" the canal.

The outbreak of violence on October 29, 1956, was met with shock and opposition around the world. Taken by surprise, the Americans were furious at both the lack of consultation and the ham-fisted nature of the operation. British and European public opinion was quickly mobilized against the attacks, and Eden in particular faced criticism for an exercise that was seen more as colonial bungling than as a courageous stand against dictatorship. What had seemed to the Israelis, the French, and the British to be a brilliant manoeuvre turned overnight into a dramatic political challenge.

Widely respected in Washington and London, Pearson was equally well known in the corridors of the United Nations. He had been elected president of the General Assembly in 1952. His breezy and avuncular style, which belied his acute intelligence, made him well liked among delegates. Pearson shrewdly saw a peacekeeping force as accomplishing two objectives—building the credibility of the United Nations and getting the Suez invaders off the hook. But he also had to persuade the Egyptians to allow foreign troops on their soil, something Nasser only reluctantly allowed under two conditions: it had to be done under the UN flag, with UN uniforms and command, and with Egyptian permission that could be removed unilaterally by him.

And so the baby was born, the subject of many compromises and drafts, imperfect, but still a proud moment for Pearson and for Canada. When the General Assembly passed the resolution that established the UN Emergency Force, the delegates surrounded the Canadian desk in the forum, offering congratulations to Pearson and his team. Canada had been at the centre of the action—constructive, engaged, effective. It was a good day.

45

United Nations Emergency Force members
on patrol during Suez Crisis of 1956.
Photographer: Anonymous.

Elvis Presley rocks
Maple Leaf Gardens
in Toronto in 1957.
Photographer: Leo Harrison.

46

All Shook Up

April 2, 1957—Elvis Presley rocks Canada.

MARK REID

His hips were weapons of mass distraction, his pompadour something to adore. And that voice! Silky and seductive, with just enough edge to set young knees aquiver—at least, as much as knees were permitted to quiver in the strict societal code that ruled the 1950s.

Teenagers everywhere, including those in Canada, were captivated by Elvis Aaron Presley as he rose from obscure rockabilly singer to become the King of Rock and Roll. But parents hated his morals-eroding music, vastly preferring Frank Sinatra's whimsical musings on love to Elvis's "All Shook Up."

His appearance on *The Ed Sullivan Show* in 1956 was one of the most watched events in television history—both in the United States and in Canada. By 1957 Elvis had performed more than three hundred concerts in the United States. At each, his pelvic gyrations had set American fans spinning. North of the border, the King's young Canadian subjects could only stare in envy. When would we get an audience with rock royalty?

It finally happened in 1957. That spring, Presley's handlers arranged a tour of Canada with stops in Toronto, Ottawa, and Vancouver. On April 2, Elvis kicked off the tour with two sold-out shows at Maple Leaf Gardens. The CBC sent radio reporter Bill Beatty to cover the event.

"In many years of reporting the Canadian scene, I have never observed anything quite like this night," the bewildered Beatty said. "All you could hear were the screams. Elvis—the golden boy—standing there in his shimmering gold suit. Every time he wiggled, they screamed." Beatty described the sweaty throng as "hypnotized" by Elvis's forbidden footwork on stage. At times, the audience rose up and rushed toward the singer, forcing police to hit the lights and halt the concert until the teens could be pushed back into their seats. "You couldn't hear a thing, but you could see his lips moving," Beatty reported. Presley's singing was drowned out by "the screams, the sighs, the pounding of feet." After a frenetic finale of "Hound Dog," Elvis left the building, followed by fourteen thousand "glassy-eyed" teenagers. They stumbled through the streets, causing a massive traffic jam in downtown Toronto.

For Elvis fanatics, the Toronto concert holds a special place in the canon—it marked the last time Presley would wear his complete gold lamé tuxedo in public. The three Canadian dates also make up Elvis's one and only international tour.

Some will say a single concert can't change a country. But Elvis's appearance lit a fire under countless young Canadians. Musicians from Neil Young to Gordon Lightfoot and The Guess Who's Randy Bachman—all icons in their own right—today cite the King as a major influence. Elvis's popularity also paved the way for a host of Canadian teen idols, including one sixteen-year-old Ottawa boy named Paul Anka. In the wake of Elvis's '57 tour, Anka would top the charts with his smash hit, "Diana."

As much as parents today roll their eyes at teen idols like Justin Bieber, the Canadian pop cutie is just the latest in a line of musical artists who, like Elvis before them, hypnotize young fans with their style and image as much as with their singing. *Plus ça change . . .* When Elvis came to Canada he left us *all* shook up—and we haven't stopped shakin' since.

Slings and Arrows

February 20, 1959—Diefenbaker announces the end of the Avro Arrow program.

J.L. GRANATSTEIN

In memory the Arrow was a wondrous aircraft—supersonic speed, swept-back wings, powerful engines and weaponry, a machine far ahead of any other interceptor in the world. Even more stirring, the CF-105 Avro Arrow was the product of Canadian design and development, a touchstone of national pride. It was almost all true, but in the end it didn't matter.

Through the 1950s the Soviet Union developed nuclear weapons and the long-range bombers to deliver them on North American targets. Canada and the United States created squadrons of fighter-interceptors to stop the Soviet bombers, ideally intending to shoot them down as far north, as far away from the cities of the heartland, as possible. They even integrated their air defences in the North American Air Defence Agreement and built radar chains across the top of the continent. It cost billions, but survival was at stake.

The Arrow, intended to be the Royal Canadian Air Force's new interceptor, began its life in 1953, when the RCAF sought six hundred supersonic fighters, and the Liberal government of Louis St. Laurent agreed to finance construction of prototypes. After the Russians showed off their bombers in 1954, the government raised the ante to twenty-nine Arrows for $190 million, soon adding $70 million more to develop an engine. John Diefenbaker's Progressive Conservatives took power in June 1957 and revived the Arrow program with more funds and a bigger initial order. The real difficulty, rising costs aside, was that technology had started to overtake the project. The United States had begun rapid development of surface-to-air missiles, and even more frightening, the Soviet Union in 1957 had launched a satellite that heralded a future of intercontinental ballistic missiles.

The Arrow's problems continued to mount. The Avro plant at the Toronto suburb of Malton employed fourteen thousand people, and cancellation was certain to have major political implications. The navy and army needed new equipment and worried that the Arrow would use up the available funds; even the RCAF worried that the Arrow would prevent acquisition of other needed aircraft. The government tried to sell its futuristic fighter to friendly governments to lower unit costs. None were interested: the Arrow was a short-range two-seater that cost far too much compared to other roughly comparable U.S. designs. The Americans hinted that they might buy Arrows for the RCAF, but the government didn't want charity and refused.

Finally, on February 17, 1959, the cabinet took its courage in hand and decided to cancel the CF-105 contract. Three days later the prime minister announced the decision: Canada was to acquire American-made nuclear-tipped Bomarc missiles instead of the Arrow. Immediately, a huge public furore erupted. Avro fired all its workers that very day, the best aircraft designers immediately finding jobs in the United States space program. The Opposition charged the government with selling out Canadian technology, and the Tories never recovered.

But Diefenbaker had been right. The Arrow was a fine aircraft but far too expensive for a small nation to develop on its own. Canada had been priced out of the high-tech defence business.

Test pilot Janusz Żurakowski is hoisted onto the shoulders of officials after the inaugural Avro Arrow flight.
Photographer: Anonymous.

47

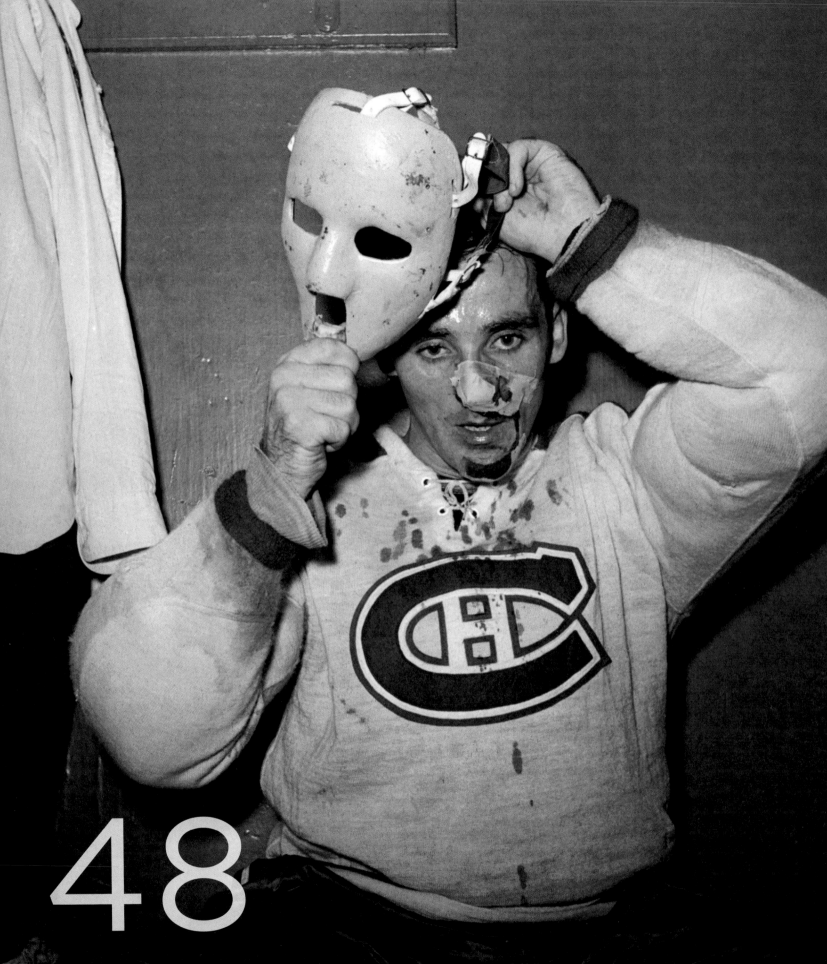

48

Montreal Canadiens goalie Jacques Plante dons a face mask for the first time during a 1959 NHL game.

Saving Face

November 1, 1959—Montreal's masked man changes hockey.

DON NEWMAN

He won six Stanley Cups and seven Vezina trophies as the best goaltender in the National Hockey League. The all-star netminder was also the first to control a game by leaving his crease to play rolling pucks on the end boards. But Jacques Plante's game-changing moment came on November 1, 1959, during a mid-season tilt between his Montreal Canadiens and the rival New York Rangers.

Hit with a booming shot that broke his nose and left a gaping cut on his face, Plante was forced to the dressing room. When he returned, no one in the crowd could see the tape job and stitches the team's trainers had used to pull together the damage—because Plante was wearing a protective face mask.

In 1930 goalie Clint Benedict had briefly worn a leather protective covering over his nose after being hit by a puck. After his nose healed, the protection disappeared. Plante, meanwhile, had been wearing his mask for about four years in practice, and was determined to change the very way the game was played. Plante played in the era of bare-knuckled hockey. No players wore protective helmets, and skaters cut by pucks or sticks were expected to return to the ice as soon as the bleeding stopped and their wounds were stitched. Teams carried only one goalkeeper. If he was cut during play, the game was halted just long enough to sew him up and get him back on the ice.

Plante's coach, the legendary Toe Blake, didn't like him using a mask at all and forbade the netminder from wearing it in games. In fact, the night before the fateful November 1 game, Plante had been cut and stitched up, and then returned to the game. But on this specific night, the severity of the cut—plus his success as a star on a team full of stars—convinced Plante to defy his coach. And he got away with it. The Canadiens won

that night, and Blake grudgingly agreed to allow Plante to wear his mask in games until his injury healed. The team then went on an eighteen-game winning streak, so Blake kept his complaints to himself. In March, however, Blake asked his goalie to play a game against Detroit without his mask. Plante reluctantly agreed—and the Canadiens lost 3–0. The next game, Plante's mask was back for good.

At first Plante was the only goalie willing to wear a mask. But over the next decade, fewer and fewer netminders played barefaced. And it wasn't just goalkeepers' equipment that changed. Eventually the NHL decreed that all players—at every position—had to wear helmets. Today, many position players wear protective face visors as well. As for goalkeepers, they all now wear full-coverage masks that bear colourfully painted symbols and team insignias that personalize their protection.

There is nothing more Canadian than hockey. It took a star player with a sense of invention and self-protection, and also the courage to defy his coach and the traditionalists in the game, to change hockey—and in doing so, change Canada.

Road Warriors

September 3, 1962—The Trans-Canada Highway is completed.

DANIEL FRANCIS

At a few minutes past three o'clock on the afternoon of September 3, 1962, standing among the glistening peaks of the Selkirk Mountain Range in British Columbia, Prime Minister John Diefenbaker tamped down the final square of asphalt in the Rogers Pass roadbed and declared the Trans-Canada Highway officially open. A band played "God Save the Queen," and the assembled dignitaries and onlookers sought shelter from the hot sun beneath a festive canopy, where they enjoyed a late lunch.

The project of a national highway had been launched in 1911 by a small group of motorcar enthusiasts calling themselves the Canadian Highway Association. Now, after a half century of political squabbling and daunting construction challenges, it was finally possible to drive an all-weather road from St. John's, Newfoundland, to Victoria on Vancouver Island without having to veer south of the border or expose your automobile to the perils of rutted gravel tracks—or it would be, once Newfoundland finished paving its section. A great national project, a second "national dream," was complete.

When Diefenbaker boasted that the highway brought "a renewed sense of national unity" to the country, a sceptical listener might have raised an eyebrow. The Chief was ignoring the years of infighting and constitutional wrangling that had plagued the project since its inception. Still, the highway was a great accomplishment. At more than 7,700 kilometres, it crossed six time zones, had taken 20 million person-days to build, and today remains the world's longest continuous transnational highway. It represented the triumph of national determination over provincial parochialism and unruly geography.

The highway made Canada accessible as never before. Its completion touched off a scramble by young Canadians to see their country, as if they had been waiting for a starter's gun. Hitchhiking across the Trans-Canada became a rite of passage for the younger generation. The shoulders of the highway were crowded each summer with long-haired adventurers in tie-dyed T-shirts, determined to experience their country. It was no accident that the resurgence of national pride that marked the 1960s and culminated in the 1967 centennial celebrations followed on the heels of the highway.

The Trans-Canada plays an essential role in the economic life of the country. The road delivers almost all the products we use in our daily lives, not to mention the tourist dollars spent by motorists visiting the country. But beyond dollars and cents, most Canadians have a story to tell about how the road has played a part in their lives. It has been the setting for many personal adventures, and for some of our most compelling national dramas. Who can forget Terry Fox on his heroic run for a cancer cure, or Rick Hansen driving his wheelchair across the country on the last leg of his Man in Motion World Tour in 1986–1987? When Canadians wish to draw attention to a cause or accomplish something together as a nation, they seem irresistibly drawn to the highway.

The Trans-Canada has never become the iconic symbol of national unity that the transcontinental railway once was. Instead it reveals just the opposite: that Canada is a diverse country of many landscapes, many communities, and many points of view. It is by revealing this diversity to us that the Trans-Canada Highway has made its most important contribution to our national character.

Workmen clearing the right-of-way for what will become the Trans-Canada Highway in northern Ontario, circa 1940.
Contributor: Ralph Larson.

49

PART THREE

IDENTITY CRISIS

1964–1980

Countries are falling apart everywhere else, so why shouldn't Canada?

—MALCOLM MUGGERIDGE, 1977

In 1967 the world came to Montreal for Expo and was dazzled by our kaleidoscopic vision of the future, replete with miniskirted hostesses, far-out architecture, celebrity visitors, and even a monorail. Historian Pierre Berton famously called our centennial "the last good year." The description was apt, for the afterglow of Expo soon dimmed, and optimism was replaced by profound concern for the future of the country.

Many of the challenges stemmed from our proximity to the United States. Two years after Expo, in March 1969, Prime Minister Pierre Trudeau gave a speech in Washington, D.C. "Living next to you is in some ways like sleeping with an elephant," he quipped. "No matter how friendly or even-tempered is the beast . . . one is affected by every twitch and grunt."

The American audience responded with laughter, but the truth was that Trudeau wasn't joking. He knew Canadians couldn't avoid being affected by the turmoil in America. Out of the growing quagmire of Vietnam came the challenge of dealing with draft dodgers and war deserters. Assassinations of key American public figures, from President John F. Kennedy to the Reverend Martin Luther King Jr., fuelled a deepening cynicism toward the political systems of both nations. Scenes of Black Americans being attacked in the Deep South, simply for demanding their civil rights, shocked most right-minded Canadians and forced them to reconsider Canada's own treatment of minorities.

The late sixties and early seventies were times of seismic changes. In Alberta the launch of tar sands production set the province on a path to new prosperity. But it also upset the delicate economic and political balance between the provinces. Canada had always split along east–west lines, but western oil money exacerbated the gulf between have and have-not provinces.

For some segments of society, it was a time to rise up. Women marched in the streets to call for equality with men and for reproductive rights. First Nations demanded compensation for lands lost long ago. In Quebec a cadre of violent separatists took the notion of rising up to the extreme. A Front de libération du Québec mail-bombing campaign that began in 1963 would metastasize by the decade's end into brazen kidnappings and cold-blooded murder.

Even showcase events like the Montreal Summer Olympics were overshadowed by concerns about cost overruns. With alienation growing in the West and a newly elected separatist government in Quebec, Canadians everywhere had cause for concern.

A century earlier, the Fathers of Confederation had united to consolidate and expand the country. By the 1980s a new generation was desperately trying to find ways to keep it from falling apart.

What we needed was a hero, someone who could unite the country in common cause. And we got him—a young man from British Columbia who believed that he could help cure cancer by running across Canada. His tenacity was inspiring and his Marathon of Hope would move an entire nation.

—Mark Reid

50

An Africville boy poses in front of a house in the community that is slated for demolition.

Photographer: Bob Brooks.

Africville Forever

January 16, 1964—Halifax votes to demolish Africville.

LAWRENCE HILL

Nova Scotia has the oldest Black communities in Canada. In 1783 three thousand Black Loyalists who served the British on the losing side of the American Revolutionary War sailed from Manhattan to settle in the province. Denied the land and equality they had been promised in exchange for wartime service, many sailed a decade later to Sierra Leone.

Another two thousand Blacks arrived in Nova Scotia after serving the British in the War of 1812. They, too, struggled to obtain promised land grants, and eked out a difficult existence in Preston and Hammonds Plains. Historians note that in the 1840s, a few of these families created the community of Africville on land overlooking the Bedford Basin in the north end of Halifax. Interestingly, the Africville Genealogy Society asserts that Blacks began living there half a century earlier, in 1798.

The people of Africville carried on in poverty but with their own dignity for at least 125 years, despite many insults to their community. For instance, the city disposed of night soil (human waste) in pits next to Africville in 1858, opened a dump within a hundred metres of its homes a century later, and refused to provide sewage treatment, running water, or police and fire services.

But the people had a lively community. Some men worked on the docks and on coal barges. Others hauled waste, found jobs as railway porters, and served with the Allies during the two world wars. Women cooked and cleaned in Halifax homes, and sewed bags in a nearby bone-meal plant. People raised chickens and goats and fished in the Bedford Basin. Some foraged in the dump next door. The Baptist church formed the heart of their community. Portia White, the famous singer, taught in the Africville school. George Dixon, the champion boxer, came from Africville. Jazz maestro Duke Ellington's second wife, Mildred, came from Africville, and he visited from time to time.

On January 16, 1964, Halifax city council voted to expropriate the land of Africville and provide compensation to the four hundred residents, who dreaded the loss of their community but negotiated reluctantly with the city. They asked to be relocated together nearby, but instead were scattered throughout Halifax. The city used garbage trucks to haul out the residents' personal possessions and bulldozers to flatten their homes and church. Aaron "Pa" Carvery, at seventy-two, was the last holdout. His insistence on staying until the bitter end so frustrated civic officials that they summoned him to city hall and offered him an open suitcase stuffed with cash, but still he refused the bait. Finally, he was evicted in January 1970.

The magnitude of Africville's loss emerged only after its destruction. The forcible relocation deprived citizens of important relationships and the pride of owning land and living together in their own century-old gathering place.

Paradoxically, the neglect and demolition of Africville helped to make it the most famous Black community in Canadian history. It is the subject of Canadian jazz legend Joe Sealy's Juno Award–winning *Africville Suite* and Shelagh Mackenzie's film documentary *Remember Africville*. For twenty-five years, the Africville Genealogy Society negotiated with the city for reparations. Finally, in 2010 the city issued an apology and committed funds to build a replica of the Seaview African United Baptist Church, as well as an interpretive centre to tell the story of Africville for generations to come.

© 2011 by Lawrence Hill Creative Services, Inc.

On the Double-Double

May 17, 1964—Canada warms to Tim Hortons.

PAUL JONES

Imagine asking Canadians to name the brand of doughnuts eaten onscreen by Bob and Doug McKenzie, the SCTV hosers who defined 1980s Canadianness. Need more clues? By the mid-1970s this doughnut chain had more locations than any other. And in 1994 it featured conspicuously in a CBC news story heralding our world-beating doughnut consumption. Most Canadians would by now be piping up, "Tim Hortons". *Bzzzzzzt*. Sorry. There's no way of sugarcoating this: the correct answer is Country Style.

Although the hegemony of Tim Hortons now seems preordained and eternal—indeed, "always Tim Hortons"—national-icon status was a long time coming. As Tim Hortons executives are fond of saying, "We are a forty-five-year overnight success story."

It didn't hurt that the business was co-founded by the eponymous Tim Horton (born Myles Gilbert Horton), a hockey Hall of Famer who embodied the taciturn masculine virtues of small-town Canada. After Horton's untimely death, the chain was aggressively built by the initial franchisee, Ron Joyce, a former police officer. (How perfect is that?) Product innovations boosted business: for instance, the Timbit (thankfully not the Mylesbit) in 1976. Then, in 1986, came the country's most successful marketing contest: RRRoll Up the Rim to Win. This promotion subtly shifted attention to coffee, a far more important product for building customer loyalty. Thanks to shrewd marketing, doughnut stores were transforming themselves into coffee shops, and in 1995 Tim Hortons opened its one thousandth location in Canada.

Sixteen years later, there are more than three thousand stores, capturing a staggering 60 percent of the fast-food coffee market. What propelled the company to such unprecedented success? Some credit its saccharine "true stories" advertising campaign. Explicitly depicting its connection to the lives of real Canadians, Tim Hortons wrapped itself in both the flag and the mantle of everyday life. Timmy's became the place where Joes and Janes of all stripes interact, talk, and laugh—even if only for the time it takes to guzzle a coffee. Appropriating and simultaneously redefining Canadian identity for its own purposes, the campaign not only illustrated the extreme loyalty of customers but also inserted Tim Hortons into the narrative of their routines and relationships. Tim Hortons was no longer a brand to be consumed, but the essence of life in Canada. Kitschy, but effective: in 2006, when the Canadian Forces wanted to bring a piece of Canada to Kandahar, it was Tim Hortons they called, giving new meaning to the phrase "home, sweet home."

Not everyone agrees with the wisdom of "locating national identity within mundane, sensual consumptive desire," as one academic put it—especially when we're talking Dutchies or double-doubles. But Canadians are a pragmatic people. And if the ritual of an okay cup of coffee gets you through a wintry day, is that such a bad thing?

Here's my Tim Hortons "true story." Act 1: Our four-year-old son, eager for a sugar fix and happy to forgo syllables to that end, blurts from the back seat, "Hey, there's Hornuts!" Act 2: Unsurprisingly, "Hornuts" becomes the permanent nickname for Tim Hortons in our household—first laughingly, then wryly, and with the passage of time, matter-of-factly. Act 3: Years later I am chairing a corporate meeting and suggest unthinkingly that we could really use some Hornuts. *Exeunt omnes* with much hilarity. A new cycle of Tim Hortons stories begins. Eat your heart out, Country Style.

Ron Joyce, owner of the Tim Horton chain, celebrates the opening of a new doughnut shop in Hamilton in March 1977.

Photographer: Anonymous.

51

Marshall McLuhan, shown circa 1974, coined the phrases
"global village" and "the medium is the message."
Photographer: Yousuf Karsh.

52

Early Warning

May 25, 1964—Marshall McLuhan's Understanding Media *is published.*

PHIL KOCH

Edmonton-born, Winnipeg-raised, and eventually Toronto-based, Marshall McLuhan was for a time among the most sought-after thinkers in the world. The charismatic university professor was profiled in popular magazines, appeared on CBC, NBC, and BBC television, and offered advice to educators, business leaders, scientists, and politicians.

Besides making unique if sometimes mystifying analyses about the state of the world as he found it—for instance, he said General Electric was "in the business of moving information," not making light bulbs—McLuhan was always willing to extend those analyses into the future. His focus, if you can call it that, was the study of media and communication, which for McLuhan included just about everything. His breakout book, *Understanding Media*, contains chapters on language, the telephone, radio, and television, but also on clothing, clocks, weapons, and many more "extensions of man," as the book's subtitle called them.

McLuhan's star was rising when he appeared at a Toronto press conference on May 25, 1964, to announce the book's publication. His research into "how technology affects culture and vice versa" had already been reported in U.S. newspapers, but *Understanding Media* established his international reputation and is considered to be among the best statements of his ideas.

Canadian news reports of the book's launch focused on his views about Quebec. In his typical manner, McLuhan boldly told reporters that because of television—which, like other media, has effects that often escape notice—separatists did not understand what they really wanted: more involvement in Canadian society. Arriving as television took hold of the public consciousness, *Understanding Media* explained how the medium affects children and how it suited former U.S. presidential candidate John F. Kennedy better than his rival, Richard Nixon. The book also featured McLuhan's enigmatic phrase "the medium is the message"—less often remembered than "the global village," but perhaps his key insight. He wrote that "the 'message' of any medium or technology" is not its content but rather "the change of scale or pace or pattern that it introduces into human affairs."

Variously referred to as a guru, a prophet, and the "oracle of the electric age," McLuhan's focus on media and the social changes they produce gave him a better sense of the future than many of his contemporaries. He is sometimes credited with having foreseen the Internet. McLuhan described electronic media as extensions of the central nervous system but feared their "hidden and perhaps insidious effects." He regarded experimental art—and also his own work—as an "early warning system" and a "means of training perception" against the prevalent "somnambulism." Yet the technological future he imagined wasn't altogether bad. He predicted that a "closed circuit" would one day obviate the need to access filing cabinets and allow people to work from home.

While academics decried his lack of rigour and consistency, McLuhan accepted his reputation for wordplay and jargon, saying these were ways of provoking his audiences to change their thinking. The audience he most cared about was students. He believed the television generation was being forced to learn the compartmentalized thinking characteristic of the age of print, and he looked for new methods of educating both children and adults about the effects of media.

Understanding Media was first conceived as a syllabus for educating grade eleven students. In its pages, McLuhan gave us new ways to talk about the massive technological changes taking place in the world.

Flag Flap

December 15, 1964—Canada embraces the Maple Leaf.

PETER MANSBRIDGE

An eleven-pointed red maple leaf centred on a white square and bordered by two vertical bands of red. The Canadian flag is so familiar to us, and seems so right, that it's hard to imagine it was born only after a bitterly divisive national debate.

In 1964 Prime Minister Lester Pearson made it government policy to come up with a new flag. For ninety-seven years Canada had confused everyone by using two flags, neither ever legally adopted—the Union Jack and the Canadian Red Ensign. Few doubted we needed a flag to call our own, but there was scorching disagreement on what the new flag should look like.

The battle lines were clear. On one side were those who wanted to keep elements of our colonial past— some version of the Union Jack, maybe with a fleur-de-lys. These were primarily older Canadians, most of whom could trace their ancestry to Great Britain. On the other side were those who wanted something uniquely Canadian. These were generally younger people, and those who had no family ties to the British Empire. There was no middle ground in the debate. Pearson took enormous public abuse. At a Canadian Legion convention in Winnipeg he was booed loudly and heckled persistently. Fighting most vociferously against any radically new flag was John Diefenbaker. The former prime minister told Parliament there would be a new flag only "over my dead body."

The government set up a committee, which held more than forty meetings and looked at more than two thousand designs. Many were silly, of course, with Mounties and beavers prominent. The committee narrowed the choices to three, and then picked one. For two draining weeks, and through 250 emotional and patriotic speeches, the House of Commons debated the flag, until finally, at 2:15 a.m. on December 15, 1964, MPs voted 163 to 78 for that red maple leaf. Even some of Diefenbaker's Conservatives voted for the new flag.

Canada now had an unmistakable national symbol. No more confusion about which flag was ours. No more sharing a flag with the United Kingdom, or part of the flag with current and former colonies such as Australia, New Zealand, Fiji, and Bermuda. The Maple Leaf is instantly recognizable in even the most remote parts of the planet. So many countries have flags that leave you guessing about ownership. France has three vertical stripes of blue, white, and red. The Netherlands has three horizontal stripes of red, white, and blue. Or is it the other way around?

Just as the Statute of Westminster made Canada legally independent of Britain in 1931, so the new flag made Canada symbolically independent. The Maple Leaf tells the world that Canada isn't just proud to stand on its own but insists on doing so. Though the flag divided Canadians in 1964, it has since united us. The Canadian flag has been sewn onto the backpacks of so many of us as we travelled the world that it has become a cliché. Every citizen seems stirred by the sight of the Maple Leaf. In a country not given to open displays of patriotism, it's the flag that causes us to say, "That's mine."

53

Supporters of the Red Ensign rally on Parliament Hill in 1964.

Photographer: Ted Grant.

54

By 1966, when Joni Mitchell performed again at the Mariposa Folk Festival, she was already a star.

Photographer: Julian Hayashi.

Blue Muse

August 6, 1965—Joni Mitchell shines at the Mariposa Folk Festival.

RONA MAYNARD

My friend was mourning another breakup, and I knew exactly what to tell her: "You're having a Joni Mitchell moment." Among women of a certain age, that's code for the boundary between desire and disappointment, between wanting to wreck your stockings in some jukebox jive with Mr. Almost Right, whose kisses make your mind see-saw, and travelling on alone. Joni mapped that place like no one else. Especially on her touchstone album *Blue*, she made it feel okay to wander those emotional thickets. There was something exultant in her sorrow, in her open-hearted longing for connection even as she rued the cost. She wanted what we all wanted, a passionate partnership of equals bringing out the best in each other, no need for a piece of paper from the city hall to keep them tied and true. She insisted it was not too much to ask.

Ever since my generation came of age, we've been bonding through the language Joni gave us. Leather and lace: a cool way to dress. Woman of heart and mind: the only kind of woman to be. Paving paradise and putting up a parking lot: the blight of our times. We loved Joni's shrewd eye for the ways of men. Who else would observe a bedmate picking up her scent on his fingers while admiring the waitress's legs? But of course men found plenty to love about her too. That zest for naughty sex! That sporting spirit! (A handsome devil named Carey stole her camera on a Greek island, but she still penned a jaunty tribute to him.)

And oh, that unflinching honesty. When Joni probed romantic debacles, she didn't let herself off the hook like pretty well every other pop songwriter. She faced her own jealousy and selfishness. "I love you when I forget about me," she sang. When she rounded a creative corner toward jazzy social critiques, I was one of those who missed the blue, consoling Joni. Yet I had to admire her courage. She didn't need my loyalty, any more than she had needed the men she'd left behind. And when had Joni ever pandered to audience expectations? As far back as her breakthrough performance— at the Mariposa Folk Festival on August 6, 1965—she was pushing limits. In the heyday of the protest-song era, which urged listeners to the barricades, the twenty-two-year-old from Saskatchewan took her audience back to a familiar childhood marvel—catching a dragonfly in a jar—and wove from that image "The Circle Game," a tender meditation on innocence lost.

At heart Joni never really changed. I wanted her as the soundtrack for my life, but now I read her lyrics—correction: her poems—and see the through-line that joins "The Circle Game" to all her enduring songs. Whether her subject was lovers getting lost in a no-win quarrel or half a million baby boomers trekking to Woodstock, she was asking us to care for one another and the earth, calling us back to the same garden.

I'm old enough to remember when Joni told *Time*, without a trace of irony, "I feel like I'm married to a guy named Art." How thrillingly nervy, I thought (it was 1974). And as it turned out, he was Mr. Right.

Canadian Chorus

January 1, 1967—Gordon Lightfoot debuts the "Canadian Railroad Trilogy."

MIKE FORD

Canada's optimistic centennial year, 1967, announced to the world that the future was very bright—and it was starting right here. One Canadian artist, however, summoned his considerable creative powers to turn 180 degrees and look back. Gordon Lightfoot's masterpiece song "Canadian Railroad Trilogy," which debuted on national television on January 1, 1967, was a soaring proclamation that Canada's sunny present had an extraordinary past, a past that demanded our attention.

Much credit must go to the CBC for commissioning the piece and for making an event of its debut, complete with a live "music video" that provided visual accompaniment to the song's epic sweep. But it was Lightfoot who responded beyond all expectations. He knew he'd need a broad canvas to tell the story of the building of the Canadian Pacific Railway—the Confederation promise that linked this land from coast to coast and arguably made the nation's existence possible.

The Orillia-born-and-bred musician, whose career was just then exploding into international success, created a stirring three-part anthem to the iron road's construction, evoking not only the energy, motivations, hardship, and toil of the era, but also wonder at the majestic expanse of land and history upon which the story unfolds. Pierre Berton, author of *The National Dream*, once remarked that it took him 450 pages to do what Lightfoot did in a seven-minute song.

The song's tale of national adventure carries a historical message: look what can be done. It is a message as relevant to twenty-first-century Canada as it was to the centennial year. On a cultural level, it carries an equally provocative message: look what can be *sung*. What remains breathtaking today is the audaciousness of the Canadian songwriter, on the cusp of international acclaim and reward, summoning his powers to create something for, and entirely about, *here*. Some say it made him English Canada's national troubadour. Perhaps the only comparison is the creative dam-burst effected in Quebec by Gilles Vigneault's "Mon Pays."

A century ago in this country, it was normal to hear songs about local exploits—provided one was sitting around a work camp wood stove. With the rise of radio and television, Canadian stories proved to be all but invisible in popular song. But Lightfoot's broadcast rekindled the fire for the satellite age and inspired countless artists to do the same—to sing in depth about here—career consequences be damned. True, the commercial market seems to support little more than the occasional Canadian place-name dropping, but beyond that—from summer music festivals to CBC Radio competitions and to a multitude of MP3 collections—there exists a phenomenon that "Canadian Railroad Trilogy" helped initiate: a new way of being a musical artist, or music listener, in Canada.

Today the song inspires still, and continues to raise questions. Where is the composer who can mirror the spirit of Canada today in song? Who in the media will champion such a tune? Who will listen? And will it still be heard a half century later? On New Year's Day, 1967, Gordon Lightfoot set the bar high indeed.

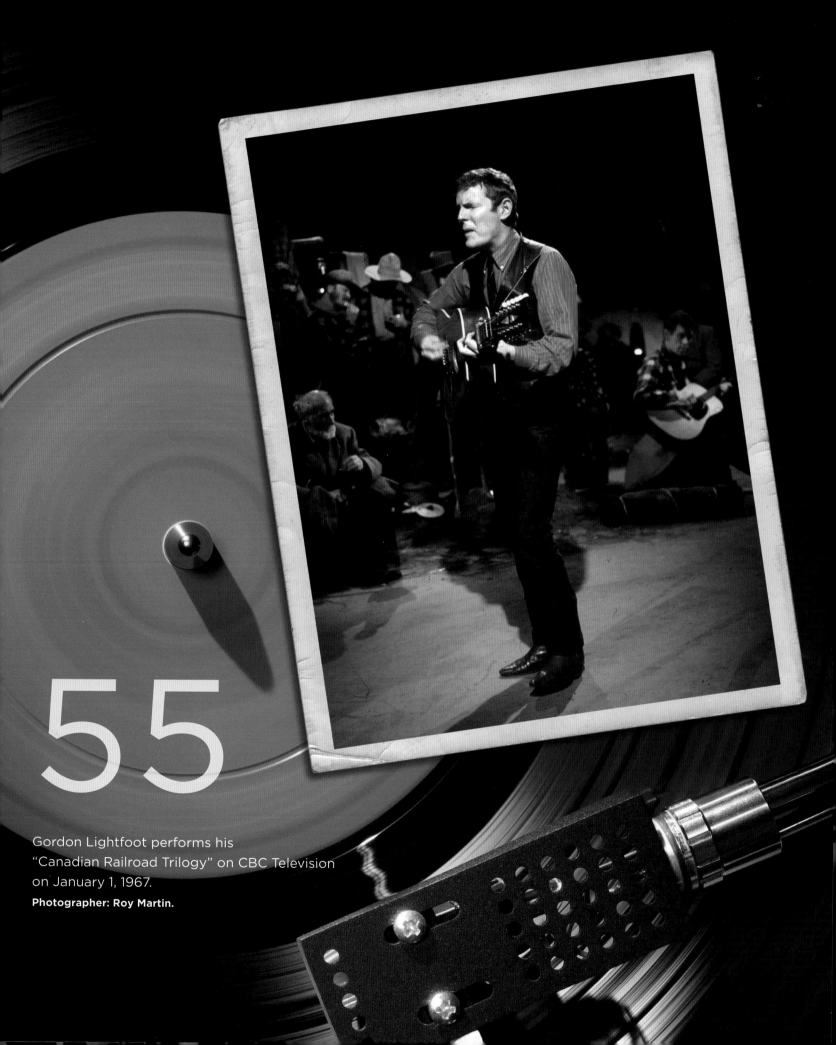

55

Gordon Lightfoot performs his
"Canadian Railroad Trilogy" on CBC Television
on January 1, 1967.
Photographer: Roy Martin.

56

Mr. Dressup, played by Ernie Coombs, was best friend to generations of Canadian children.
Photographer: Fred Phipps.

Kids' Stuff

February 13, 1967—Mr. Dressup *airs on Canadian television.*

JILL FORAN

At its finest, a television program can serve as a unifying force, a shared cultural experience that links viewers through time and place. For a certain segment of English-speaking Canadians, *Mr. Dressup* was such a show. The mere mention of it can unleash a torrent of childhood memories and spark lively debates over which aspect was the best: the puppet pals Casey and Finnegan, the Tickle Trunk, the crafts and songs, the tree house, the gentle demeanour of the show's eponymous host.

Created and played by Ernie Coombs, the character of Mr. Dressup first debuted in 1964 on the CBC children's television program *Butternut Square*. When high production costs prompted the series' cancellation two years later, Coombs and puppeteer Judith Lawrence set out to build a new show with a much simpler structure: just the kindly Mr. Dressup, a couple of puppets, and some very basic props. The magic was in its simplicity.

On Monday morning, February 13, 1967, Mr. Dressup—with his horn-rimmed glasses and ready grin—welcomed young viewers into his creative world for the first time. Over the next three decades, preschool children across Canada and in parts of the northern United States tuned in every weekday for a half hour of imaginative play. For many of us it was a mid-morning appointment not to be missed.

The draw was undeniable. In Mr. Dressup we found an adult friend who spoke directly to us, on our level, with no pretension or lecturing. He sparked our curiosity and encouraged us to be confident in ourselves. Over the course of an episode we watched, captivated, as he drew pictures and made crafts. We relished the sound of his scissors cutting through construction paper, and marvelled at what he could create with just some tape

and a paper-towel tube. Thanks to his gentle encouragement, we believed we could do it too. We listened, rapt, as he chatted with Casey and Finnegan or one of his other puppet friends. We delighted in that moment when he finally opened the lid to his big red Tickle Trunk and pulled out a costume. And we got to do it all over again the next day.

In 1996, after thirty-two years of playing Mr. Dressup, Ernie Coombs retired. The program's last original episode aired on February 14, 1996, but reruns continued on CBC Television for another ten years. Parents were pleased that even amid the growing number of high-tech, aggressively commercialized entertainment options for children, *Mr. Dressup's* lo-fi format kept kids tuning in.

But really, it shouldn't have come as a surprise. For the young and the young at heart, there is no greater gift than a safe place that gives us the licence to let our imaginations run free.

On September 18, 2001, Coombs died of a stroke that he had suffered days earlier. Tributes poured in from colleagues and peers, as well as from average Canadians who had grown up with *Mr. Dressup*. As one man told CBC.ca, "Mr. Coombs, in my thirty-four years, I have had lots of heroes . . . hockey players, rock stars, and others. You were my first. . . . You taught a young boy of about three how to discover new worlds by simply using his imagination."

The Future Is Here

April 27, 1967—The opening of the Montreal world's fair.

PHIL KOCH

Expo 67 was the shining star of the country's centennial year. The six-month celebration announced a coming of age for Montreal, Quebec, and Canada, and it took place before the eyes of the entire world.

While there were many concerns in the lead-up to the fair, most doubts were forgotten on the brilliant opening day, April 27, 1967. The official ceremonies—attended by a few thousand invited guests, dignitaries, and members of the media, and broadcast to 700 million viewers and listeners worldwide—gave Canadians a new sense of what we could achieve.

It wasn't at all clear that things would turn out that way. In fact, Montreal initially lost its bid to host the 1967 world's fair but was handed the opportunity when Moscow backed out in 1962. With less time to prepare and build, organizers nonetheless took on an ambitious plan that included a grand theme—Terre des Hommes/Man and His World—the participation of sixty-two countries, and the creation of the fair's main site in the middle of the St. Lawrence River.

Besides the construction of Île Notre-Dame and expansion of Île Ste-Hélène out of millions of tonnes of rock and earth, the city also set to work on a new metro system, additions to the Place des Arts complex in the city centre, and several other major building and infrastructure projects.

It is easy to understand how the task's completion could have seemed at best improbable and at worst a potential embarrassment for the country. So when over a million visitors poured into the site on the first weekend, Montrealers and all Canadians had good reason to be proud.

The 50 million people who visited Expo that year included world leaders and royalty. Top arts and cultural groups from around the world performed in Montreal throughout the summer. But the highlight was undoubtedly the site itself and the many marvels it contained.

Expo 67 was all about a modern, cosmopolitan vision of the future. Provincial, regional, industrial, and thematic pavilions sat beside those of other countries and parts of the world. Visitors encountered an array of foods, displays, and entertainments, and they moved around the site on futuristic modes of transport such as monorails. Design elements and signage aimed for ease of understanding, but also for interaction, discovery, and spontaneity in a kind of utopian urban experience.

Spectacular and innovative architecture included Buckminster Fuller's geodesic dome for the United States pavilion and Moshe Safdie's nearby Habitat 67 housing project. Large- and multi-screen film projections were tremendously popular. Even the Christian pavilion showcased grand multimedia experiments that seemed destined to expand visitors' minds as well as their horizons.

The sixties were also a time of new possibilities for women and youth—represented memorably, for many visitors, by the miniskirt- and go-go-boot-wearing official hostesses—as well as for an emerging Québécois culture.

Canadian filmmaker Roman Kroitor said of the National Film Board's Labyrinth pavilion, "The ideal effect would be like a very real, very vivid dream which you don't really understand. You know only that something inside it is explosive and important." He could have said the same for Expo as a whole.

57

Visitors to Expo 67 enjoy a ride at La Ronde.
Photographer: Anonymous.

John Diefenbaker glares at Progressive Conservative party president Dalton Camp in November 1966. (Camp is seated next to Robert Stanfield, far right, who would go on to replace Diefenbaker as leader.)
Photographer: Anonymous.

58

ARTHUR MALONEY FOR PRESIDENT
PARTY UNITY - L'UNITÉ

Dumping Diefenbaker

September 9, 1967—Progressive Conservatives turn on The Chief.

TIM COOK

John Diefenbaker's glare in this November 1966 photograph could peel paint from a wall. His dagger eyes are pointed at his hated enemy and one-time friend, Progressive Conservative party president Dalton Camp. Camp had called for a leadership review at the 1966 convention, which would eventually lead to Diefenbaker's replacement on September 9, 1967, by Robert Stanfield. What had gone wrong? Why were the Conservatives set to dump the man who had almost single-handedly brought the party back from the political wilderness a decade earlier?

As a young man, Dief had been a brilliant lawyer but a terrible politician. A Great War veteran, he had a track record in the 1920s and 1930s of five defeats in a row, at federal, provincial, and municipal politics. He finally cracked the code and was elected as a member of Parliament in 1940. He took control of the party in 1956. Running as a populist and an underdog in the 1957 federal election, Diefenbaker captured the imagination of voters with his odd but compelling speaking style. A good dose of venom was also directed at the ruling party Liberals, who seemed smug, complacent, and elitist.

Prime Minister Diefenbaker achieved some success over his seven years in power. He provided greater recognition for First Nations, as well as the right to vote; he offered an exciting if unattainable vision of the North; he introduced the impotent if still important Bill of Rights; and he exhibited moral bravery in standing up to the South African government for its odious policy of apartheid. But there were problems. Many problems. Defence issues in the Cold War remained hideously complicated. Diefenbaker's decision to scrap the Avro Arrow was unpopular, and his waffling over whether to equip Bomarc missiles with nuclear warheads split his party, eventually paralyzing it.

During the October 1962 Cuban Missile Crisis, President John Kennedy was calm and cool, showing force and resolve. Dief was distracting and embarrassing, to both Americans and Canadians, as he seemed unable to commit the country to action and did not know his own mind. In the end Canada was seen as not pulling its weight in supporting the Americans, and opinion polls savaged the bewildered Diefenbaker. The Kennedy administration did not forget, and did its best to undermine Diefenbaker.

Canadians were fed up; Dief lost the 1963 election but staggered on, steadily slipping, increasingly bitter. Another defeat in 1965 created a sense of urgency among Conservatives to replace The Chief. Sympathetic followers and friends tried to reason with Diefenbaker that it was time to hand over the reins. He refused. Disillusioned followers drifted away, while conspirators rose in number and influence, positioning themselves in the party. It was only a matter of time before they struck; by 1966 Diefenbaker had been knifed in the back, and he lost control of the party the next year. Most felt it was justified, although all agreed it was a sad end to the strange reign of John Diefenbaker.

The party faithful took solace in his replacement, the competent Robert Stanfield. Their dreams were dashed when Liberal leader Pierre Trudeau rode a wave of mania to destroy the Tories in 1968. Dief watched it all grimly, an MP in the House until his death in 1979.

Black Gold

September 30, 1967—Alberta's oil sands open for business.

DON MARTIN

It was hardly the idyllic setting for profound prophesies. The Fort McMurray sky was a threatening grey. The thermometer registered unseasonable cold, even for northern Alberta, and the wind-whipped rain drove the six hundred invited guests under inflatable tents. They were there to kick-start the world's first commercial plant dedicated to extracting bitumen from oozing sand, and were about to glimpse the future.

Alberta's premier and the project's patriarch each took the stage to frame the Athabasca oil sands as much more than an engine for Canada's economy. It was, they argued, a cornerstone of global energy. "No other event in Canada's centennial year is more important or significant," thundered Premier Ernest Manning. "It is fitting that we are gathered here today to dedicate this plant not merely to the production of oil, but to the continual progress and enrichment of mankind."

Heady stuff, even for a politician just two months away from retirement. Then J. Howard Pew, the eighty-five-year-old founder of Great Canadian Oil Sands Limited, took to the podium. "It will be the means of opening up reserves to meet the needs of the North American continent for generations to come. No nation can be secure in this atomic age until it can be amply supplied with petroleum," he declared.

It may have sounded like hyperbole at the time, given the modest startup output of forty-five thousand barrels per day at a per-barrel cost far above the world oil price. But fast-forward four decades and the "red-letter day" predicted by Manning has delivered far beyond expectations. Mines in northern Alberta collectively capable of producing about 2 million barrels of bitumen per day are in operation or have cleared regulatory approval. The gooey Fort McMurray motherlode has become Canada's largest export, most of it to the United States but with the dangling promise of extending exports to Asian markets if a proposed pipeline is punched through the Rockies to British Columbia.

More than $500 billion will have been invested in multiple projects by 2020. The economic boost they will deliver goes far beyond Alberta, with 20 percent of the spinoffs going to Ontario and other forecasts suggesting that up to sixty cents of every oil sands dollar will benefit the rest of Canada.

Of course, it wasn't a smooth transition from pilot project to megaproject. Fluctuating world oil prices often called into question the economics of the difficult extraction process. Costs soared as production hiccups plagued the one-of-a-kind project, forcing engineers to invent unique technology that could handle the abrasive and superheated separation of black gold from its sandy prison. The setbacks and complications quickly underlined why the industry had for so long ignored the oil sands in favour of conventional crude.

But with an estimated bitumen reserve of 1.75 trillion barrels waiting to be extracted in a world of declining conventional oil reserves, expansion of the oil sands continues relentlessly and, in the view of environmentalists, recklessly. While giving Canada's reputation an environmental black eye globally, the reclamation of tailings ponds is accelerating, carbon sequestration is moving into place, and research has found ways to reduce water and natural gas consumption.

What started on the cold, wet morning of September 30, 1967, put Canada on a new economic track— from bold prophecy to red-letter reality.

The oil sands project near Fort McMurray, Alberta, circa 1976.

Photographer: Doug Griffin.

59

60

American war resisters involved in the American Deserters Committee, February 1970, Montreal.
Photographer: Bruno Massenet.

Gimme Shelter

May 22, 1969—Canada welcomes war resisters.

ANDY BARRIE

In 1969 I was a twenty-four-year-old draftee based at Fort Sam Houston, Texas. My unit was made up entirely of conscientious objectors. We were trained as combat medics, but we knew that if we shipped to Vietnam it would be our job to put wounded soldiers back on their feet so they could do the shooting we wouldn't do. There was no way, in the words of Buffy Sainte-Marie, that I'd let my body be "a weapon of the war." But beyond that certainty, I—and thousands like me—had no idea where to turn.

We all knew about the draft dodgers who had made their way to Canada, but deserters were a different story. In February 1969 five York University students posed as deserters at different border crossings and were denied entrance into Canada. The ensuing uproar, in addition to mounting pressure from the United Church and the NDP, resulted in Manpower and Immigration Minister Allan MacEachen issuing an internal memo on May 22, 1969, that opened Canada to war resisters: "Desertion . . . potential or actual—will not be a factor in determining the eligibility of persons applying for landed immigrant status in Canada." Eight months later, my orders to Vietnam came through— and I crossed the border into Canada.

It should be remembered that this was only two years after Canada's centennial, a time of explosive pride in all things Canadian (and, inevitably, resistance to many things American). Treating American war resisters as undesirable criminals became a sovereignty issue. As one letter to MacEachen asked, "Since when is it Canada's job to enforce U.S. laws?" Add to this the sizable brain gain that U.S. immigrants represented, and it's clear that the governing Liberals might have acted as much from political expediency as from high-minded morality. MacEachen's memo

marked a significant about-face for the government. Only months before, Pierre Trudeau had responded to a question about U.S. deserters this way: "Surely a person who deserts from the armed forces of the U.S. is guilty of a criminal offence and accordingly would be inadmissible to Canada on that ground alone." In 2010 the Conservative government used the same rationale to deny entrance to U.S. deserters from the Iraq War.

As for Canadians, their views seem to have shifted since Vietnam. A Gallup poll in 1969 showed a strong majority wanted to close our borders to American war resisters, but the opposite was true during the second Iraq war, which began in 2003. In both cases the governments of the day went against popular opinion.

Nobody knows how many Americans came to this country during the Vietnam War, or how many stayed when the war ended. We were dodgers, deserters—and in some cases, we were entire families. (For example, famed urbanist Jane Jacobs moved her family to Canada to prevent her son from being sent to Vietnam.) If we who came to Canada have had a lasting impact, it is in reminding this country that it was and is anything but the "fifty-first state." And when Prime Minister Jean Chrétien declined Washington's 2003 invitation to wage war on Iraq, I'd like to think he recalled that day in May 1969 and questioned again the wisdom of allowing Canada to march to another nation's drummer.

Rights Fight

May 11, 1970—The Abortion Caravan shuts down Parliament.

PENNI MITCHELL

Drawing strength from the U.S. civil rights movement and anti–Vietnam War protests, women in the late 1960s were determined to end sex discrimination. Chief among the demands of the women's liberation movement was the right to safe, legal abortion. In Canada more than thirty-three thousand back-street abortions were being performed each year. Some estimates put the number at more than a hundred thousand. And while women with means could travel to the United States, where abortions were safer, most Canadians faced risky procedures at home that could maim or possibly kill them. Botched abortions remained a leading cause of female hospital admissions.

Justice Minister Pierre Trudeau's Criminal Law Amendment Act, 1968–69 made contraception and homosexuality legal for the first time. Yet Trudeau's famous "no place for the state in the bedrooms of the nation" bill forced women seeking abortions to plead their case before a hospital therapeutic abortion committee, a stipulation viewed as patronizing. In 1970 anger over the law transformed women's fury into the pivotal event known as the Abortion Caravan. Seventeen women from the Vancouver Women's Caucus set out on a road trip to confront Trudeau, now prime minister.

Taking their cue from the 1935 cross-Canada On to Ottawa Trek to protest unemployment camps, the women set out with two cars and a coffin-topped van bearing the slogan "Smash Capitalism." When they hit Alberta, they were surprised that media listened to them, reporting on their cause. At each stop along the way, the protesters performed guerrilla theatre in the evening and listened to local women discuss their illegal abortions. Many had never spoken about it before. Those discussions cemented the philosophical underpinnings of the pro-choice movement, which would not see hospital committees disbanded for eighteen years.

By the time it reached Ottawa, the Caravan drew five hundred supporters. On Monday, May 11, 1970, thirty-five of the protesters "dressed up" as respectable women in order to get inside the parliamentary gallery. They borrowed nylons and some wore gloves—a tactic to distract security guards from finding the chains stuffed in their purses. Once inside, the protesters chained themselves to the gallery, a nod to suffragists who had chained themselves to the British House of Commons to obtain the vote. Then one of the protesters started giving a speech. Others chimed in, shouting for abortion on demand.

Some of the chains didn't hold, but it didn't matter. The women closed down the House of Commons for more than thirty minutes—the first time in its century-old history—as guards hauled them off. Outside, meanwhile, nearly one hundred protesters in black headscarves carried a coffin representing the estimated ten thousand women who had died from "butcher shop" abortions. They burned a placard bearing the words of Canada's abortion law. Ten women were taken into police custody, but none were charged. National media coverage of the Abortion Caravan helped galvanize the demand for abortion. The women's movement had become an unstoppable force.

61

Abortion is our Right!

Corps
N'est pas
la propriété
de l'état

Pour Nous

Members of the Abortion Caravan protest in Ottawa after shutting down Parliament.
Photographer: Peter Bregg.

62

A newsboy holds up a newspaper reporting the invoking
of the War Measures Act.
Photographer: Peter Bregg.

Desperate Measures

October 16, 1970—Trudeau invokes the War Measures Act.

PETER C. NEWMAN

On October 22, 1970, rumours of war were being passed around Ottawa like after-dinner mints. I was attending a cocktail party at the home of the Liberal trade minister, Jean-Luc Pépin, a target of the Front de libération du Québec, since he was one of the province's most outspoken federalists. In his professorial way Pépin was going on about the mayhem raging in his home province. "Revolutions are all the same," he was saying. "Acts against the old order are invariably preceded by the disintegration of inward allegiances. The images of kings topple before their thrones."

"Well, yeah, I suppose, but what about Mike here?" asked John Munro, one of Trudeau's better ministers, voicing the concern we were all feeling. Mike was an army private from Bell Island, Newfoundland, who had been assigned to guard the Pépins against the forces of evil stalking the trimmed hedges of Rockcliffe.

We were more than two weeks into the FLQ's war against Canada and our first line of defence was Trooper Mike. It was raining, and Pépin had invited the soldier into the house to warm up with a hot toddy. After asking our host to "cut de sweet stuff, gimme de rum," Mike was feeling no pain. "I's de boy to squash dem crazy frogs," he volunteered, which caught the attention of Jean-Luc, among others. When conversation slowed, he took this as a signal to fill the silence with Newfie humour. "De boys up in Gander," he confided, "wants Quebec to separate, just so's we kin drive to Toronto in half de time."

Somebody saved the situation by turning up the television just as Montreal's police chief came on, looking sweaty and dishevelled. "We're raiding blind," he confessed. "We've run out of leads."

For some silly reason, I kept repeating to myself Social Credit party leader Bob Thompson's malapropism: "If this thing starts to snowball, it will catch fire right across the country." The snowball had become an avalanche.

Someone changed the television channel to catch the CBC news and called for quiet. The announcer's voice filled the room, attempting to strike a tone somewhere between authoritative and calm, but barely disguising his underlying panic. A communiqué from the FLQ claimed that two more kidnappings were under way. The Canadian army, swarming over Montreal, had turned the city into an armed camp. Another forty Montrealers had been rounded up and jailed. It was Canada's first experience with domestic terrorism. We felt spooked and betrayed. Didn't these badly dressed, unshaven revolutionaries realize this was Canada, for goodness' sake? We don't do revolutions.

On October 5, British trade commissioner James Cross had been kidnapped by the FLQ. Five days later, Quebec labour minister Pierre Laporte had been snatched by another FLQ cell while playing touch football with his sons. On October 13, Pierre Trudeau assured his place in history and in the hearts of Canadian federalists. When asked how far he would go to defeat the FLQ, even at the cost of their civil rights, he shot back, "Just watch me!" His cheeky defiance was for show; his brute strength—vividly attested by the implementation on October 16 of the War Measures Act—was for real.

And watch him we did, to the exclusion of all else.

Fight for Equality

December 7, 1970—The Status of Women report is released.

NELLE OOSTEROM

When Prime Minister Lester B. Pearson—with great reluctance and after much prodding—announced in early 1967 the establishment of a Royal Commission on the Status of Women, many people wondered what the heck for. The *Globe and Mail* declared that "a commission studying the lack of legal rights for women would probably be able to wind up its business in an afternoon."

It turned out to be a long afternoon. What began as an inquiry that few in the media took seriously—one male columnist snickered at the idea of "women's briefs" being presented at the hearings—became a movement that gained momentum as it crossed the country. In packed hearings women who had never before had a place to air their grievances finally had a forum where they could be heard. The tone of the coverage slowly turned from cheap ridicule to grudging respect. It was apparent that something big was in the air.

The small number of angry young radicals who took to the streets yelling into bullhorns—such as the handful of protesters who showed up at Toronto's Nathan Phillips Square on August 26, 1970—was but the tip of the iceberg of women's discontent. The commission gave space to legions of women who couldn't, or wouldn't, go marching as "women's libbers."

Many of the women who showed up for the hearings were barely aware of the women's liberation movement, which was then in its early stages in Canada. The presenters tended to be with clubs and associations that represented teachers, businesswomen, professionals, homemakers, and the like. Among the inequalities they drew attention to were marital property rights—a particular issue for farm women, who usually had no claim to the farms they worked on.

The hearings—which were held in fourteen cities over a ten-month period and chaired by CBC broadcaster Florence Bird—heard mostly from white, educated, middle-class women. However, some First Nations women did come forward, speaking of poverty, discrimination, and lack of education for themselves and their children.

Although it seems strange today, the commission heard little about violence against women—at that time it wasn't much spoken of—and not a single one of its 167 recommendations addressed that issue. The biggest issue of the time was actually child care. Women made up about a third of the workforce in 1970. Decent daycare for working mothers was the demand of the day. Sadly, it still is today, when women now make up half the workforce. A national system of affordable, regulated daycare has yet to become reality.

However, many of the recommendations tabled in Parliament on December 7, 1970, were eventually implemented in full or in part: employers could no longer discriminate based on gender or marital status; equal-pay laws were strengthened; maternity leave became part of the Labour Code; women could serve alongside men in the RCMP and the armed forces; birth control and abortion became more accessible. While many will argue that much work remains to be done, historians today see the commission's 1970 report as the blueprint that guided the entrenchment of women's rights in Canada.

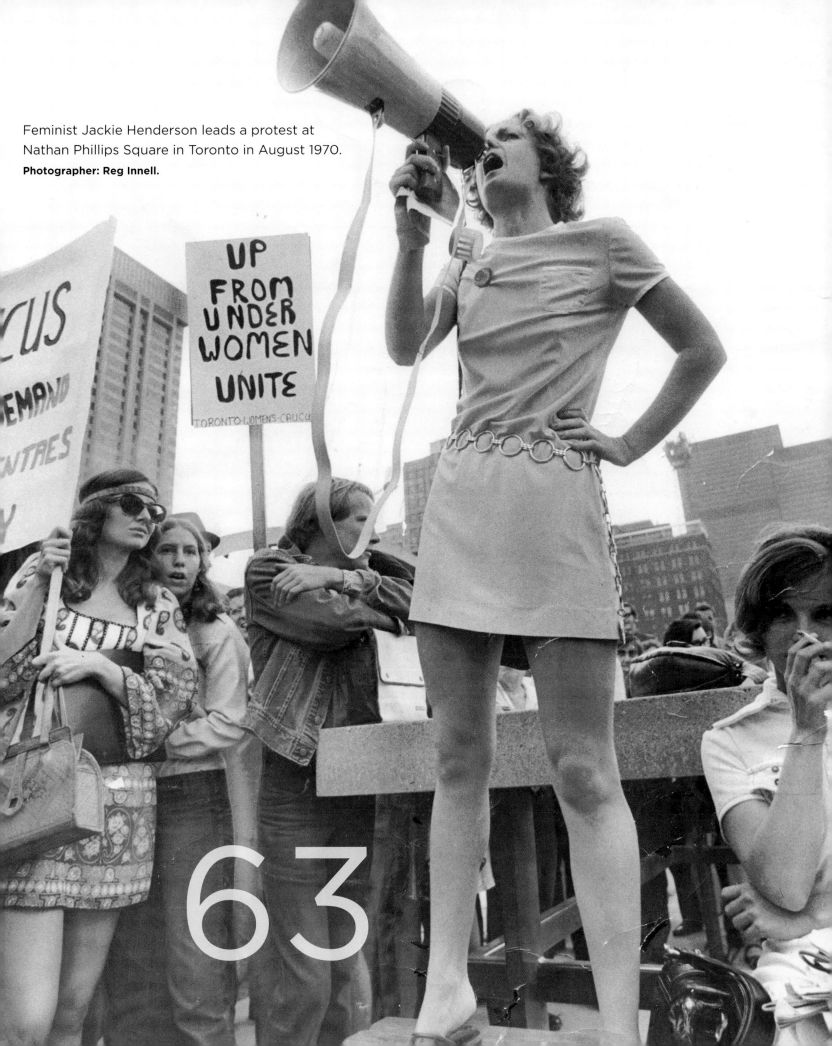

Feminist Jackie Henderson leads a protest at Nathan Phillips Square in Toronto in August 1970.
Photographer: Reg Innell.

63

64

Team Canada goalie Ken Dryden is stormed by Soviet skaters during the 1972 Summit Series.
Photographer: Fred Ross.

Canada Gets Iced

September 2, 1972—Shocking Game 1 loss in the Summit Series.

KEN DRYDEN

On September 28, 1972—in the afternoon in St. John's, Trois-Rivières, Brandon, and Medicine Hat; in the morning in Nanaimo and Dawson City; at night in Moscow, where it happened—Paul Henderson scored the "goal of the century." Twenty-six days earlier, the Canada–Russia Summit Series had begun in Montreal.

Hockey had originated less than a century before, also in Montreal. In the decades since, the National Hockey League was formed and radio had brought the Montreal Canadiens and Toronto Maple Leafs into the imaginations of Canadians in all nine provinces (and Newfoundland). After the Second World War communities everywhere constructed "memorial arenas" and more kids played, more often, and for longer. At the time almost every NHL player was Canadian, and even if, as professionals, they couldn't play the best "amateurs" from other countries in the world championships or the Olympic Games, it didn't matter. Originators and developers of hockey, we were also its foremost practitioners—by far. That is, until the 1950s, and especially the 1960s.

In 1946 the Soviets played their first hockey game. In 1954 they won the world championships. This was the time of the Cold War. Would the communist East or the democratic West win the future? Two aspects of these different ways of life—the space race and sports—were beyond the manipulation of propaganda because we could see them with our own eyes. In the 1972 Summit Series, for the first time able to use NHL players, we would show that West was best. With almost no indoor arenas, the Soviets had developed their game in gyms and on playing fields. They had heavy, club-like sticks and wobbly skates. We had a hundred years of history and hundreds of thousands of players. We had

the equipment, the facilities. Then, in Game 1, we lost 7–3. But wasn't this always what happened to us at any big moment? *Typically Canadian, eh?*

Canada won the Summit Series—barely. But by 1981, when the Soviets beat us 8–1 in the Canada Cup final, our time at the top seemed over. Then a strange thing happened. The NHL opened up to more European and American players. Canadians began training more, both on and off the ice. A skinny kid from Brantford, Ontario, named Wayne Gretzky—his father-teacher greatly influenced by the Russian and European style—transformed the NHL with his passing and open-ice play.

The result, nearly forty years after that Game 1 loss, is that we are the best—not because we started decades ahead of everyone else but because we've learned. The English invented soccer and dominated its first century. They had their "Montreal 1972 moment" at Wembley in 1953 against the Hungarians, losing 6–3. They have made their league the place where the world's best players now play, but unlike Canadians in hockey, the English have seen the world's best countries leave them in the dust. They didn't adapt. We did. *Typically Canadian, eh!*

The truth is, you don't learn when you win. You learn when you lose. On September 28, 1972, we won a game and a lifetime memory. On September 2, we lost and began to learn, and learned that we could learn. September 28 didn't change Canada. September 2 did.

Owe, Baby!

January 29, 1973—Montreal's mayor vows a debt-free Olympics.

RICHARD W. POUND

Almost three years after Montreal's improbable winning bid to host the 1976 Olympic Games, defeating the two superpowers of the day, the financial picture was far from rosy. The massive costs of Expo 67 were still fresh in political minds in 1973, and in Ottawa the Liberal minority government was unwilling to risk defeat by appearing to direct more funds to Montreal. Yet the costs of security—following the massacre during the Munich Games the previous year—were obviously going to increase, and the city's announced budget of $325 million for the Games was clearly insufficient. In fact, little progress had been made on the infrastructure required to organize the Games.

It was time for the City of Montreal to step in to calm the fears and reassure the naysayers. Jean Drapeau was the charismatic, energetic, ambitious, and enigmatic mayor of the city. It was his vision to have a world exposition in Montreal and his dream to host the Olympic Games. Everyone knew the organization of the Games was his project. He would make a statement to calm the situation.

Never one to miss an opportunity for a good line, on January 29, 1973, he uttered the phrase that would become famous. The Olympics could no more have a deficit, he said, than a man could have a baby. This was pretty brave talk from someone who had scribbled the total budget on the back of an envelope, who could not get capital funding from federal programs, who was heading toward the ruinous cost of a covered stadium, and who had not yet succeeded in obtaining legislation to permit an Olympic lottery.

Drapeau played into the hands of a sceptical press by insisting on a single budget, which did not differentiate between capital infrastructure projects and the operational costs of the Games themselves. There was no reason for anyone to expect that Olympic spectators and broadcasters should pay for extensions to the metro line, road improvements, and capital facilities that would be used for decades, not just for the two weeks of the Games. But every item of expenditure was lumped together and the public was misled into thinking that the Olympics were bankrupting the city. Added to this was municipal mismanagement of many projects, eventually leading the Quebec government to step in to ensure that facilities promised by the city for use during the Games were delivered on time. It was fortunate that the stadium did not have to be covered for the Games, since the entire mast and roof structure was not completed until much later.

In one respect Drapeau had been correct. The Games portion of the activities did, in fact, generate a profit. It was larger per capita than that of Los Angeles in 1984, widely regarded as the most financially successful Games in history. Indeed, had the federal government not gratuitously surrendered the immensely profitable Olympic lottery to the provinces, the proceeds would soon have paid off even Montreal's infrastructure investments.

Instead Drapeau was widely regarded as a financially irresponsible laughingstock—deliciously harpooned by Aislin's epic cartoon in the *Montreal Gazette*, which depicted the mayor pregnant and holding a phone, desperately trying to reach abortion doctor Henry Morgentaler. Montreal continues to try to shed the reputation of hosting the costliest Olympics ever.

65

Montreal Mayor Jean Drapeau unveils a model of the proposed Olympic Stadium in January 1975.

Photographer: Anonymous.

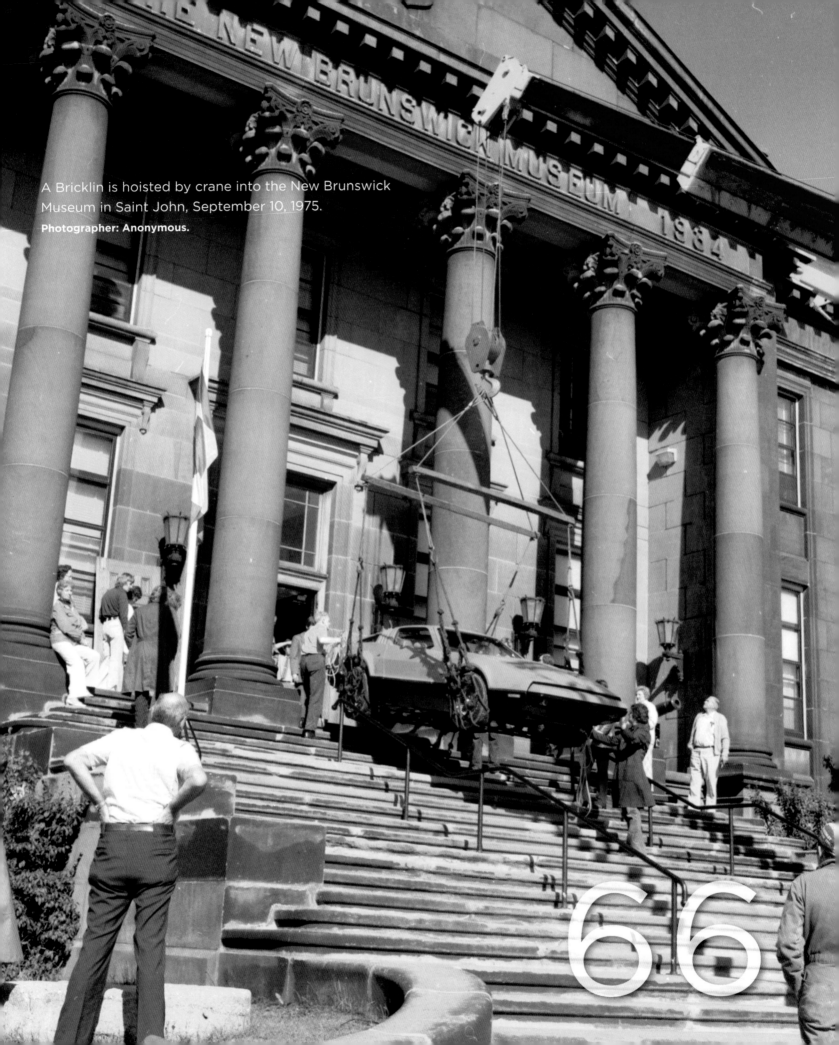

A Bricklin is hoisted by crane into the New Brunswick Museum in Saint John, September 10, 1975.
Photographer: Anonymous.

66

Driven to Distraction

September 25, 1975—New Brunswick's sports-car dream stalls.

MAURICE BASQUE

Richard Hatfield was premier of New Brunswick from 1970 to 1987. His government continued his predecessor Louis J. Robichaud's work of transforming the province into an inclusive, bilingual state, more open to its dynamic Acadian minority. Hatfield really enjoyed the Acadians—their fun-loving nature, their eagerness to party to the wee small hours. They were so different from residents of his native Hartland, firmly located in the Protestant belt of New Brunswick.

No surprise, then, that the doll-collecting, disco-hopping premier fell under the spell of American automotive entrepreneur Malcolm Bricklin. A smooth talker if there ever was one, Bricklin had some experience in introducing imported cars to the North American market. But Bricklin had bigger dreams. He had created a new sports car with an acrylic body and doors that opened upward, looking like seagull wings. The Bricklin SV-1 (which stands for "Safety Vehicle One") was ahead of its time in safety, design, and urban chic, but its production needed millions of dollars. Where would Bricklin find someone with enough chutzpah to bankroll the project?

Enter Premier Hatfield. Convinced his mostly rural province, with no experience in car manufacturing, would be the ideal place to produce the futuristic chariot, he signed a deal with the carmaker. After many delays, the Bricklin was officially launched in June 1974—not in New Brunswick but at the Four Seasons Hotel on Park Avenue in New York City. "Disco Dick" was already a well-known connoisseur of the Big Apple's nightlife. The beautiful people of Manhattan were surprised by the car's revolutionary look and its unique building material, but like the box of fresh Atlantic salmon Hatfield had brought with him, the Bricklin failed to make a lasting impression.

New Brunswickers, on the other hand, never forgot the Bricklin. Customers did not rush to purchase it (only 2,854 were produced), and on September 25, 1975, the company fell into receivership, leaving a $23-million debt in the hands of the Hatfield government. The Bricklin fiasco would be one of many personal public embarrassments that would haunt Hatfield during his last years as premier. Marijuana was found in his suitcase on the royal plane during Queen Elizabeth II's visit to New Brunswick in its bicentennial year in 1984. And if that wasn't enough, rumours persisted that he had used cocaine with young male university students, rumours that were also linked to the perception that he was a closet homosexual. In the provincial election of 1987, the Liberal Party under Frank McKenna won all fifty-eight seats in Fredericton's legislature. The party was over for Hatfield. He was appointed to the Senate in 1990 and died the following year of a brain tumour.

In death, Richard Hatfield and the Bricklin affair became the stuff of legends. Books were written on the subject, documentary films were produced, Canada Post issued a commemorative stamp in 1996, and in 2003, the Royal Canadian Mint struck a twenty-dollar sterling-silver commemorative coin. A Bricklin International Owners Club was created, and in 2010, a musical entitled *The Bricklin: An Automotive Fantasy*, produced by Theatre New Brunswick at the Fredericton Playhouse, was a hit. It showed Richard Hatfield boogying on stage in front of a Bricklin. For eternity, "Tricky Dicky," the scion of a Baptist Conservative political dynasty, would now fly on the wings of a Bricklin, enjoying the spotlight he had craved in life.

Death-or-Life Situation

July 14, 1976—Canada abolishes the death penalty.

LESLEY PARROTT

In 1976 it felt like I was living the Canadian dream. Since emigrating from Scotland to Canada eleven years earlier, I had established myself in the advertising world. I was happily married and had, in 1974, given birth to a much-anticipated and truly adored baby daughter, Alison.

When legislation to abolish the death penalty was passed in 1976, I didn't give it much thought. The last executions had been carried out in 1962, and I was surprised that capital punishment had *ever* been legal in Canada. In my view, it did not seem to fit with the attitudes and values of my newly adopted country.

The vote in the House of Commons, though, had proven divisive. Members of Parliament voted their conscience, crossing party lines to abolish the death penalty by a narrow margin. Some credited Prime Minister Pierre Trudeau's last-minute plea for swaying the minds of Liberals and Conservatives alike: "Those who vote against the bill . . . cannot escape their personal share of responsibility for the hangings which will take place if the bill is defeated."

In 1987 capital punishment once again dominated headlines. A free vote loomed before Parliament, provoking intense public debate. This now commanded my full attention, as by this time my life had changed irrevocably. In July 1986 our darling daughter, Alison, had been lured from our home, raped, and murdered. Immediately following her murder, I was moved to state publicly that "I did not believe in the death penalty last week and I certainly don't now."

I did not want Alison's death to be used as a reason for restoring the death penalty. So in the spring of 1987, as the debate intensified, I felt compelled to participate. I spoke out in the media and wrote to MPs, beseeching them not to vote for this bill. I personally met with my own MP, who did change his mind on the issue, and I heard back from many others; most were appreciative of my stance, given my deeply personal experience.

It's been argued that capital punishment makes victims' families feel that justice has been duly served. But I couldn't comprehend how premeditated killing by the state could ever be condoned. In my mind, it would only continue the cycle of needless violence. For this act to be done in the name of my country—and on behalf of my daughter—seemed outrageous. Then there is the possibility of wrongful convictions: David Milgaard, Donald Marshall, and Guy Paul Morin, among others. Had they been executed, it would have been an unforgivable public sin.

I came to realize that revenge is a bitter pill that often burns deeply only in our own souls. I wanted to find ways for me to heal, for our society to heal, and for Alison to be remembered with love. Therefore, I was very pleased when the 1987 motion to reinstate the death penalty was defeated by a vote of 148 to 127.

Deeply complex issues are involved in keeping society safe from dangerous and repeat offenders. Life imprisonment has to mean just that. Simplistically, taking a life for a life lowers our country's dignity and values, and it would certainly not make Canada a better or safer place.

67

Protesters march in Toronto on the night of Canada's last executions, December 11, 1962.
Photographer: Barry Philp.

68

LE PARTI QUÉBÉCO

OUI

Independence Anxiety

November 15, 1976—The Parti Québécois soars to power.

BRIAN YOUNG

What a dramatic moment in Quebec history, with the diminutive René Lévesque celebrating the first victory of the Parti Québécois! A popular television journalist, Lévesque founded the party in 1968 around the contradiction, as he put it, that "French Canada was an authentic nation, but a nation without sovereignty." His call for an independent Quebec confronted Pierre Elliott Trudeau's federalist vision of a French Canada from coast to coast. Quebec, Trudeau insisted, "cannot say it alone speaks for French Canadians."

As a result of the Quiet Revolution, the Quebec state expanded greatly after 1960, taking control of schools and hospitals from the Catholic Church, nationalizing the remaining private electric companies, and using capital from the Quebec pension and automobile insurance funds to control massive public works projects such as hydroelectric dams. The PQ victory of November 15, 1976, came on the heels of a charged decade that had included Expo 67 in Montreal, Trudeau's introduction of official bilingualism across Canada in 1969, the October Crisis of 1970, the Common Front strikes in Montreal in 1972, and on going French-language insecurity, particularly around Italian immigration into Montreal and the community's preference for English schools.

Quebecers increasingly came to see the Quebec government, rather than Ottawa, as their "national" government. Those in favour of independence in Quebec rose from 5 percent in 1966 to 41 percent a decade later. In the 1976 election the Parti Québécois won 71 of the 110 seats in the Quebec National Assembly. With this mandate Lévesque set out to extend reforms begun in the Quiet Revolution, appointing powerful ministers like Jacques Parizeau in finance, Jacques-Yvan Morin in constitutional matters, and Camille Laurin in culture and language questions.

Bill 101—the 1977 Charter of the French Language—was the cornerstone, with French legislated as "the normal language of work, education, communications, and business." Access by immigrants to English education was severely restricted, bilingual signs were prohibited, and French was given priority in government and business. In 1977 Quebec, which already had diplomatic missions in Europe, opened offices in the United States. A year later, through an agreement with Ottawa, the province took on a much stronger role in the choice of its immigrants. Quebec roundly rejected the multiculturalism promoted by Ottawa in favour of a pluralist society that gave priority to French language and culture. A generation of nationalist artists, supported by the ministry of culture, produced an extraordinary body of films, plays, music, and literature.

The euphoria of 1976 did not last. The failure of two referendums on sovereignty in 1980 and 1995, Quebec's exclusion from the constitutional agreements around the Charter of Rights and Freedom of 1982, the defeat of the Parti Québécois in 1985, and the failure to ratify the Meech Lake Accord in 1987 saw to that. By the beginning of the twenty-first century, Quebecers faced a future in which they remained deeply divided over independence.

Madonna of the Ice Fields

March 22, 1977—Brigitte Bardot protests the seal hunt.

TINA LOO

Why choose Paris in the springtime when you could be in St. Anthony? That was the decision French bombshell Brigitte Bardot made when she joined a group of animal rights activists in the northern Newfoundland town to protest the seal hunt in March 1977. Bardot's presence signalled a turning point in the anti-sealing campaign, especially for more militant groups like the International Fund for Animal Welfare. Committed to ending the hunt, in the mid-1970s IFAW began to phrase its opposition more in the emotional language of animal rights than in the dispassionate arguments of science. Like their fellow travellers in Greenpeace, the members of IFAW had become more media savvy. IFAW hoped that Bardot's star power would be bright enough to illuminate the carnage occurring on the whelping grounds.

On March 22, the fading starlet and her guides headed to the ice fields to search for seals—and for photo ops. IFAW's shift in goals, messaging, and tactics was all contained in a single image that circled the globe. An oddly disturbing and potent combination of sex, death, maternal love, and mascara, the image of Bardot cuddling a harp seal pup appealed to everyone. Men, women, and children pledged their support—and funds—to the cause, which by the mid-1970s had found itself short of cash and momentum thanks to its own success.

Those successes were rooted in a campaign directed at Canadians, calling for scientifically based conservation and more humane killing methods. In response, during the 1960s Ottawa subjected the hunt to licensing, limits, and on-site inspection. By the early 1970s the effectiveness of the campaign was such that mainstream campaigners like the World Wildlife Fund withdrew to focus on more pressing issues, leaving IFAW with a big problem: the seals might have been saved, but the animal rights agenda was at risk. Then, thanks to the woman whom journalist and Newfoundlander Rex Murphy dubbed the "madonna of the ice fields," IFAW raised $1.3 million in 1977 while the price for sealskins plummeted. Even the hardbitten politicians of the European Community weren't immune to her influence: Bardot's appearance led them to ban the importation of whitecoat seal products in 1983.

Newfoundlanders were powerless in the face of the parade of "cleavage scientists" who found their way to the floes. All they had to counter Bardot was Premier Frank Moores, some scientists, and a slogan: "Save the Cod, Kill a Seal." The Inuit fared no better: the Canadian government was ineffective in making the case for hunting as a cultural right.

Few who supported the end of sealing had any idea of the impact of their actions on the people who depended on the hunt. In the end IFAW's success in stopping commercial sealing was built first on exploiting the gulf between producers and consumers that lies at the root of many of the environmental problems we continue to confront, and second on feeding the same "star-maker machinery" that created a demand for furs in the first place.

Brigitte Bardot hugs a whitecoat seal on the ice of the Gulf of St. Lawrence in March 1977.
Photographer: Miroslav Brozek.

69

70

Pierre Trudeau pirouettes behind Queen Elizabeth
at Buckingham Palace, May 7, 1977.

Photographer: Doug Ball.

Just Watch Him

May 7, 1977—Trudeau pirouettes behind the Queen.

MARGARET WENTE

There had never been a leader like him. Pierre Trudeau was anti-conformist, cheeky, and irreverent—just like the youthful crowds who adored him. His calculated pirouette behind the unsuspecting Queen at a G7 conference in London on May 7, 1977, captured the spirit of the times: we were a colony no more; Canada had come into its own.

Trudeau was our Kennedy—a youthful, virile prime minister who made the grey and dull Canada of our youth seem almost sexy. He dated Barbra Streisand and wed a flower child. He flipped off diving boards. He paddled northern rivers in a fringed buckskin jacket. Trudeau had no taste for the polite evasions of public life. He once referred to members of Parliament as "nobodies" and told Opposition members to "fuddle-duddle" themselves. During the FLQ crisis of 1970, when pressed about how far he would go in suspending civil liberties to maintain order, he said, "Just watch me." We never stopped.

Trudeau did more than transform our image of ourselves. He transformed our institutions. For years he battled to patriate the Constitution, a task he finally completed five years after that naughty pirouette. With that, Canada officially cut the apron strings to Britain and won complete sovereignty as an independent country. He expanded access to abortion, made divorce easier to obtain, promoted women's rights, and decriminalized homosexuality, leading a wave of social change that has made Canada one of the most tolerant nations in the world.

To the extent that we regard our nation as liberal, progressive, and tolerant, Trudeau's values have become Canadian values. He entrenched bilingualism and multiculturalism. His Charter of Rights and Freedoms, which was designed to protect individuals and minorities against the state, greatly expanded the freedoms of Canadians and has become a cornerstone of Canadian law. As pollster Michael Adams wrote, "Love him or hate him, we are all Trudeau's children."

There's a dark side to the story, of course. By the time he left office in 1984—after fifteen years in power—Canadians were thoroughly sick of Pierre Trudeau. Westerners never forgave him for his ruinous energy policies, which confiscated billions from the coffers of Alberta. His flower child bride had long since fled, taking much of the Trudeau magic with her. The economy had turned sour, and even those who'd cheered loudest in the early days were fed up with his aloofness and his arrogance.

His critics have called Trudeau a boastful exhibitionist—always on the lookout for the calculated gesture. I prefer to regard him as an early master of the photo op. There are more iconic photos of Trudeau than of all our other prime ministers put together—the young, hip politician with a rose in his lapel; the unflinching leader standing his ground before a separatist mob; the nose-thumbing rebel sliding down the banister at Buckingham Palace; and many others.

The pirouette itself had been planned and rehearsed. Nothing personal, of course—Trudeau liked the Queen. It was the aristocratic pomp and protocol that he couldn't stand. We all got the message, and we loved it. The era of deference was over. And we were free, at last, to be ourselves.

Stand Tall

March 31, 1978—Stompin' Tom Connors sends back his Junos.

OLD MAN LUEDECKE

Stompin' Tom Connors had a good point to make in 1978 when he sent his Juno Awards back. He believed that Canadian radio didn't want to play Canadian music—certainly not his—and that too often, Junos were given to artists who had left Canada to work and live in the United States or elsewhere.

Prior to the 1978 Juno Awards, Connors withdrew his name from contention, drawing heat for his decision. Two days after the ceremony, he called a press conference. It was March 31, 1978, and Connors, standing before a group of reporters, said, "I feel that Junos should be for people who are living in Canada, whose main base of operations is Canada, [and] who are working toward the recognition of Canadian talent in this country." Before him on a table were his six Junos—awards, he said, he was "once proud to receive, but am now ashamed to keep." With that, he packed the Junos in a cardboard box and sent them in a taxi to the offices of the Canadian Association of Recording Arts and Sciences, which ran the awards. Connors also vowed not to perform live again until the music industry began to support homegrown talent. Few believed he would carry through with the threat—but he didn't perform again for more than a decade.

In 1978 Stompin' Tom took a stand for made-in-Canada music. Since then, his cause has been taken up by subsequent generations of artists, including—somewhat by accident and partly by design—me. It's a simple notion: that great music can be made here and exported to the world.

I grew up during a great bloom of made-in-Canada musical success. In high school, I made mix tapes stuffed with bands like the Hip, Skydiggers, and Blue Rodeo, inking in badly drawn maple leaves on the tapes' spines. Today I make my living playing music and, like Stompin' Tom, do it from within Canada. I know many other artists who are also fighting through the music-business muck to create something real. I'm proud of my music, and work hard to get it heard both in Canada and around the world—although I'm sure it would never have made it on commercial radio back in 1978, when Stompin' Tom was kicking up a fuss, just as it doesn't now.

We have a wonderful and nourishing myth in this country about "the Canadian songwriter." Although based in part on the brilliant art of a select group of Canadians who found astronomical success south of the border, the myth has helped give us generations of good songs and encouraged many young musicians to take up the cause. Thanks to technology, musicians today can connect with audiences worldwide while living and working in Canada. If you can create something valuable—and if you don't crave massive success—you can usually squeak by.

My grandmother had an expression: "The quiet good goes on." Few of us have stood for independent music in as bold a fashion as Stompin' Tom. (I haven't returned the two Junos I've won for best traditional folk album.) But all Canadian musicians should thank Tom Connors for the elbow room he created for us to express our individuality, independence, and our pride in Canada. Stompin' Tom helped make us all believe that we can create music that's relevant to ourselves—and to the world.

71

Stompin' Tom Connors performs in 2005 prior to an NHL game between Toronto and Ottawa.
Photographer: Frank Gunn.

72

A Vietnamese refugee cries tears of joy after meeting her Canadian sponsors in Ottawa.
Photographer: Drew Gragg.

Sanctuary

August 6, 1979—Ottawa gives asylum to the boat people.

BEVERLEY TALLON

They crammed in rusty, overcrowded boats, some fleeing the Communist takeover of South Vietnam and many expelled by their country. These were the so-called boat people, who came to Canada in 1979 and 1980. Unlike their predecessors—mostly urban, middle-class Vietnamese—the boat people were a diverse economic and social group of Vietnamese and ethnic Chinese, Cambodian, and Laotian people.

Almost sixty thousand refugees would seek sanctuary in Canada during this time. Some almost drowned during their escape. They endured typhoons, pirate attacks, starvation, and illness. Many people didn't make it. Some had already spent months, sometimes years, in makeshift relief camps.

Organized efforts to help the boat people began as early as June 1979. Marion Dewar, the newly elected mayor of Ottawa, saw the refugees as people in crisis, not foreigners clinging to boats. She decided that Ottawa and its citizens needed to help. With the support of local church and citizens' groups, as well as immigration officials, she approached the media to launch Project 4000—a plan to recruit local citizens to sponsor refugees to Canada. On July 7, 1979, the *Ottawa Citizen* ran a series of sponsorship request forms in its pages, urging its readers to support the boat people. Some two hundred sponsorship groups formed as a result of it.

Meanwhile, the Canadian government was formulating its own response to the humanitarian crisis. In July 1979, the federal government had launched a new joint sponsorship program: it would accept one government-sponsored refugee for each person who was sponsored by a private citizen. Response was mixed. Some Canadians did not want more new immigrants, fearing they would topple the country's delicate economic balance. But many church and corporate groups, plus private individuals, opened their arms and their wallets to the newcomers.

In Ottawa citizens began to rally behind the cause. A public meeting for Project 4000 held in mid-July at Exhibition Hall in Lansdowne Park resulted in a huge turnout. Mayor Dewar was thrilled: "The feeling was so positive, it was electric. I expected a lot of opposition but it wasn't there." From these leaps of faith, the pieces of Project 4000 were put in place. On August 6, 1979, the first two hundred refugees arrived at Ottawa's airport. Citizens and government would eventually go on to sponsor close to 3,700 boat people, and other communities would also step forward to welcome refugees.

Today, Canada is one of the most multicultural countries in the world. Since the Second World War the country has opened its doors to refugees and others dispossessed by war and violence. Hungarians, Ugandans, Chileans, and recently Haitians are among the many nationalities to have joined Canada's cultural makeup.

The adjustments for the newcomers are enormous: from learning an unfamiliar language to negotiating new surroundings. A friend of mine—one of the boat people—rarely speaks about his past. Perhaps the experience is still too traumatic to discuss. I know him as a cultured man who wears fine monogrammed shirts. But life as he knew it changed dramatically when the Vietnam War ended. As he once told me, "I arrived with only the shirt on my back."

The long tradition of immigration has brought a rich blend to Canada's culture and economy, and immigrants like my friend will continue to be the country's future.

Journey's End

September 2, 1980—Cancer halts the Marathon of Hope.

DEBORAH MORRISON

On August 31, 1980, my family and I were driving west along the highway just east of Thunder Bay on the final day of our long trip home from a summer vacation in Quebec. It was late Sunday afternoon, and we slowed our car as we noticed flashing lights up ahead of us, followed by the unmistakable gait of Canada's legendary marathoner. I remember saying to my mom, "Hey, look—that's the guy who's running across Canada to raise money for cancer! That's Terry Fox!"

My sisters and I peered over the back seat and watched Fox recede in the distance. I remember it looked like a hard and lonely mission. He was running by himself, with police escorts ahead and a van behind him, just as we had seen in so many photos and videos. The modest caravan kept as far to the right of the road as it could to allow cars and freight trucks to pass.

Although Terry Fox had captured the hearts of many Canadians as he worked his way through Ontario during the summer months, he was at that time far from the household name he is today. In the car, our family speculated about that. We wondered how many western Canadians were following his Marathon of Hope, how long it would take him to reach Vancouver, and how big his campaign would become. Having reached the halfway point—conquering the tough roads around Lake Superior, and at that point exceeding his original goal of $1 million by raising $1.7 million—this determined young man would indeed finish the journey, we were sure.

Two days later, on September 2, 1980, I wept as I watched his television interview from a hospital gurney outside a waiting ambulance. A devastated Terry Fox confirmed that the cancer had returned and his run was over. All of Canada was devastated too. Terry said, "I hope with what I have done, I have been an inspiration.

That people will take off and continue where I have left off here." Canadians couldn't bear the thought that Terry's tireless determination might not be enough to carry him to the finish line. He moved us to respond in ways we never imagined we could.

Overnight, his fight became our fight. Within hours of the news story, tens of thousands of dollars were raised by radio call-in shows and individual pledges to the Canadian Cancer Society. Within a week, tens of millions were pledged through corporate campaigns and a nationally televised marathon. And by the time of his death, on June 28, 1981, $24 million—representing his revised goal of a dollar for every Canadian—had been raised.

Although many offers were made to complete his run, Terry always refused them, determined one day to return and finish it himself. The one exception was Four Seasons owner Isadore Sharp's proposal to establish an annual running event to be held across Canada. Terry agreed, so long as the race would always be non-competitive. Thirty years later, the annual Terry Fox Run has collected over $550 million and involves more than thirty countries around the world. The event takes place every September, typically right after Labour Day weekend, to honour when Terry's Marathon of Hope ended—and ours began.

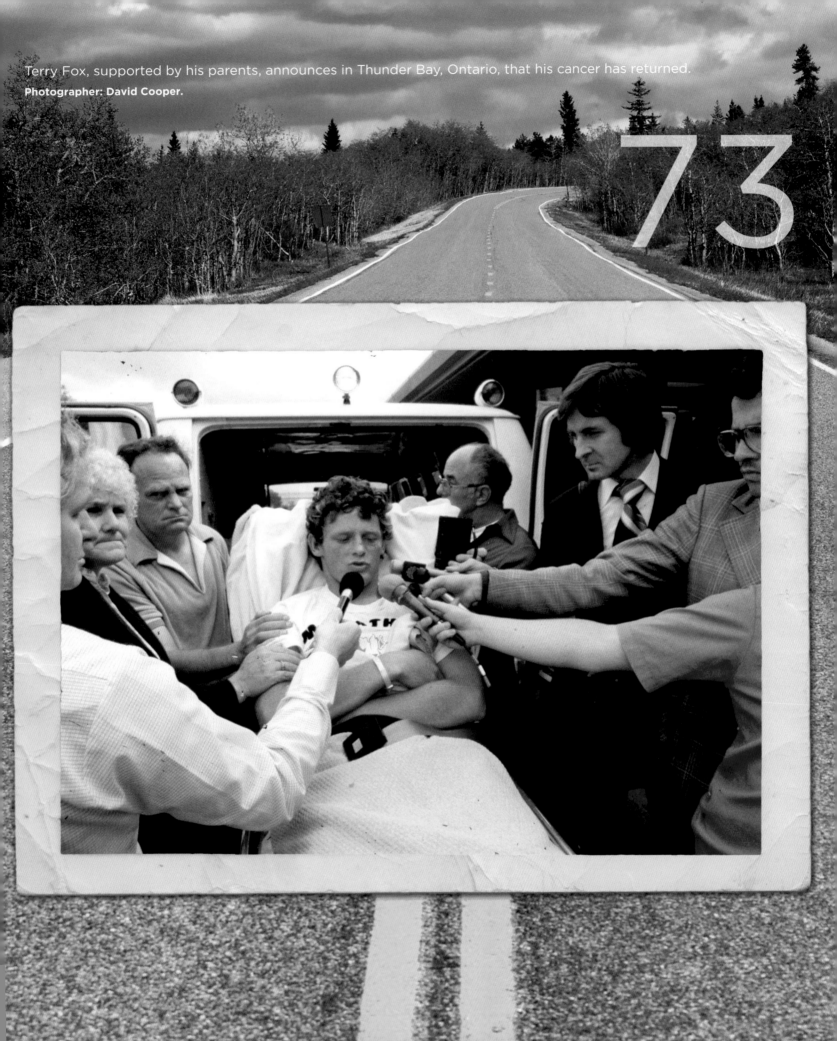

Terry Fox, supported by his parents, announces in Thunder Bay, Ontario, that his cancer has returned.
Photographer: David Cooper.

73

74

Edmontonian Brian Brunke, wearing a Pierre Trudeau mask and an oil barrel, protests the National Energy Program in 1980.
Photographer: Anonymous.

Power Failure

October 28, 1980—The National Energy Program infuriates Westerners.

PETER LOUGHEED

The attempted introduction of the federal National Energy Program on October 28, 1980, changed for all time the nature and substance of Canadian federalism. In tandem with the constitutional revision of 1982, it created a Canada in which the provinces are equal with the federal government on most major economic and social issues.

When Pierre Trudeau returned to power in 1980—defeating Prime Minister Joe Clark's minority government—he had won a majority but had practically no seats in Western Canada, and none in Alberta. After successfully combating separatists during the Quebec referendum, Trudeau turned his focus on Alberta. Concerned that the province had such a strong financial position from its oil and gas revenues, thereby allowing it to act independently from the federal government on financial matters, Trudeau initiated discussions with me directly in July 1980 at his summer residence in Harrington Lake, outside Ottawa.

The meeting did not go well. Trudeau proposed a new energy policy that amounted to a takeover of provincial ownership rights. I responded that the policy would threaten Confederation—especially as it was concurrent with the prime minister's attempt to amend the Constitution to create an almost centralized state, essentially controlled by the federal government.

On October 28, 1980, the federal government presented its budget, which included the proposed National Energy Program. The NEP would give Ottawa overriding authority over oil and natural gas. The main provisions were federal oil taxation at the wellhead and a federal natural gas export tax. In addition, there was a "back-in" provision through which the federal government would pick up a 25 percent interest in any previous discoveries on federally owned land through the newly created and federally owned Petro-Canada. This created a sour attitude in the international investment community, particularly in the United States. As David G. Wood states in his book *The Lougheed Legacy*, the NEP was among the biggest fiascos in any public policy program in Canada's history.

In Alberta our initial response was to inform Albertans via a half-hour television program that the provincial government would "turn down the taps" and reduce, in three stages, the province's crude oil production by a very substantial 180,000 barrels per day. The last stage would take place in September 1981. Next, we challenged the natural gas export tax in the courts. We considered the tax illegal because one government in Confederation cannot tax another. Our test case was successful at both the Alberta Court of Appeal and the Supreme Court of Canada. Clearly, the NEP could not stand unchanged.

Negotiations between Alberta and Ottawa resulted in an agreement that the prime minister and I signed on September 1, 1981. The deal reaffirmed Alberta's ownership of its resources, increased the price of oil and thus the financial return to the province, and removed the federal export tax on the sale of Alberta-owned natural gas to non-Canadians. Alberta compromised as well—for instance, by accepting the federal wellhead tax and a natural gas liquids tax.

In 1985, the newly elected prime minister, Brian Mulroney, worked with Alberta to dissolve all aspects of the NEP. The program caused a chain of reactions, perhaps the most long-lasting being the strong and sustained antipathy toward the federal government that many older Western Canadians have.

PART FOUR

INTO THE FUTURE
1981–PRESENT

Perhaps, then, Canada is not so much a country as magnificent raw material for a country; and perhaps the question is not "Who are we?" but "What are we going to make of ourselves?"

—ALDEN NOWLAN, 1971

There were so many things to admire—and even envy—about Canada at the close of the twentieth century. We enjoyed democratic freedoms and a stable economy. Our natural areas were vast and unspoiled. We consistently ranked among the ten best countries in which to live, according to United Nations surveys. So the twentieth century hadn't belonged to Canada. The Americans had claimed that crown. But we had staked a place near the top: we were a major middle power, punching far above our weight in terms of influence on the world stage.

Despite this, Canada entered the 1980s as a nation searching for its identity. We survived the first Quebec referendum on sovereignty but emerged wounded and raw. We were officially bilingual, but in reality the centuries-old solitudes of English and French remained.

All the while, a new Canada was emerging—one that was multicultural and increasingly urban. As western oil fuelled the country's economy, increasing numbers of Easterners, particularly from Atlantic Canada, decided to go "down the road" to find work.

We beamed over our technological achievements, taking pride as the American space shuttle relied on the Canadarm to conduct its missions. But beginning in the mid-eighties, we were jolted back to earth by a series of tragedies that would have lasting repercussions. We were shocked by the 1985 Air India disaster and by the 1989 massacre of women students in Montreal.

Incredibly, in the mid-nineties we found ourselves again on the brink of separation. It had begun in 1990, when Prime Minister Brian Mulroney opted to "roll all the dice" on Canada, with disastrous results. The death of his Meech Lake Accord further splintered the country along regional and linguistic lines, resulting in the 1995 referendum, which was barely won by the federalist side.

As we rushed toward the new millennium, the pace of change was staggering. In the 1960s computers had filled entire rooms. Now laptops and hand-held smartphones were becoming commonplace. The era of social networking, googling, and tweeting had arrived. Marshall McLuhan's bold prediction of a "global village" was unfolding around us. Canadian talent—from Bryan Adams and Céline Dion to Margaret Atwood, Rohinton Mistry, and Wayne Gretzky—was no longer ours alone. We shared our constellation of stars with the world.

Then came September 11, 2001. The 9/11 terrorist attacks in the United States forced us to rethink the decades-old myth of Canadian soldiers as peacekeepers. We now faced an enemy without borders or national ties. We sent troops to Afghanistan to fight in a "war against terror." We cracked down on security—at borders, at airports—and also increased the powers of government to monitor and arrest us.

As we head deeper into the twenty-first century, the old tale of Canada, based on two "founding peoples" with last names like Macdonald and Cartier, seems outdated. Today, we're writing a new story—not yet complete—about an increasingly cosmopolitan nation still seeking its destiny.

—Mark Reid

75 Quebec Premier René Lévesque shrugs off Prime Minister Pierre Trudeau at a first ministers conference, September 9, 1980.
Photographer: Drew Gragg.

What's Cooking?

November 2, 1981—The kitchen conference saves the Constitution.

DON NEWMAN

It came down to three men huddled in the kitchen of an old railway station just off Parliament Hill in Ottawa that had been transformed into a government conference centre. Away from prying eyes, federal justice minister Jean Chrétien, Ontario attorney general Roy McMurtry, and his counterpart from Saskatchewan, Roy Romanow, were engaged in secret negotiations to put an end to nearly a decade of constitutional wrangling.

All through the night of November 2, 1981, the three politicians jousted until they finally agreed on a deal to break the provincial logjam preventing the patriation of the Constitution. It was a pivotal moment for the country, but ominously, no one from Quebec had been invited to attend.

For years Canadians had been talking about and trying to patriate the Constitution from the British Parliament at Westminster. But without an agreement on how to make future amendments, the British North America Act of 1867 remained the primary law of the land. Complicating the situation was Prime Minister Pierre Trudeau's wish to add a Charter of Rights and Freedoms to a Canadian Constitution. The premiers generally opposed the plan, fearing that it would weaken the powers of provincial legislatures. Quebec, which was governed by Premier René Lévesque and his separatist Parti Québécois, was especially concerned. Their government was still smarting from the referendum loss of 1980 and was in no mood to compromise.

After a failed attempt to reach a deal in 1980, and under the direction of the Supreme Court, the premiers and Trudeau met in Ottawa in November 1981. Going into the meeting, Trudeau had only two premiers onside—Ontario's William Davis and New Brunswick's Richard Hatfield. He faced opposition from Lévesque and the remaining premiers, the so-called Gang of Eight.

At the conference, Trudeau surprised the Gang of Eight by proposing to patriate the Constitution immediately with no changes, no Charter, and no amending formula. Trudeau's plan called for a further two-year period to debate finer details like an amending formula. At that time, the results would be put to a national referendum. Lévesque liked the plan, but the rest of the Gang of Eight did not.

Trudeau's goal of splitting the Gang of Eight had worked. The other premiers thought Lévesque had abandoned them. Behind the scenes, though, Trudeau knew the separatist premier would never agree to a new Canadian Constitution. And so he secretly sent his justice minister, Chrétien, to work out a compromise with his ally Ontario and with Saskatchewan, who represented the now-split Gang of Eight. The deal they settled on gave increased powers to the provinces, as well as a dual method of amending the Constitution. And crucially they added a "notwithstanding clause" that permitted provinces to ignore court orders requiring them to change laws to conform to the Charter.

And where was Lévesque during all this? Soundly sleeping at a separate hotel across the Ottawa River in Quebec, away from the other premiers. The next morning he arrived at the conference to find himself the odd man out—betrayed, he said, by his fellow premiers, who in turn said he had betrayed them.

The kitchen conference of 1981 enabled Trudeau to bring the Constitution "home" to Canada. But it alienated nationalist Quebecers. Three decades later, the document still doesn't have Quebec's signature. And among nationalist Quebecers the kitchen conference is still bitterly referred to as "the night of the long knives."

Ocean Danger

February 15, 1982—Disaster strikes Newfoundland's offshore oil industry.

NELLE OOSTEROM

For many people in Newfoundland and Labrador, the memory of the *Ocean Ranger* disaster is still vivid and raw. They recall waking up on the morning of February 15, 1982, to the unbelievable news that the world's biggest, most advanced oil drilling rig had disappeared into the freezing waters of the Atlantic in the teeth of a fierce winter storm. All eighty-four men on board perished. Dreams of an easy path to oil prosperity for Canada's poorest province died with them.

Perhaps what stung the most was that the *Ocean Ranger*'s sinking had been preventable. Two other nearby rigs survived the storm with barely a scratch. Sloppy safety procedures, design flaws, poor training, and pressure to maximize profits combined to sink the *Ranger*, according to the Royal Commission into the disaster.

The sinking came just three years after oil was found in the Hibernia field off the Grand Banks. That discovery was huge—all of a sudden Newfoundland had a shot at Alberta-like oil prosperity. Goodbye to the futility of making a go of the rapidly disappearing cod fishery. Hello, petrodollars.

Mobil Oil of Canada, which held the leases for the region, contracted the New Orleans–based Ocean Drilling and Exploration Company to drill delineation wells to map out the size of the field. ODECO's *Ocean Ranger* arrived in Newfoundland in November 1980. Eager locals clambered aboard for well-paid work. But some soon came to call their floating workplace the *Ocean Danger*. Workers told of an unusually high number of minor accidents and injuries, of being under tremendous pressure to perform, of poor training. Only a week before the disaster, the rig nearly toppled over because an ill-trained crewman accidentally opened a valve in one of the ballast tanks.

On the evening of February 14, a massive wave up to six storeys high washed over the rig, smashing through a porthole in the ballast control room. Water poured in, wreaking havoc with the computer system that controlled the rig's balance. As the commission would ask later, why was a sensitive computer system placed so close to a porthole and not sealed against water damage? The rig began to list badly. A few hours later, all hands abandoned ship. Lifeboats fell apart in the maelstrom as they were lowered in gale-force winds. One lifeboat carrying about thirty-six crewmen remained intact but capsized just as a rescue boat came tantalizingly close to hauling it in. No one survived.

Lessons learned from the disaster led to enhanced safety regulations and improved design. In fact, Newfoundland and Labrador has become a world leader in training for disasters at sea. After a brief hiatus, drilling continued. Oil and gas now account for about 15 percent of the province's gross domestic product and, in 2010, helped fuel what was the highest rate of economic growth of all the provinces.

Yet prosperity and pride have not erased the lingering anger and mistrust that are still palpable at the *Ocean Ranger* memorial service, held each year at St. Pius X church in St. John's. In 2010 the Reverend John Dinn reminded people in his sermon that "faceless oil companies are only concerned with profit. That may not be nice to say here today, but it's true. It's true."

A young Newfoundland girl prays at a memorial service for victims of the *Ocean Ranger* disaster.

Photographer: Boris Spremo.

76

Diana, Princess of Wales, dazzles a group of young fans during the 1983 Canadian royal visit.
Photographer: David Cooper.

77

Lady Love

June 14, 1983—The People's Princess dazzles Canada.

MARK REID

There's a part in all of us that wants to believe in fairy tales. And so, when Prince Charles married Diana Spencer in 1981, we saw it as a storybook romance come to life.

Two years later, a new chapter was written when the couple arrived for an eighteen-day tour of Canada. From the moment the royals landed in Nova Scotia, on June 14, 1983, we were transfixed. "It was love at first sight," the *Globe and Mail* gushed on its front page. With her blonde hair, blue eyes, and shy demeanour, Diana dazzled the thousands who flocked to see her. Her charm was captivating—and even New Brunswick's premier wasn't immune. In Saint John, Richard Hatfield shocked many when, during a toast to the couple, he declared, "Your Royal Highnesses, we have heard and read the lies; today it was wonderful to meet and know the truth." Charles later said he was left speechless by the reference to the tabloid tales dogging the couple, while Hatfield chalked his gaffe up to being "totally drunk on her charm."

Day after day Canadians eagerly enjoyed the latest glamour shots of the princess: laughing with a tuxedoed Pierre Trudeau at a state dinner in Halifax; chatting intimately with a little girl in a wheelchair in St. John's; politely enduring wolf whistles from teenage boys in Ottawa. During the tour the royal couple marked the first birthday of their son, William, with a telephone call, while Charles confided during a speech that he and Diana hoped to have more children. This confession, one newspaper noted, caused the crowd to cheer and clap, while "Diana . . . blushed and looked downward." Thanks to the royal visit of 1983, approval ratings for the monarchy soared in Canada, stemming, at least momentarily, the tide of republican sentiment.

Canada's relationship with the monarchy is tortuous. From the Statute of Westminster in 1931 to our new flag in 1964 and the patriation of the Constitution in 1982, we have slowly but inexorably severed our ties to Britain. We retain our governor general, and the royal presence is still felt in our legal and parliamentary systems and seen on our currency. But our enthusiasm for the royals continues to wane; one poll in late 2010 suggested that almost half of Canadians consider the monarchy a relic. Monarchists in this country are hoping a new royal romance—that of Prince William and his bride, Kate Middleton—can turn things around. The fairy tale begins anew.

One thing's clear—our love affair with Lady Diana was real. Women dreamed of being like the princess; men dreamed of dating her. And when she died in a car crash in August 1997, we were stunned. Flags flew at half-mast. Mourners laid flowers at the British High Commission in Ottawa and at the Princess of Wales Theatre in Toronto. CBC Television brought us news of the tragedy, and during the broadcast, when a Regina woman was asked why she was so distraught, she spoke for all of us: "Because she's part of the family."

You Had an Option, Sir!

July 25, 1984—The Mulroney–Turner debate delivers a knockout blow.

PETER MANSBRIDGE

Every televised leaders' debate in every federal election follows the same pattern. In the days before, there's a great buildup of anticipation. The titans clash! The election is at stake! And then in the immediate aftermath, everyone agrees nothing happened.

Except once.

On July 25, 1984, Liberal prime minister John Turner and Progressive Conservative leader Brian Mulroney had the debate everyone dreams about: the debate that changes everything. Going into that night, the polls agreed that John Turner led the race. By most accounts he had a comfortable nine-point lead. For the first hour and a half of the debate, Turner and Mulroney exchanged barbs, and most journalists were getting ready to call it a draw. Suddenly, Turner brought up the subject of patronage. It was a baffling decision since he was obviously vulnerable on the topic. It was he who had made several distasteful patronage appointments when he first became prime minister. Turner said he had "no option."

Mulroney pounced without hesitation. "You had an option, sir!" he exploded. And he went on to excoriate Turner so completely that the prime minister was left mumbling helplessly, a picture of defeat broadcast from coast to coast to coast.

Now it was the Conservatives with the nine-point lead in the polls. Allan Gregg, the Conservative pollster at the time, told Mulroney it was the greatest single change in the numbers since polling began in Canada. A few weeks later, Brian Mulroney became Canada's eighteenth prime minister. He won 211 seats, more than any party ever had before, or since. No one doubted the turning point of the campaign. "You had an option, sir" is now part of our political lexicon.

Everything Brian Mulroney was able to achieve as prime minister came as a direct result of that riveting moment, in that debate, on that night. It's possible, of course, that some other prime minister, at some other time, would have adopted the policies that he pursued—free trade with the United States, the GST, the Meech Lake Accord, the Charlottetown Accord. But we'll never know that.

What we do know is that the consequences of a single debate reverberated for almost nine years—longer, really. Mulroney was so unpopular at the end of his term in office that the Progressive Conservatives collapsed in the election following his resignation. That led to the election of Jean Chrétien and his Liberals, but also to the rise of the Reform Party, then the Canadian Alliance, and eventually the complete disappearance of the Progressive Conservatives.

That July night in 1984 also changed election debates in this country. We'd never seen such an electric exchange between party leaders. The media loved it, of course. But the politicians, and especially their advisers, weren't nearly so thrilled. They now saw that months, even years, of careful policy planning and platform building could be undone in an instant. Front-running campaigns now try to negotiate the rules of debates to minimize the risk of a so-called knockout punch. They don't want that punch even thrown, let alone allowed to land.

It's routine now to hear commentators lament that Canadian election debates are boring. Blame 1984.

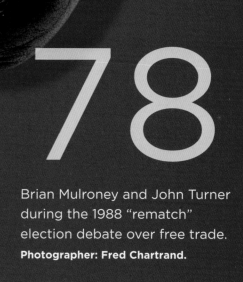

78

Brian Mulroney and John Turner during the 1988 "rematch" election debate over free trade.
Photographer: Fred Chartrand.

VJs Jeanne Beker and J.D. Roberts, shown with Louise Garfield of the Toronto group The Clichettes, celebrate the launch of MuchMusic in August 1984.
Photographer: Tibor Kolley.

79

Generation Much

August 31, 1984—MuchMusic takes over the tube.

DENISE DONLON

On August 31, 1984, J.D. Roberts and Christopher Ward burst through a paper screen displaying projections of wacky graphics, chroma-keyed fireworks, and swirling M's, followed by the first video ever made—filmed in 1922 by Eubie Blake. It was fantastic!

MuchMusic—the brainchild of television producers John Martin and Moses Znaimer—was unlike anything ever seen on Canadian TV: musically ambitious, unconventional, loud, irreverent, and *live*. No scripts, no sets, no teleprompters. It was original, streetwise, risky, and rude. And—what a delight!—unabashedly Canadian.

Mistakes happened live on air, and the artists and the audience loved its raw energy. At any given moment, viewers at home might see superstars like Rush, Duran Duran, Maestro Fresh Wes, or The Parachute Club chatting with VJs Erica Ehm, Michael Williams, and Laurie Brown. With big rock hair, spandex, and shoulder pads, Much was the coolest of Canadian places. As David Bowie once remarked to me during the chaos of the groundbreaking MuchMusic Video Awards, "This place is amazing. It seems to be run by children!"

MuchMusic's gonzo style owes much to Citytv's *The New Music*—Canada's *60 Minutes*–style music-journalism program. Started in 1980, one year before the launch of MTV, it featured music journalists Jeanne Beker, J.D. Roberts, and Daniel Richler, and later Laurie Brown, Jana Lynne White, and me, gallivanting around the world to document emerging musical trends. We made it our mission to engage with pop and rock icons with a fresh, journalistic, yet fun approach. Anyone who watched Jeanne Beker interview Andy Summers in a (rapidly disappearing) bubble bath, or Daniel Richler jockeying with Lou Reed, knew this was a new style of music television.

Culturally speaking, MuchMusic was significant to our young audience because we had style *and* substance. We covered political conventions and federal elections from a youth perspective. We produced shows on racism, and we challenged images of violence and sexuality in music videos on shows like *Too Much 4 Much*. We explored HIV/AIDS awareness between airings of Madonna and Guns N' Roses videos. And we invited the audience into the studio to participate forcefully in a medium they saw as their own.

We were the first mainstream broadcaster to put a float in Toronto's Pride Parade. The influence of that action—and others—was to send a strong message of support for diversity to a generation we hoped would be more tolerant and inclusive than those that came before.

Much's issue-oriented material got us worldwide attention. Artists, as well as our audience, loved and respected us for being authentic, edgy, and having a conscience. We didn't come off as preachy, since every issue we examined and took a stand on came from the music: REM was campaigning for Greenpeace; Peter Gabriel was touring for Amnesty International; Bob Geldof was organizing Live Aid; Little Steven was singing against Sun City; and Bryan Adams and David Foster were recording "Tears Are Not Enough."

Before Facebook or YouTube—hell, before the Internet!—there was MuchMusic. "The Nation's Music Station" was the touchstone, arbiter, and trusted navigator of youth culture in Canada. It meant so much to so many because Much gave voice to the times. The early days of MuchMusic were a wild, non-stop, adrenalin-charged ride—and we loved every minute of it.

Courting Disaster

June 23, 1985—Terrorist bomb destroys Air India Flight 182.

KIM BOLAN

When a bomb built in British Columbia downed Air India Flight 182 on June 23, 1985, it devastated the families and friends of the victims. Canada was also forever changed. Until then, we had thought of ourselves as a tranquil nation, best known for our peacekeeping efforts abroad and our ability to get along at home, regardless of language or cultural barriers. Sadly, the image was more myth than reality.

Extremists in British Columbia's Sikh community were plotting to commit acts of terrorism. Their plan—which targeted two jumbo jets owned by the government of India—might have been stopped if warnings coming from moderates within the community had been heeded. Leading up to the attacks, police had received calls about violent militants among local Sikhs. Canada's spy agency was told the extremists were seeking revenge against India for its 1984 attack on the Golden Temple.

In April 1985 Ujjal Dosanjh—the future B.C. premier and federal Liberal health minister—was a crusading Vancouver lawyer. Beaten for speaking out against the extremists, he sent a letter to Prime Minister Brian Mulroney warning of dire consequences if the federal government didn't deal with the growing threat. He received no reply, and later claimed he wasn't taken seriously because of his ethnicity.

On June 23, 1985, Canadians awoke to terrible news. A suitcase loaded in Vancouver had exploded at Tokyo's airport. Tagged for an Air India flight, it had killed two baggage handlers. Barely an hour later, Air India Flight 182 exploded off the coast of Ireland, killing all 329 people aboard.

The majority of the victims were Canadians of Indian origin. But Mulroney's first response was to call Indian prime minister Rajiv Gandhi to express condolences. Nobody wanted to admit this was a Canadian tragedy. There was very little mystery as to who was responsible. News reports immediately linked the bombing to a B.C.–based group, Babbar Khalsa, and its leader, Talwinder Singh Parmar. But it would take twenty years before a B.C. court would formally declare the long-dead Parmar the mastermind of the terrorist plot. The same judge would acquit two of Parmar's associates. A third associate, Inderjit Singh Reyat, pleaded guilty to aiding the bombing and received a five-year sentence on top of a ten-year term he had served for the Narita bombing.

The victims' families had expected guilty verdicts all around and were devastated by the acquittals. Numerous problems had plagued the trials of the accused. Witnesses were threatened. A newspaper publisher, Tara Singh Hayer, was assassinated after giving sworn statements to the police implicating one of the accused.

Following the acquittals in March 2005 and an outcry from victims' families, the federal government launched an inquiry into the Air India disaster. The inquiry found that the RCMP and the Canadian Security Intelligence Service had committed several mistakes both before and after the bombings. The agencies were plagued by infighting and a lack of information sharing, and had been unable to reach out to moderates within the Sikh community.

In January 2011 Inderjit Singh Reyat—having already served his sentence for his role in the bombings—received an additional nine-year sentence for committing perjury during the Air India trials of Ripudaman Singh Malik and Ajaib Singh Bagri. It was welcome consolation for those who had waited so long for the truth to come out.

80

Relatives of Air India victims gather in June 2010 for a memorial marking the twenty-fifth anniversary of the bombing.

Photographer: Julien Behal.

81

A victim is rushed to hospital after the shootings at
l'École Polytechnique on December 6, 1989.

Photographer: Shaney Komulainen.

Montreal Massacre

December 6, 1989—A gunman targets women at l'École Polytechnique.

STEVIE CAMERON

For some people it was the day President John F. Kennedy was shot. For some it was the day Diana, Princess of Wales, died in a Paris hospital after a terrifying car crash. Others remember the day the space shuttle blew up or the day the Twin Towers came down in New York. But the date many Canadians remember best is December 6, 1989—the day Marc Lépine carried a rifle into l'École Polytechnique in Montreal, separated the women engineering students from their male colleagues, and then shot fourteen of them simply because they were, as he screamed at them that afternoon, "feminists!" We remember watching the ambulances tearing into the campus, the stretchers flying by the weeping, disbelieving students, and the frantic parents running past them to look for their girls.

Canadians sat up late that night to watch the television news, appalled and shocked. The next morning, in offices and schools and public institutions, there was silence and grief; across the country women wept and men felt somehow responsible in ways they couldn't understand. There were so many things people had to come to terms with: Marc Lépine's hatred of women, the inability of the male students to help their classmates, the violence of the attack, the senselessness of it. It became a sensational international story, and because he killed himself as well that day, Marc Lépine was not there to explain what drove him to such rage.

As Canadians tried to manage their grief and anger, as governments tried to respond, things happened that changed our country. Violence against women became a mainstream issue for both men and women at every level of society. Men began wearing white ribbons to show their support for ending violence against women. Communities across the country, small towns and villages and large cities, put up memorials to honour the dead women, and then, every December 6, held memorial services attended by both men and women. Many institutions, such as Toronto's Women's College Hospital, hold annual memorial services for their staff members.

Two years after Lépine shot the young women in Montreal, Parliament designated December 6 as an annual National Day of Remembrance and Action on Violence Against Women. As well, the federal government took several other steps to protect women, including raising the age of sexual consent from fourteen to sixteen and strengthening laws to assist women who are victims of violence. More recently police and provincial governments have begun to look at ways to protect Aboriginal and immigrant women, who suffer more violence than other groups.

In 1995 Parliament also passed Bill C-68, requiring people who owned or bought rifles and other long guns to register their weapons, a move that brought howls of protest from hunters across the country. It took until 2003 for the registration of long guns to become mandatory. Today the Conservative government is trying to undo the law, despite efforts by Canadian police chiefs who support it. And in 2010, for the first time, the families of the women who died in the massacre refused to take part in the National Day of Remembrance ceremony because of the government's determination to end the long-gun registry. They have not forgotten—indeed no one can forget—what happened on December 6, 1989.

Under Fire

March 7, 1990—National Gallery scorched by controversial art purchase.

PAUL JONES

Most Canadians saw red when they learned on March 7, 1990, that the National Gallery of Canada had purchased American artist Barnett Newman's *Voice of Fire* for almost $1.8 million. Rarely in the field of human endeavour—according to talk radio— had such an egregious abuse of the public purse been perpetrated by an overfunded and out-of-touch arts establishment. Clearly the curators were hostage to an elitist, anti-human aesthetic, and were also very likely the hoodwinked patsies of New York sharpies.

One person told Global TV the painting looked like "something my son'll do in daycare." The *Kamloops Daily News*, tapping the heartland's fury, harrumphed about "the work of—uhm—art" and invoked the memory of P. T. Barnum and his dictum about suckers. Oddly, the first official voice of protest had come from within the arts community. A lobbyist for Canadian artists, apparently unaware of the gallery's multi-year financing strategy, whinged to the *Toronto Star* that too large a chunk of the annual budget was going to purchase a work by an American.

Cometh the hour, cometh the man. Tory MP Felix Holtmann, not previously noted for his interest in the arts, declared that he would soon hold hearings at which gallery officials would be called to account for their profligacy. A spokesman for Deputy Prime Minister Don Mazankowski insinuated that a cabinet committee might annul the purchase—notwithstanding that payment had been made in 1989 with full legal approval by no fewer than three supervisory bodies. Meanwhile, cultural nationalists contorted themselves to find a posture in which they could rebuff icky populist support, embrace curatorial independence, and outstretch their open palms.

Throughout this laff riot, gallery officials remained remarkably low-key—mild, even—in the face of outrage. Were they shell-shocked? Did they count on time and legality being on their side? Or maybe, like Newman (who had died in 1970), they thought that art should speak for itself.

Here's what I wish someone had said.

On technique: "Barnett Newman was a craftsman recognized by peers as 'profoundly involved in technique,' including the minutiae of canvas preparation, medium, palette, and brushwork. Anyone who thinks a child or MP could have painted *Voice of Fire* is misinformed."

On artistic significance: "Stand close to *Voice of Fire* and study the painting. You will soon feel unfamiliar emotions. Some people cry. Others become reflective. The upward sweep of the canvas (5.4 metres high) envelops the viewer in what the artist called a 'dome.' The seemingly solid fields of colour shimmer and then dissolve into composite shades. Sensory stimuli flood to a less rational, older part of the brain. Rarely will you have been so moved by a work of art."

On the painting's relevance to Canada: "As is widely known, *Voice of Fire* was originally commissioned for the U.S. pavilion at Expo 67, but Newman's connection to Canadian art goes back much further. The artist divulged in 1947 that his aesthetic sensibility was influenced by British Columbia's Kwakiutl artists, who believed an abstract shape was a living thing and therefore a 'real rather than a formal "abstraction" of visual fact.' Would that every work in the National Gallery was so grounded in Canada!"

Was the painting a waste of tax dollars? Arguably, no expenditure of the Mulroney era has yielded such a generous return on investment. At auction today *Voice of Fire* would conservatively fetch six to eight times the purchase price.

82

The purchase of *Voice of Fire* in 1990 provoked a firestorm of controversy.
Photographer: Pat McGrath.

Manitoba MLA Elijah Harper, shown here with arm raised, played an instrumental role in killing the Meech Lake Accord.
Photographer: Wayne Glowacki.

83

Distinct Disappointment

June 23, 1990—The Meech Lake Accord sinks.

PETER MANSBRIDGE

In 1982, when Canada patriated its Constitution, Quebec was the only province that didn't sign on. The province was legally bound in any case, but there was a feeling that the country would be better off, more whole, if Quebec joined the family. Over many years there were on-again, off-again meetings to try to make that happen. But it didn't happen, and Canadians had become used to failure.

Then, one late night in April 1987, Prime Minister Brian Mulroney and all the premiers stunned the country by agreeing to the terms of reconciliation. At the heart of the agreement was a clause that recognized Quebec as a "distinct society."

The Meech Lake Accord then had to be ratified by the Parliament of Canada and the legislatures of all ten provinces within a three-year period. Quebec ratified on June 23, 1987. If the rest of the politicians had simply gone home and ratified the deal just as quickly, Canadian history would have gone down an entirely different path. But they didn't, and over time the ratification process became a debate fought with profound bitterness. Opponents of the Accord said the distinct society clause gave Quebec special status, which they found unacceptable. Supporters of Meech said the clause had only symbolic meaning and this was the best chance to settle the national unity question once and for all.

Not only did Canada change on the day Meech died, but Canada is still changing because Meech died. June 23, 1990, was full of political intrigue. In Manitoba, as the three-year ratification period was just hours from slamming shut, a Cree member of the legislature, Elijah Harper, denied the House unanimous consent for a vote on the Accord. He was protesting the exclusion of Aboriginal concerns. Ottawa came up with a rolling-deadline strategy that might have allowed Manitoba to vote later. But the other province up against the deadline, Newfoundland, rejected that strategy and cancelled the vote in its legislature. Two provinces were now out, and the Accord was well and truly dead, with profound consequences.

Elijah Harper had awakened Aboriginal political awareness. You can draw a line from Harper to the standoff a few weeks later at Oka/Kanesatake, Quebec, between Native people and the Canadian military, and to major land claim settlements that have happened since. Meanwhile, on the same day the Accord died, Jean Chrétien won the Liberal Party leadership at a convention in Calgary. Chrétien had been anti-Meech. His main rival, Paul Martin, had been pro-Meech. The enmity built up over that issue between the two men never healed. When Martin became prime minister, he ruled a divided party and was beaten in the 2006 election by Stephen Harper.

And where did Harper come from? He was a founding member of the Reform Party, which was born as a reaction to, and rejection of, Brian Mulroney's "special" treatment of Quebec. Inside his party, Mulroney paid a price for trying to win last-minute support for Meech. Lucien Bouchard, a member of Mulroney's cabinet, said the prime minister was appeasing English Canada in his efforts and betraying Quebec. He quit cabinet, and a month later formed the Bloc Québécois. And that party has skewed Canadian politics ever since.

Hook, Line, and Sinking

July 3, 1992—The cod fishery collapses.

RICHARD FOOT

Fishermen across Newfoundland knew the moment of truth was coming. Their catch rates had been declining for years. Still, when federal fisheries minister John Crosbie announced on July 3, 1992, a moratorium on the northern cod fishery in Newfoundland, the news struck his province like a kick in the teeth.

While the rest of Canada basked in the afterglow of the country's 125th birthday, Newfoundland faced economic and ecological disaster. Mobs of angry fishermen and fish plant workers had hurled insults at Crosbie as he toured the province the day before the dreaded announcement. "There's no need to abuse me," Crosbie told his angry accusers. "I didn't take the fish from the goddamn water!"

The moratorium, which was extended to the rest of Atlantic Canada the following year, triggered the largest industrial layoff in Canadian history. Thirty thousand people lost their jobs almost immediately, and a $700-million enterprise—the mainstay of both Newfoundland's economy and its cultural identity—was wiped out overnight. For the province it was akin, observers said, to Ontario losing its entire auto industry in a single stroke. It wasn't merely a commercial ban. No one was allowed to jig even a single cod simply to put on his or her supper table. "It's just inconceivable," said Premier Clyde Wells, "that we could ever have reached a stage where it is illegal to catch a codfish two hundred miles off the island of Newfoundland."

It was cod that first brought Europeans to Canada. Crewmen who sailed on Giovanni Caboto's historic voyage to the New World in 1497 took home tales of a "new found land" whose waters were so thick with cod they could literally be scooped from the sea in baskets. So began a transatlantic saltwater gold rush by Britain, Spain, France, and Portugal that led eventually to the first English settlement in North America and the founding of Newfoundland's myriad outports.

The exploitation of the Grand Banks cod stocks lasted more than four hundred years. The fishery grew—along with the size, appetite, and efficiency of factory-freezer trawlers—peaking in 1968, when more than 800,000 tonnes of cod were taken in one year. The decline then came quickly. By the late 1980s the destruction of one of the planet's great food resources was almost complete.

The collapse of the cod fishery cost Ottawa an estimated $4 billion in compensation for fishermen and led to an exodus of Newfoundlanders to Ontario, Alberta, and elsewhere. In the decade after the moratorium, the province's population fell by 10 percent. The closure also fuelled a lasting mistrust of Confederation and resentment toward the federal government, which many blame for mismanaging the fishery and for failing to halt the continued presence of foreign fishing fleets on the international portions of the Grand Banks.

By 2010 Newfoundland's overall fishery had magically become healthy again, thanks to retooling and a new focus on shrimp, crab, and other shellfish stocks. People were also being lured home by the wealth and promise of offshore oil. In the years since the moratorium, small, limited cod fisheries have also opened up in places—but the famous outports remain mostly empty today, the painful memories are still fresh, and the teeming schools of fish that built a province and inspired so much wonder have yet to return.

Fishermen at Placentia Bay, Newfoundland, ponder the future
in the wake of the cod moratorium.
Photographer: Bridget Besaw.

84

85

Joe Carter celebrates with his Toronto Blue Jays teammates after winning the 1992 World Series.
Photographer: Rusty Kennedy.

Having a Ball

October 24, 1992—Toronto Blue Jays win the World Series.

STEPHEN BRUNT

It is all contained in that descriptive phrase: *national pastime*. More than just a game. Something that runs so deep in a culture, is so interlaced with the history of a place, that it has become a touchstone. Even if baseball wasn't really all of that by 1992, even if the sport had long before been supplanted by football as the favourite athletic diversion of the United States, the myth at least was still very much alive.

For a Canadian team to win the World Series for the first time was therefore a very big deal indeed—an especially big deal in this country, where so much of our national identity is tied up in a complicated, often contradictory relationship with our powerful neighbours to the south.

Baseball had been played in Canada even before the modern rules were codified in the nineteenth century. And for decades before the Montreal Expos began life in 1969, minor-league teams had been part of our national sporting fabric. That said, from their snowy beginning in 1977, a large part of the attraction of the Toronto Blue Jays, as they climbed from expansion awfulness to contending status (setting attendance records), was that they put a Canadian city on the same field as the New York Yankees and the Boston Red Sox—playing, and soon enough dominating, what we regarded as the definitive American game.

Following an agonizing stretch of near misses, the Jays captured the American League pennant in 1992 and headed for a World Series matchup against the Atlanta Braves. No, there weren't any Canadians on the roster, and those Blue Jays could hardly be cast as plucky underdogs, given that they carried the highest payroll in the major leagues. Still, it felt like the mouse was finally kicking back at the oblivious elephant, a sentiment symbolized perfectly before Game 2, when at

Atlanta's Fulton County Stadium, a U.S. Marine Corps Color Guard marched onto the field carrying the Canadian flag upside down. The Jays won that game with a late comeback to even the best-of-seven series 1–1. They won the next two to take a stranglehold, and then, after failing to close out the series at home in Game 5, travelled back to Atlanta. In Game 6, on October 24, 1992, a Dave Winfield double in the top of the eleventh inning drove in the decisive runs for the Jays. Toronto's Mike Timlin fielded Otis Nixon's bunt with a runner in scoring position and threw to first for the final out.

Back home, the celebration began from coast to coast. A Canadian team sat atop the American national pastime. A sweet moment, a defining moment, and a different moment from all those great hockey triumphs past because we had beaten the other at their own game, rather than defending against them in ours. No crisis of American confidence ensued. It's not in their nature—though at least a few writers pondered what it all meant to have such a storied title held outside the country's borders. But here, for a little while, you could sense that little extra swagger in our step. Look at us. *Your* national pastime—*our* champions.

Bloody Shame

September 16, 1993—Tainted blood scandal sparks inquiry.

RICHARD FOOT

It was a day of hope for thousands of Canadians, amid the fear and anger that had enveloped their lives. After years of mounting evidence that Canada's blood supply had infected people with HIV and hepatitis C, the federal government announced, on September 16, 1993, a full public inquiry into the screening system and the growing national tragedy it had spawned.

"It's long overdue," said Marlene Freise, an Ontario woman who became HIV positive after receiving a blood transfusion as therapy for anemia in the late 1980s. Freise and other victims had been knocking their fists against a political brick wall for years, calling for an inquiry without success—until now.

The tainted blood scandal was Canada's worst public health disaster. About two thousand hemophiliacs and transfusion recipients contracted HIV and AIDS; another twenty thousand people who received blood products contracted hepatitis C, a potentially fatal liver disease. At least three thousand victims died as a result, and thousands more still struggle with their infections today. The scandal cost various governments and agencies billions in compensation. It also gutted Canadians' faith in the blood system, as well as our assumption that governments could be trusted, at the end of the twentieth century, to safeguard public health. The Canadian Red Cross Society, which had run the blood program since the end of the Second World War, was stripped of its responsibility and reduced to near bankruptcy.

The federal Krever Inquiry, as it became known—overseen by the tall, steely Ontario justice Horace Krever—pursued the roots of the scandal for four years. Krever fought successfully for the right to publicly name those who had failed to safeguard the system, but ultimately his report assigned no personal blame for the tragedy. Rather, it showed in clear, horrifying detail the bungling of Red Cross administrators and government regulators, who failed to screen out high-risk blood donors, who used imported blood products from places such as U.S. prisons at the height of the AIDS crisis, and who made a series of flawed decisions aimed at saving money—but that ended up costing lives.

Krever also criticized political leaders for first denying the tragedy and then failing to apologize and offer adequate compensation to victims. He called it a "public health disaster that was unprecedented in Canada . . . caused by a systematic failure of mistakes that victims paid for with their lives, with their futures, with their dreams." Krever said all victims of tainted blood should be compensated. The federal government disagreed, sparking outrage among some hepatitis C victims. Years of legal wrangling ensued. In the end a number of compensation funds were put in place—some volunteered by governments, others won through the courts—totalling about $2.7 billion. By 2010 thousands of Canadians were still collecting compensation, or waiting to have their claims resolved. Meanwhile, a new independent public agency, Canadian Blood Services, was created to run the country's blood system and impose strict new donor-screening rules.

The RCMP also laid criminal charges against the Red Cross and its officials, plus a number of doctors from Health Canada and a U.S. blood supply company. Only the Red Cross pleaded guilty as an institution to distributing a contaminated product—and paid a $5,000 fine. All of the individuals charged in the scandal were eventually acquitted.

86

A man walks by crosses placed on Parliament Hill in 1998
to protest the tainted blood compensation scheme.
Photographer: Tom Hanson.

87

Jack Rabinovitch, shown in 1999, founded the Giller Prize
in memory of his wife, Doris.
Photographer: Phill Snel.

The Write Stuff

November 2, 1994—The Giller Prize celebrates our finest fiction.

CHARLOTTE GRAY

Jack Rabinovitch really knew how to throw a party. He booked Toronto's classiest venue, the Four Seasons Hotel ballroom, ordered a grand dinner and an open bar, and invited 230 friends. "It was black-tie, glitzy and fun—but it worked," he said in 2010, recalling the presentation of the first Giller Prize, on November 2, 1994. The day after, newspapers across Canada carried stories on the Giller Prize dinner and the winner of the $25,000 award. The excellence of Canadian writers was finally acknowledged in the popular press in their own country. And in imitation of Rabinovitch's initiative, several other awards (such as the Charles Taylor Prize for literary non-fiction) were subsequently established to celebrate Canada's literary culture.

Until 1994 the only national literary prizes were the Governor General's Awards for Literature, administered by the Canada Council. These awards, presented at a dowdy dinner in March, received little publicity and had little impact on sales. Rabinovitch, a successful developer, and his old school friend Mordecai Richler from Montreal, decided "we didn't have to be dependent on government to support Canada's great writers. We could do it our way." Rabinovitch's wife, Doris Giller, a flamboyant and popular literary journalist, had died the previous year, and a literary award named after her seemed the perfect memorial.

The Giller Prize recognized the extraordinary flowering of literature in the previous half-century. In 1948 American and British books swamped the tiny Canadian market: English-language publishers in this country issued a mere fourteen books of fiction and thirty-five works of poetry and drama. By the 1990s Canada was awash with home-grown, Canadian-published authors, a handful of whom were picking up international awards: Margaret Atwood won the Arthur C. Clarke Award in 1987 and would go on to win the Man Booker Prize in 2000; Michael Ondaatje was awarded the Man Booker Prize in 1992 for *The English Patient*; and Carol Shields won the Pulitzer Prize for *The Stone Diaries* in 1995. Yet within Canada, sales remained sluggish.

That changed rapidly after the first Giller dinner, strategically scheduled during the pre-Christmas publishing season, during which 70 percent of books are sold in this country. At the inaugural dinner, there was glamour and tension: guests made informal pools on the five short-listed authors while watching short videos about them. Finally, the high-profile jury, which included Mordecai Richler and Alice Munro, announced the winner: M. G. Vassanji. Thanks to the excitement and hype, sales of his novel *The Book of Secrets* soared.

Since then, the Giller has become the literary occasion of Canada. In 2005 the Bank of Nova Scotia became the major sponsor (it is now the Scotiabank Giller Prize): in recent years the Four Seasons Hotel ballroom has strained to accommodate 490 guests, and a total of 2.8 million Canadians watch broadcasts of the event. The impact on sales for the winner is extraordinary: Linden MacIntyre's *The Bishop's Man* had a sales spike of nearly 340 percent in the week after it won the 2009 award, and the previous year, sales of Joseph Boyden's *Through Black Spruce* jumped 560 percent.

Jack Rabinovitch has never deviated from his original intention—to boost Canadian talent. Each year, he makes the same plea to his guests: "For the price of a dinner for two in this town, you can buy all five short-listed books. So buy them, eat at home . . . and read them."

Gold Standard

July 27, 1996—Donovan Bailey owns the podium in Atlanta.

BRIAN WILLIAMS

The Winter Olympic Games are officially the games of ice and snow. Being a cold-weather country, Canada is certainly competitive in the glamour sports of winter.

It is a somewhat different story in the Summer Games. The centrepiece is the men's 100 metres in athletics. And prior to the centennial Games, in Atlanta in 1996, Canada had won only one gold medal in the 100 metres.

Nelson Mandela once said, "Politics divides a country, sport unites." There is no question that hockey has long united this country. And our recent success at the Vancouver 2010 Winter Games highlights that Canada's new can-do attitude has extended far beyond the rink. Few realize, however, that it was Donovan Bailey—at the 1996 Games in Atlanta—who planted the seed of the pride and passion that would change how Canadians felt about themselves and their country.

For Bailey, and for the nation, the Atlanta Games were first and foremost about redemption. Bailey prepared for and competed in Atlanta under the shadow of the Ben Johnson steroid scandal eight years earlier. Even though Donovan Bailey competed clean, he was always under a microscope of suspicion and never truly received the recognition he deserved. The scrutiny extended far beyond Canada, because the men's 100 metres is arguably the most competitive sports title in the world.

In the post-Vancouver 2010 era, we hear so much about a new confidence and pride among our athletes. This is the essence of the Own the Podium program, credited—and for good reason—with the amazing performance of the Canadian team in Vancouver. Well, Donovan Bailey was Own the Podium before the program was a twinkle in the eyes of Canadian sports officials. Not only did Bailey possess unique athletic ability, but also, like most sprinters, he was supremely confident. As he famously stated following Atlanta, simply participating was not an option—he had been determined to win the Games' glamour event. At the time, this attitude was new and not always well received by Canadians. To put it simply, it was un-Canadian.

With his July 27 performance, and the now famous victory photograph as he crossed the finish line on that Saturday night in Atlanta, he had indeed set in motion a change in our country.

The exclamation point on this new attitude came exactly one week later. On a typically warm Saturday night in Georgia, Bailey and his teammates, Bruny Surin, Glenroy Gilbert, Robert Esmie, and alternate Carlton Chambers, won the gold medal in the 4-x-100-metres relay—an event that had been dominated by the United States in the modern Olympics.

For some, Bailey's triumph in the 100 metres rankled. Following his gold-medal performance, some American commentators maintained that the title of the "World's Fastest Man" belonged not to the winner of the 100 metres, as had been the case for one hundred years, but to the winner of the 200-metre race, who just happened to be American Michael Johnson.

This further fuelled Canadian passion and pride, and led to a 150-metre match race between Bailey and Johnson in 1997 at Toronto's SkyDome, which Bailey easily won.

88

Donovan Bailey wins the gold medal for the men's 100 metres at the 1996 Summer Olympics in Atlanta.

Photographer: Doug Mills.

89

Research in Motion director Eric Ritter, right,
demonstrates a BlackBerry device in 2007.

Photographer: Mark Lennihan.

The CrackBerry

January 19, 1999—BlackBerry addiction begins in Canada.

DEBORAH MORRISON

Timing is everything in business. No one knows this better than Canadian technology pioneers Mike Lazaridis and Jim Balsillie, co-executive directors of a Waterloo-based company called Research in Motion.

In the late 1990s the Internet was in its infancy. People were just discovering its potential to increase the flow of information. High-powered executive types began to lug around an array of digital accessories—pagers, mobile telephones, PDAs (electronic organizers), and laptop computers—that made their businesses more portable. With each device they acquired a new phone number, email address, or contact point. It became confusing to manage.

Founded in 1984, RIM was a key player in the industry, developing wireless pagers and electronic messaging services for radio devices. Lazaridis had already anticipated the growing dependence on email (his business card had included an email address since 1984), and he foresaw the need for convergence and portability—one single handheld device that could deliver it all, wherever and whenever. Balsillie's business development and marketing acumen would be pivotal to RIM's success.

The first BlackBerry devices, so named because their patented full QWERTY thumb-keyboard resembled the fruit, were launched throughout corporate North America on January 19, 1999, with a consumer version available by August that same year. It was hugely popular with corporate IT departments, which could finally offer fully secure end-to-end delivery of an integrated email service for travelling employees. It became the hip device literally and figuratively, the defining measure of how central you were to the flow of information.

Its addictive guarantee of instant, "always on, always connected" access to email went viral. By the end of 2000 more than 32 percent of data-handheld users were "berry-ing" each other. Since then the market has been flooded by lighter and faster smartphones; the number of things you can do on them continues to grow.

The BlackBerry epidemic has changed our world. Its promises of greater mobility and increased productivity have certainly been fulfilled. A 2007 Ipsos Reid study revealed that the average BlackBerry user worked an additional 250 hours responding to emails and keeping work flowing during downtime. And downtime could be anywhere—in a 2004 AOL study 59 percent of all handheld users admitted they'd sent text messages from the bathroom. Indeed the device's ease of use has made it increasingly hard for people to put it down. "BlackBerry thumb" joins "carpal tunnel syndrome" on a growing list of repetitive strain injuries. A dramatic rise in accidents due to "intexticated driving" has led to outright bans on handheld use in motor vehicles in many countries. Indeed, Webster's dictionary named "CrackBerry"—used to describe BlackBerry addiction—its 2006 word of the year.

One other impact hits closer to home. Within a year of BlackBerry's launch, Mike Lazaridis donated $100 million to establish the Perimeter Institute for Theoretical Physics at the University of Waterloo. It was the largest charitable gift ever made in Canada. The institute will see leading scientists contemplate the potential of computing—exploring quantum techno-possibilities like transferring data at the speed of light and teleporting. The day may come when we are able to speak into our BlackBerries and say, "Beam me up, Scotty!"

*Sent from my wireless BlackBerry device.

Canadian Mosaic

April 1, 1999—Nunavut is born.

BEVERLEY TALLON

The map of Canada has been redrawn time and time again. In 1841 Ontario and Quebec joined together as the Province of Canada. In 1867 these two provinces banded with New Brunswick and Nova Scotia to form the Dominion of Canada. Over the next six years, the provinces of Manitoba, British Columbia, and Prince Edward Island joined the alliance, along with the Northwest Territories. Eventually, that territory was carved up, creating the Yukon Territory in 1898, and Saskatchewan and Alberta in 1905.

When Newfoundland and Labrador (originally called just Newfoundland) joined in 1949, many Canadians probably thought that would be the last addition to Canada. They were wrong—there was one last territory to take shape.

In the early 1960s the federal government began considering further division of the Northwest Territories. John Parker, a former N.W.T. commissioner, was appointed to oversee the creation of the new territory—Nunavut. At the time, the Northwest Territories consisted of two main regions: the west, with a Dene, Métis, and non-Aboriginal population; and the east, with a population that was 85 percent Inuit. After much discussion and debate, the residents voted in May 1992 on an official boundary for the new territory.

A key goal of the eastern Inuit was to obtain rights to self-government and self-determination. On October 30, 1992, an accord detailing those rights was signed by the federal and territorial governments, as well as by the Tunngavik Federation of Nunavut, a group formed to represent the eastern region's land claim negotiations. On July 9, 1993, Parliament passed the Nunavut Act. Almost six years later, on April 1, 1999, Nunavut officially became a territory of Canada—the largest Aboriginal land claim settlement in Canadian history,

and also the last great frontier in the Canadian patchwork quilt. Paul Okalik, a thirty-four-year-old Inuit lawyer, became its first premier.

Canada's newest territory faced immediate challenges, from staffing a government to dealing with the region's high rate of unemployment and numerous social problems. At the beginning of the twenty-first century, the future of the North is uncertain. Blessed with great mineral wealth, Nunavut holds the promise of jobs and major investment in its resource industries. But the Arctic climate is being changed by global warming. It is affecting the land, the ecosystem, and the traditions and lifestyle that are a crucial part of Inuit cultural identity.

In 2009 Nunavut celebrated its tenth anniversary. At the time, Chuck Strahl, Canada's minister of transport, infrastructure, and communities, said, "When people talk about territory, they often speak in terms of land, and that is the very name that was chosen for this new territory—Nunavut, 'our land.' This territory is more than land; it is the people on the land who form the heart of what Nunavut is about."

It will be up to the future generations of Nunavut, with the support of their fellow Canadians, to chart the way forward.

Children play in Iqaluit during Queen Elizabeth's 2002 visit.
Photographer: Paul Chiasson.

90

A former Nortel employee attends a protest against the loss of pensions in Toronto in 2009.
Photographer: Mark Blinch.

91

Boom and Bust

February 15, 2001—Nortel's nosedive hits the Canadian tech sector hard.

JOE MARTIN

On February 15, 2001, Nortel Networks issued a press release warning of a slowdown in the market. CEO John Roth concluded, "No other company is as well positioned in the market today with our leading portfolio and management bench strength as Nortel Networks."

If only that had been the case. Back in 2000, Nortel's stock had traded as high as $124.50 per share. In the intervening months it had plummeted by more than 75 percent, to thirty dollars. The day after Roth issued his guidance, trading volume jumped more than tenfold, and the value plunged a further third in one day. By 2002 Nortel had been reduced to a penny stock with a low of sixty-seven cents per share. And thousands in North America, Europe, and Asia had lost their jobs.

Despite the signs, many Canadians saw Nortel as too big, and too successful, to fall. But Nortel was one of many companies caught up in the irrational exuberance of the last years of the twentieth century. The dot-com boom was caused by the expectations of the "new economy" of computer software, telecommunications, and Internet firms. But the dot-com bust saw the stock market plunge and the industry hit by massive layoffs.

Several factors contributed to the boom in the telecom-equipment manufacturing sector. There was a major change to the regulatory environment in the United States, where Nortel had a large presence, at the same time that wireless technology and the Internet had become pervasive in the economy. This led to billions of dollars of demand—a bubble—as telecom companies placed huge purchase orders at a level that could not and would not be sustained.

As a consequence of earlier bad decisions, Roth—who became CEO in the late 1990s—decided to make some huge gambles to catch up, acquiring new companies such as Bay Networks. The gambles did not pay off. Nortel's revenue, which reached $45 billion Canadian in 2000—a level no other Canadian company has attained since—declined precipitously into bankruptcy in 2009.

In 2000 Nortel was the largest Canadian-based, non-financial, non-resource company with a global reach, employing ninety-five thousand workers. In January 2009 the company filed for bankruptcy. The human cost of Nortel's collapse has been severe, with massive job losses and concerns over the fate of employees' pensions.

At its peak Nortel represented Canadian engineering excellence, global competitiveness, and leadership. Its demise reduced Canada's reputation of global competitiveness in technology. Nortel's failure affected all the stakeholders, from its employees to its investors. Even before the company was bankrupted, Canada had a net deficit in its trade in high-technology products, and that of course increased. The good news is that in 2010, more than five thousand patents were issued to Canadian firms and individuals by U.S. authorities—showing that Canadian ingenuity and inventiveness can survive even a major corporate collapse.

Terror's Toll

September 11, 2001—The "War on Terror" begins.

J.L. GRANATSTEIN

Everyone with a TV set watched as first one, then another airliner deliberately flew into the twin towers of the World Trade Center in New York. Soon after, viewers saw the Pentagon on fire, another passenger plane having crashed into the headquarters of the U.S. military. A fourth aircraft crashed into a Pennsylvania field, diverted from its intended target in Washington by angered, courageous passengers.

Within mere hours, the world knew that nineteen al-Qaeda hijackers had seized control of the four airliners and staged a merciless assault that killed some three thousand men and women, including hundreds of firefighters and police officers and twenty-four Canadians working in or visiting New York City. Al-Qaeda is a Muslim terrorist organization dedicated to driving the United States out of the Middle East, and while it had struck embassies and naval vessels before, 9/11 was its most daring and successful attack.

The American government reacted quickly. All air traffic was shut down, leaving hundreds of aircraft en route to the United States from Europe and Asia in mid-flight. Would, or could, Canada let these planes land? Some four hundred aircraft were over the Atlantic, half of them past their halfway point. These last were ordered to continue, and Canadian aviation authorities, improvising quickly, arranged for airports at Halifax, Gander, St. John's, Goose Bay, and other sites to land two hundred aircraft and their thousands of passengers. Similar arrangements were made on the West Coast for transpacific flights, two of which had to be escorted by fighters with orders to shoot them down if necessary. Fortunately, it wasn't necessary. Canadians opened their homes to the stranded passengers. Tiny Gander, with its population of 10,000, took in more than 6,600 passengers and housed, fed, and consoled them until the skies reopened.

On September 14, 100,000 Canadians gathered on Parliament Hill for a national day of mourning. But already the Canada–U.S. border was tightening, the traffic slowing in a tense security atmosphere. Some in the United States mistakenly thought the hijackers had entered the country from Canada, and that belief lingered for years. Ottawa scrambled to upgrade the nation's security, implementing an anti-terrorism plan, passing tough legislation, and spending billions.

And late in 2001, when the United States attacked Afghanistan—where al-Qaeda, sheltered by the Taliban government, had planned its terrorism—Canada decided to deploy a battalion of the Princess Patricia's Light Infantry to fight there for six months. President George W. Bush had declared a "War on Terror," and Canada's involvement in the Afghan War—a decade-long commitment, as it turned out—was under way.

While Canadian support for the United States was strong, it was not unanimous. Critics talked of U.S. policy being "soaked in blood," and they linked American (and Canadian) support for Israel with Muslim anger. Still, Canadians rallied to their neighbour's side. Al-Qaeda had Canada on its target list. Most people sensibly believed North Americans had to stand together.

Fire erupts from the World Trade Center after a second airplane hits the New York landmark.
Photographer: Chao Soi Cheong.

92

A poster in Toronto protests a planned May 2009 visit by former American president George W. Bush.
Photographer: Chhobi.

03202003
DATE: MAY 29, 2009
NAME: GEORGE W. BUSH
DOB: 07/06/1946
CHARGE: WAR CRIMES

GEORGE BUSH IS COMING TO TORONTO
WAR CRIMINALS NOT WELCOME HERE!
Friday, May 29
Metro Toronto Convention Centre, 255 Front Street West
(the location of George Bush's speaking engagement)
3:00pm to 5:00pm – Unwelcome Bush activities, including music, drumming
shoe-tossing (bring your

Coalition of the Unwilling

March 17, 2003—Canada opts out of the Second Gulf War.

JOEL RALPH

As tension in the House of Commons grew, Stephen Harper, the leader of the Official Opposition, rose to open Question Period. It was March 17, 2003, and the last ultimatum for Iraqi president Saddam Hussein to disarm had passed. The United States and Britain were readying their forces for a massive invasion of Iraq. Harper had already told the House, "The time has come for Canada to pledge support to the developing coalition of nations . . . to ensure the safety of millions of people in the region from Iraq's suspected weapons of mass destruction." Now the Opposition leader wanted to know Canada's position on the eve of war.

Acknowledged by the Speaker, Prime Minister Jean Chrétien rose and made it perfectly clear. Attempts at the United Nations to form a new resolution authorizing the use of force against Iraq had failed. "If military action proceeds without a new resolution of the Security Council," Chrétien said, "Canada will not participate."

While the New Democrats and Liberals cheered the decision, Canadian Alliance MPs continued to pepper the prime minister with questions. But the decision had been made and the government required no further action. In fact, the prime minister defended the need not to have a vote of the House of Commons on the issue, arguing, "When Parliament announces a policy such as this one, the prime minister is entitled to assume he has the support of the House of Commons."

Two days after Canada opted out of Iraq, the Americans and British launched their blistering attack on Saddam's regime along with a handful of Polish and Australian soldiers, from the only two other nations willing to send troops in the initial assault. Another forty-four nations, ranging from Spain to Mongolia, pledged a wide array of support as part of the "coalition of the willing." The Anglo-American forces quickly brushed aside Saddam's troops. With only a few sharp confrontations, most official resistance quickly crumbled, oil facilities were seized largely intact, and by May 1 American president George W. Bush had declared "mission accomplished" aboard the USS *Abraham Lincoln.*

How quickly things turned. After watching the victory in Iraq descend into a years-long quagmire of violence and terror, it's hard to imagine that Canadian soldiers could have been placed into this desert sandstorm. Another government, on a different day, could easily have sent Canadians to war. But military support was never what the United States or Britain needed from Canada. They didn't need much, or get much, from anyone. What they needed was legitimacy for a war constructed on shoddy intelligence and justified through a series of half-truths.

A March 2003 poll conducted for the *Toronto Star* and *La Presse* of Montreal found that 71 percent of Canadians backed Chrétien's decision to keep Canada out of Iraq. For those Canadians, joining the invasion force would have lent legitimacy on the international stage to an unauthorized military action. And that was something many Canadians weren't willing to give.

Par-fection

April 13, 2003—Golfer Mike Weir dons the green jacket.

SANFORD RILEY

I was twelve years old when my grandmother introduced me to the Masters. Each year, she and I would spend the Easter weekend glued to the television set as the drama unfolded on golf's most important stage. One of four major championships, the Masters is steeped in tradition. Winners, among them many of the greatest players in the history of golf—Hogan, Nelson, Palmer, Player, Nicklaus, and Woods—receive a coveted green jacket and a lifetime invitation to play in the event. Each year all the great champions return to Augusta, Georgia, to savour the recognition that comes with being a Masters champion.

In those early years, my grandmother and I cheered on the great Winnipeg golfer George Knudson, who was a perennial contender. Knudson came close on several occasions, including a runner-up position in 1969, but the stress of the back nine on Sunday inevitably seemed to get the better of him.

I continued to watch the tournament faithfully, long after my grandmother's death, hoping that there would come a time when another Canadian could challenge as Knudson had. In 2003 lightning finally struck. Mike Weir, a Canadian "lefty" from Brights Grove, Ontario, came to the Masters hot off a string of great performances, including a victory in the Los Angeles Open the month before. Augusta National, which favours long hitters, was not an ideal course for him, but Weir had a strong short game and a putting stroke that was among the best in the sport.

Weir started the tournament strongly, leading after the second round by four shots. However, a disappointing seventy-five in the third round left him among a large number of contenders heading into Sunday's final round. As the fourth round progressed, it became apparent that a journeyman professional, Len Mattiace, was having the round of his life. Mattiace started early in the day, well before the front-runners. After finishing with a sixty-five he held a clubhouse lead that looked unassailable. One by one the challengers on the course fell by the wayside—except for Mike Weir. Dealing with incredible pressure, Weir needed to make a ten-foot par putt on the eighteenth hole to secure his place in a playoff with Mattiace. That putt is something all Canadians who witnessed it will forever remember.

The playoff itself was an anticlimax. Mattiace seemed to be overcome by the realization that he might win the Masters and hit his second shot into the trees, setting up a double bogey. Weir, with the pressure off, was able to get an easy five on the hole, thereby securing his place in the pantheon of golf's legends.

Weir's victory confirmed that it is possible for Canadians to expect to be the best at any sport, no matter how improbable the activity, provided they have the basic talent, the drive, and the vision to see themselves as world champions. It also reinforced the message that in a world growing smaller and more competitive all the time, Canadians should not be afraid to reach for the top in any field of endeavour. Mike Weir showed all of us that anything is possible with hard work and a bold vision.

94

Golfer Tiger Woods helps Mike Weir don the famous green jacket
after Weir won the Masters in 2003.

Photographer: Elise Amendola.

95

Norval Morrisseau at the National
Gallery of Canada in 2006.

Photographer: Bill Grimshaw.

Shaman Artist

February 3, 2006—National Gallery gives Aboriginal art its due.

STEVEN LOFT

I remember seeing him just a few months after that day. Gaunt and frail, this once-robust man was now confined to a wheelchair. He was so weak that we all had to go out to the van he was riding in to pay our respects. He was Norval Morrisseau—the master artist and Ojibwa shaman who had changed the way Aboriginal art was viewed in Canada.

Although the work of Aboriginal artists had been appearing more and more frequently in mainstream galleries since the 1960s, *Norval Morrisseau: Shaman Artist* was the first solo retrospective of a First Nations artist in the National Gallery of Canada. The show, which opened on February 3, 2006, marked a turning point, the apogee in the trajectory of Aboriginal art in this country. NGC director Pierre Théberge said at the time, "Norval Morrisseau is one of a very few artists in the world who can claim to be the creator of a completely new art movement."

His synthesis of Anishnaabe traditions and contemporary art provided a rich visual vocabulary in which animals and humans interacted on spiritual and terrestrial planes of existence. Morrisseau's art was characterized by bold use of colour, strong "power lines," and the stories that were at the heart of his practice.

He was born in 1932 and raised by his grandparents on the Sand Point Reserve in northern Ontario. After a serious illness that almost killed him, he was given the name Copper Thunderbird from a healer in his community. Thereafter, he signed all his paintings with that name in Cree syllabics.

From his first sold-out exhibition at the Pollock Gallery in Toronto in 1962 until the last few years before his death in 2007, Morrisseau was a prolific and committed artist, a man convinced of his destiny and his power to interpret and portray Anishnaabe culture.

He conveyed a sensuality, a sexuality, and a spirituality that people had never before seen in Aboriginal art, and he taught Aboriginal artists not to be afraid to view themselves in relation to their history, their mythology, and their contemporary realities.

Morrisseau's paintings were meditations on everything from the magical transformation of the shaman to the plague brought by the colonizers. He created self-defining narratives that located Anishnaabe traditions and specific historical and social dynamics within the worlds he created. He called them his "travels to the world of invention," a visual language interpreting legends of his Anishnaabe heritage and his Christian faith. The paintings "allow us to travel with him to different planes of existence," NGC exhibition curator Greg Hill says. "This is Morrisseau's gift to us."

Morrisseau was inducted into the Royal Canadian Academy of Arts in 1973 and the Order of Canada in 1978. In 1986 he was named Grand Shaman of the Ojibwa, and in 1990 Canada Post issued a stamp bearing one of his works. In 1995 the Assembly of First Nations bestowed on him its highest honour, the presentation of an eagle feather.

Morrisseau once said, "My art reminds a lot of people of what they are. They heal themselves." The artist died on December 4, 2007—less than two years after the opening at the National Gallery. His work introduced a generation of Canadians to new worlds of Aboriginal art and culture. Because of Morrisseau, the face of Canadian art changed that day in February—for the better.

Going (Pro)rogue

December 4, 2008—The governor general saves the Harper government.

JACQUES POITRAS

Possible, plausible, even proper: the coalition that came together in late 2008 may have been extraordinary, and it may have been driven by self-interest—a need to stop the government's plan to kill public subsidies for political parties—but it was, in parliamentary terms, absolutely legitimate.

The Liberals, the NDP, and the Bloc Québécois—the three opposition parties in the House of Commons—knew there were few alternatives if they defeated Prime Minister Stephen Harper's Conservative minority government in a confidence vote. One possibility was an election, but Canadians had voted six weeks before. Governor General Michaëlle Jean might instead call on the opposition to form a government. A planned coalition cabinet would be composed of twenty-four Liberals, including the departing party leader, Stéphane Dion, as interim prime minister, and six New Democrats. The separatist Bloc Québécois would have no ministers but would vote to keep the coalition in power until mid-2010.

Possible, plausible, proper—but not popular. The Bloc's participation was fatal to the plan. Harper attacked the potential government as one that would take its cues from separatists. He also referred to the alliance as "a coalition nobody voted for"—remarkably disingenuous, given a combined Liberal–NDP–Bloc support far greater than that for his Conservatives. As any student of British parliamentary tradition will tell you, however, voters do not elect prime ministers. They elect Parliaments—and Parliaments decide who governs.

But Harper understood that in the modern media age, the finer points of Westminster tradition mattered little. In the minds of voters, Harper's Conservatives had "won" the election because they had won the most seats. The other parties had "lost" and had no right to take office.

On December 4, Harper met with Jean and asked her to prorogue Parliament, essentially a reboot normally done at the end of a session. The goal was to buy time to let public opinion turn against the coalition, which was denounced in a Tory advertising campaign as "undemocratic," and to allow the Tories to tweak their budget. Jean kept Harper waiting two hours. She would tell reporters almost two years later the delay was done to "send a message—and for people to understand that this warranted reflection." Eventually she said yes, but on two conditions: Harper had to recall Parliament soon and come up with a budget that could pass. This prevented the establishment of a broad precedent future prime ministers could use to avoid confidence votes at will. Harper got his way, but Jean made him work for it.

Jean's decision also reflected public sentiment. Stoked in part by the Conservative ads, Canadians turned against the coalition. It may have been perfectly proper, but the public wanted neither a new election nor a coalition government. In early 2009 the Liberals wavered on the idea and the agreement collapsed.

It was a defining moment for Harper. His enemies had at one time confidently predicted he would never be prime minister. After he took office, they said he would not last very long. The coalition showdown revealed his determination to hold on to power. By February 2011, his fifth anniversary in office, Harper had eclipsed Lester Pearson as the longest-serving prime minister to lead a minority government. It was a remarkable feat, and can be traced back to that anxious meeting with Michaëlle Jean, and the dramatic collision of parliamentary tradition and public opinion.

Prime Minister Stephen Harper is eyed by Liberal Leader Stéphane Dion during
the coalition crisis of December 2008. Dion would later be dumped as party
leader, while Harper would win a majority in the 2011 federal election.
Photographer: Chris Wattie.

96

CANADA FOR HAIT

L'UNION FAIT LA FORCE

97

Rapper/singer K'naan speaks to media prior to the *Canada for Haiti* charity telethon of January 22, 2010.

Photographer: Steve Russell.

In Harmony

January 22, 2010—Canada for Haiti *telethon aids earthquake victims.*

MARK REID

On January 12, 2010, when a disastrous earthquake struck the island nations of Haiti and the Dominican Republic, Canadians felt the catastrophe on both a national and an international level. Measuring 7.0 on the Richter scale, the earthquake was amplified by poorly built infrastructure. Buildings everywhere collapsed, while roads cracked and sank into the ground. We were shocked by scenes of the Haitian capital in ruins and the bleary, dirty faces of the Haitian people as they searched the wreckage for survivors. In the aftermath, the cries of the wounded blended with sobs for the dead, a cacophony of terror and loss.

In Canada the disaster hit especially hard. Montreal and Toronto both boast robust Haitian communities, and Michaëlle Jean, who was governor general at that time, was born in Port-au-Prince. (She and her family fled to Canada in 1968 to escape the repressive Duvalier regime.)

As the federal government's relief effort took shape, average Canadians wondered how they could help. They didn't know that behind the scenes a plan was being hatched to help restore harmony to Haiti. In 1985 a constellation of Canadian stars had formed the supergroup Northern Lights and released a charity single, "Tears Are Not Enough," to raise money for famine-wracked Africa. Thanks to luminaries like Neil Young, Joni Mitchell, and Anne Murray, it raised millions for the relief effort. Now, in 2010, a new generation of artists offered their talents for a cause. Working with television producers from major Canadian broadcasters CTV, CBC, Global, and Citytv, they organized a star-studded telethon for Haiti relief.

Simulcast by all the broadcasters on January 22, 2010, *Canada for Haiti* featured performances by Somali-born rapper K'naan—whose single "Wavin' Flag" was at the time a worldwide smash hit—as well as The Tragically Hip, Nelly Furtado, and others. Our biggest celebrities, including teen pop sensation Justin Bieber, hockey star Wayne Gretzky, and actor Ryan Reynolds—*People* magazine's 2010 pick for sexiest man alive—made personal appeals for pledges. Asked why he felt compelled to take part, K'naan told CBC, "I'm like everyone else—affected by what's going on. You try to make yourself useful somehow. You do what you can. We show the best of ourselves in times of crisis."

During the telethon, Prime Minister Stephen Harper told viewers that Ottawa would match donations dollar for dollar. The public responded, flooding phone lines with promises of more than $9.4 million. A sister event broadcast in Quebec, *Ensemble pour Haiti*, raised another $6.6 million. Since then, Canada has contributed more than $150 million in relief funding. Canadian families have also stepped forward to welcome 203 adoptees and 3,600 permanent residents from Haiti.

It's estimated that more than 200,000 Haitians died in the immediate aftermath of the earthquake, and the survivors still face an uncertain future. Rebuilding the country will take decades. *Canada for Haiti* showed the international community that in times of crisis, Canadians will be there. And it reminded us at home that we are not helpless in the face of disaster when we act in chorus.

Solid Gold

February 28, 2010—Canada owns the podium.

BRIAN WILLIAMS

When Sidney Crosby scored in overtime to beat the United States and give Canada its Olympic-record fourteenth gold medal, Canadians—brimming with a new confidence and no longer apologizing for being the best—flooded into the streets as a sea of red spread out from Vancouver to all areas of the country.

From the day the Olympics were awarded to Vancouver/Whistler in 2003, CEO John Furlong had promised a Games that would unite and change the country. However, he knew that ultimate success would depend on Canadian athletes. To sports officials, this was an area of major concern. Canada was the only country to host two Olympics—Montreal in 1976 and Calgary in 1988—and not win a gold medal. Something had to change for Vancouver, and that something was the creation of the Own the Podium program. The brainchild of the late Mark Lowry (then director of sport for the Canadian Olympic Committee) and designed by Cathy Priestner Allinger (silver medallist in long-track speed skating in 1976), with support from Crazy Canuck and Olympian Ken Read, the program would give Canadian athletes the funding support that had long been enjoyed by such Olympic powers as the United States, Germany, and Russia. "Own the Podium gave Canadian athletes everything but an excuse," Read said.

The effects of the program were first seen at the 2006 Winter Games in Turin—a record twenty-four medals, sixteen won by women. Skier Jennifer Heil won the first gold medal for Canada in Turin. In December 2008, as she was preparing for Vancouver, I asked her about the pressure of competing at home. She said Canadian athletes were no longer content to simply show up and receive the uniform. They now welcomed pressure and were prepared to perform personal bests. In Vancouver, the storylines were compelling. Who

can forget skier Alex Bilodeau winning that first gold medal on Canadian soil with his family—including his brother, Frédéric, born with cerebral palsy—cheering in the finish area at Cypress Mountain? Or the courage displayed by figure skater Joannie Rochette, who competed despite the recent death of her mother. When she won the bronze medal, there was not a dry eye in the arena.

Early on, when Canadian athletes were not winning as expected, the old Canadian attitude resurfaced. Was Own the Podium arrogant? Were its objectives even realistic? It's interesting that those doubts came from Canadians. To his credit, the man who ran the program, Olympic gold medallist in rowing Dr. Roger Jackson, refused to apologize for it. He promised more medals would come. And they did—fourteen gold medals, the most by any nation in Winter Games history.

Even when Canada was struggling, something special was happening in this country. When I asked Prime Minister Stephen Harper about the changing attitude, he said this seemingly newfound pride and confidence had always been there. All it needed was an event to bring it to the surface.

On July 1, 2010, a *Globe and Mail* headline read "The Year Canada Grew Up." The catalyst was the Vancouver Olympics. Nightly, I would see thousands celebrating in the streets. Faces of every colour: new Canadians, and Canadians whose ancestors were born here. All wearing and yelling slogans that proclaimed "proud to be Canadian." We were finally comfortable with our identity. This will forever be the legacy of the 2010 Games.

Canadian medallist Jon Montgomery
celebrates his victory in men's skeleton at the
Vancouver 2010 Winter Games.
Photographer: Jeff McIntosh.

98

A police car burns in Toronto during protests against the G20 summit in June 2010.

Photographer: Steve Russell.

99

TAV56

To Serve & Pr

Arresting History

June 26, 2010—Toronto's G20 meetings set the stage for Canada's largest mass arrests.

PHIL KOCH

Heading into the June 2010 G20 meetings, news reports focused on the tremendous costs as well as the frustration and loss of income for Toronto residents, workers, and business owners due to massive security barricades erected in the city centre and expected protests. Six months later, at the release of a report criticizing both government and police actions, Ontario ombudsman André Marin said the Toronto G20 weekend "will live in infamy." He called it "the most massive compromise of civil liberties in Canadian history" and declared, "We can never let that happen again."

The beginning of the two-day event on Saturday, June 26, saw a huge police presence as thousands protested peacefully on unusually empty streets. Mid-afternoon, however, much smaller groups of vandals began to smash store windows, and several unoccupied police cars were set ablaze. Despite the mayhem, police were under orders to watch, not act. Soon after, though, large numbers of uniformed and plainclothes officers began to arrest people in different locations, including unknowing bystanders and orderly protesters in the designated demonstration zone beside the Ontario legislature, far from where acts of vandalism had taken place. Police dragged people off the ground and out of crowds. Some officers hit people with batons and shields, often from behind and without warning; others used pepper spray and rubber bullets on peaceful, unarmed citizens. After witnessing several violent arrests, including those of fellow journalists, TVOntario host Steve Paikin called it "a sad, bloody day."

Police tactics included "kettling" peaceful groups —a procedure that leaves no means of escape and is against the policy of the RCMP, the lead 2010 G20 security force. "We had to balance a very difficult set of responsibilities," Toronto police chief Bill Blair explained later. People arrested were held in a temporary detention centre lacking beds and blankets, and with open toilets but little water or food. Some had been seriously injured but went without medical attention for hours; they and others were denied medication or legal counsel. Most were released shortly after the G20 meetings ended. A large majority never faced charges.

Canadians have on occasion seen vandalism and even violence in major cities, but rarely this kind of reaction by authorities, and never so many arrests— more than 1,100. Apparent problems with police planning and training, plus hundreds of complaints, eventually prompted several investigations and a number of lawsuits. Ninety officers later faced discipline for removing their identification tags, and lawyers pushed for others to be charged for excessive violence.

With this type of incident, it often takes time for the full truth to emerge. After his arrest on November 17, 2001, during G20 meetings in Ottawa, it took David MacLaren nearly seven years to resolve his lawsuit against three police forces. He was never charged with an offence and maintains he was not part of protests that day. In June 2008, after receiving a cash payment that his lawyer called "significant," MacLaren said he hoped his difficult legal battle would cause police to adjust their policies and be more careful in their use of force.

Canadian police have a history of respect, and the RCMP has been an admired national symbol. Yet during the Toronto G20 weekend, police failed to protect the rights of many ordinary citizens. Perhaps a full public inquiry—as called for by the Canadian Civil Liberties Association and many others—will help to determine what went wrong and what can be done to avoid similar situations.

War Games

November 16, 2010—Canada extends its military mission in Afghanistan.

DON NEWMAN

Throughout the summer and fall of 2010, pressure was mounting on Prime Minister Stephen Harper and his minority Conservative government. July 2011 was the deadline for ending the Canadian military presence in Afghanistan. In Ottawa preparations were already under way to bring home the two thousand-plus military personnel serving in the Afghan mission.

In Washington concern was mounting over the prospect of Canadians abandoning the ten-year-old war with Taliban extremists. It wasn't losing the Canadian troops—as good as they had proven themselves to be—that concerned the American government. It was the optics of a neighbour, ally, and friend giving up on a war that was becoming as unpopular for Americans as it was for Canadians.

And making the Americans unhappy certainly wasn't Canada's motive when it joined the war in 2001. On the contrary, the commitment had been an attempt—in the wake of the terrorist attacks of 9/11—to convince Americans that Canada cared as much about North America's security as they did. That way, the United States would allow the Canada–U.S. border to remain open to the trade that is so vital to our economic health. The trade relationship had motivated Liberal prime minister Jean Chrétien in 2001 and continued to motivate his Liberal successor, Paul Martin, in July 2005, when he extended the mission by another two years.

Maintaining a free-flowing border was a key concern for the Harper Conservatives when the party took power in January 2006. Realizing the mission in Afghanistan couldn't be completed by the February 2007 deadline, Prime Minister Stephen Harper worked to convince enough Opposition Liberal MPs to support his minority government in extending the mission until 2009.

Flash forward to 2008. With the latest deadline to leave Afghanistan approaching, Harper appointed John Manley, a former Liberal deputy prime minister, to head a committee of eminent people to study whether the mission should again be extended. The panel recommended doing so until 2011.

The Liberals supported that decision. But by 2010—with more than one hundred Canadians killed and the toll still rising, with allegations of prisoner torture, with the Harper government withholding military documents from Parliament, and with the corruption of the Afghan government apparent—finding Liberal support to extend the mission beyond 2011 seemed impossible.

Enter the Americans, who began to exert public pressure on Canada to stay beyond 2011. In Ottawa, Liberal leader Michael Ignatieff began to openly support some form of continuing Canadian presence in Afghanistan. Harper sensed his opportunity. He at first appeared to resist, but then agreed to extend the mission again. On November 16, 2010, the federal government formally announced the details: about one thousand Canadians would stay in Afghanistan until at least 2014 to train that nation's military.

In the United States, the decision was a victory for the American administration. The Canadians were staying. And it continued the Canadian objective of maintaining easy border access to the United States. In fact, a month after the announcement, Harper was in the Oval Office at the White House, meeting with President Barack Obama. Their topic of discussion? A common security perimeter around North America that would make it easier to keep the border between the two countries open.

100

Private Nathalie Bergeron hugs her daughter farewell before departing for Afghanistan in 2002.

Photographer: Tom Hanson.

ACKNOWLEDGEMENTS

100 Days That Changed Canada is the result of months of research, writing, and editing. We are especially grateful to the fifty-six writers who contributed essays to the project. Coming from all walks of life and from myriad professional backgrounds, the contributors share a passion for Canada that shines through in their essays.

Thank you as well to Deborah Morrison, CEO and President of Canada's History, and the History Society team: Danielle Chartier, Pat Gerow, James Gillespie, Michel Groleau, Pat Hanney, Tanja Hütter, Phil Koch, Linda Onofreychuk, Nelle Oosterom, Nancy Payne, Jean-Philippe Proulx, Joel Ralph, Beverley Tallon, and Andrew Workman, our extended team of P. J. Brown, Scott Bullock, Dean French, and Brian Stendel, along with Transcontinental Printing and PrintPlus. From writing and editing essays for the book, to marketing and promoting it, to simply providing encouragement and advice, your help is greatly appreciated.

Canada's History is fortunate to have a dedicated board of directors, led by award-winning author and popular historian Charlotte Gray. Thank you to James Baillie, Tim Cook, Alex Graham, Charlotte Gray, Paul Jones, Jacques Lacoursière, Gillian Manning, Don Newman, Richard W. Pound, David Ross, and Brian Young, for your ongoing support of the History Society.

Canada's History is co-publishing *100 Days That Changed Canada* with HarperCollins Canada, and we are very grateful to Phyllis Bruce for the support and guidance she offered during the creation of *100 Days*, and also during the production of our previous bestseller, *100 Photos That Changed Canada*. Thanks also to HarperCollins' talented team of editors, designers, researchers, marketers, and publicists, including Cory Beatty, Camilla Blakeley, Neil Erickson, Laura Hughes, Charidy Johnston, Alan Jones, Barbara Kamienski, Shelley Tangney, and Noelle Zitzer.

Thank you to the photographers who contributed pictures to the book, as well as to the archives and news agencies—and especially to the many individual librarians and archivists—that provided both images and advice during our search for visuals.

Undertaking a project such as this requires the support of one's family. I want to express my deepest thanks to Mike and Susan Helm, and to Peter and Diane Reid, for their many words of encouragement over the past year, as well as Peter Reid, Jr., and Trudy Bouchie, Blair and Roxanne Keiver, and Nick and Sharon Helm. Thank you to my grandmother Dorothy Reid, for teaching me the value of history. And finally, thank you to my wife, Marianne Helm, and my children, Evan and Megan, for their unconditional love and support.

—Mark Reid

CONTRIBUTORS

Irving Abella is the Shiff Professor of Canadian Jewish History at York University and the Distinguished Senior Fellow of Canadian Studies at the University of Ottawa. The author or co-author of eight books, including *None Is Too Many: Canada and the Jews of Europe, 1933–1948* and *A Coat of Many Colours: Two Centuries of Jewish Life in Canada*, he is also a past president of the Canadian Jewish Congress and the Canadian Historical Association.

Andy Barrie was born in Baltimore, Maryland, on January 30, 1945, but says he was reborn on December 23, 1969, when, after deserting from the United States Army, he crossed the border into Canada. Doubting that he would be allowed to continue his barely begun career in radio, he was astonished to be not only welcomed but, over the next forty years, allowed to become one of the country's most listened-to voices on radio, first in Montreal and later in Toronto, where for fifteen years he was the host of the CBC's *Metro Morning*.

Maurice Basque is a historian and a Scientific Advisor at the Institut d'études acadiennes of the Université de Moncton. He has published numerous books in the field of Acadian studies and in 1995 received the France-Acadie Award for his study of the history of New Brunswick's Acadian teachers. He has participated in twenty documentary films as a historical consultant. France made him a Chevalier de l'Ordre des Palmes académiques in 2002 and a Chevalier de l'Ordre des Arts et des Lettres in 2003. He is a past president of the Association for Canadian Studies and co-president of the International Association for the Study of Canada.

Conrad Black was Chairman of the London *Telegraph* newspapers and *Spectator* magazine from 1988 to 2004, founded the *National Post*, and was the controlling shareholder of many other newspapers in several countries. He is a weekly *National Post* and *National Review Online* columnist, and a biographer of Maurice Duplessis, Franklin D. Roosevelt, and Richard Nixon. Black is a Canadian Privy Councillor, an Officer of the Order of Canada, and a U.K. peer as Lord Black of Crossharbour since 2001.

Michael Bliss is Professor Emeritus at the University of Toronto and the author of numerous books on Canadian history and the history of medicine.

Kim Bolan is an investigative reporter with the *Vancouver Sun*. She's best known for her work on the story of the 1985 Air India bombing. She was awarded the Courage in Journalism Award by the International

Women's Media Foundation for staying on the story despite death threats. Bolan has won or been short-listed for thirty-nine national and international awards. The Air India story has taken her to Punjab five times, where she met with militant Sikh separatist leaders and victims of the violence. Her book *Loss of Faith: How the Air-India Bombers Got Away with Murder* was published in 2005.

Stephen Brunt has been a sports columnist for the *Globe and Mail* since 1989 and is the author of nine books, including the national bestsellers *Searching for Bobby Orr* and *Gretzky's Tears: Hockey, Canada, and the Day Everything Changed*. His next book, about the Canadian Football League, will be published in 2012. Brunt covered the Toronto Blue Jays during their glory years, including both World Series victories. He lives in Hamilton, Ontario, and Winterhouse Brook, Newfoundland and Labrador.

Jim Burant, who holds a BA in Art History and an MA in Canadian Studies from Carleton University, worked as an archivist and manager at Library and Archives Canada from 1976 until 2011, when he left LAC to pursue independent research projects. He has presented and published widely on archival issues, the history of Canadian printmaking, photography, and the arts and has contributed to the *Canadian Encyclopedia*, the *Dictionary of Canadian Biography*, and other major publications. He has also curated exhibitions for several Canadian galleries and museums. A recipient of the 2003 Queen's Jubilee Medal, he is an off-reserve member of the Algonquins of Pikwàkanagàn First Nation.

Stevie Cameron is a successful author, investigative journalist, commentator, and humanitarian. Her investigative reports and award-winning books have brought scandals to the public eye. Cameron's most recent book, *On the Farm: Robert William Pickton and the Tragic Story of Vancouver's Missing Women*, was a finalist for the 2010 Charles Taylor Prize. Her other books include *The Pickton File*; *The Last Amigo*: *Karlheinz Schreiber and the Anatomy of a Scandal*; *Blue Trust: The Author, the Lawyer, His Wife, and Her Money*; and *On the Take: Crime, Corruption and Greed in the Mulroney Years*. She has been a contributing editor to *Maclean's* magazine, and has contributed to the *Toronto Star*, the *Ottawa Citizen*, the Southam News Service, *Saturday Night* magazine, the *Financial Post*, *Chatelaine*, and *Canadian Living*.

The Rt. Hon. Adrienne Clarkson is acknowledged to have transformed the office of the Governor General. During her career at the CBC she created and starred in numerous series, including *the fifth estate* and *Adrienne Clarkson Presents*. She holds honorary doctorates from St. Petersburg State Mining Institute in Russia, the University of Siena in Italy, and twenty-one universities in Canada. After leaving the office of Governor General, she founded the Institute for Canadian Citizenship and chairs it with her husband, John Ralston Saul. Her memoirs, *Heart Matters*, were published in 2006 and her latest book, a biography of Dr. Norman Bethune, was published for the Extraordinary Canadians series in 2009.

Margaret Conrad, OC, FRSC, is Professor Emerita at the University of New Brunswick, where she previously held a Canada Research Chair in Atlantic Canada Studies. A former chair of the publications committee of Canada's History Society, she has published widely in the fields of Canadian history and women's studies.

Tim Cook is a historian at the Canadian War Museum and an Adjunct Research Professor at Carleton University. He has published five books, including the two-volume history of Canadians fighting in the Great War, *At the Sharp End* and *Shock Troops*. His newest book, *The Madman and the Butcher: The Sensational Wars of Sam Hughes* and *General Arthur Currie*, was published by Allen Lane in September 2010. Tim is a director of Canada's History Society and a frequent commentator in the media.

Colette Derworiz is Assistant City Editor at the *Calgary Herald*. An award-winning journalist, she wrote about health, social issues, municipal politics, and education prior to becoming an editor. Colette has a BA in History from Carleton University and a Bachelor of Journalism from the University of Regina. She lives in Calgary.

Denise Donlon is one of Canada's most accomplished media executives. A former host, journalist, and producer of groundbreaking music programs for Citytv and MuchMusic, as well as the past vice-president and general manager of MuchMusic/MuchMoreMusic and president of Sony Music Canada, she joined Much-Music/Citytv in 1985. From 1986 to 1993 she co-hosted and produced MuchMusic's influential newsmagazine *The New Music*; from 2008 to 2011 she was the general manager of CBC English Radio. A strong supporter of many humanitarian and environmental causes, she holds two honorary doctorates, has been inducted into the Canadian Association of Broadcasters Hall of Fame, and is a Member of the Order of Canada.

The Hon. Ken Dryden grew up in the Toronto suburb of Etobicoke. His life as a hockey player with the Montreal Canadiens, and as a Member of Parliament, has given him the privilege of travelling almost everywhere in the country and of having people want to tell him about themselves, their families, their communities, and what they hope and fear and dream. He has written five books—about hockey, schools, politics, and the life of an average person, but really, about Canada. When people ask him where he was when Paul Henderson scored, he can say, "180 feet away" as the goalie for Team Canada.

Richard Foot is a freelance journalist based in Halifax. He is a former foreign correspondent and national affairs writer for the Postmedia Network newspaper chain and was a founding staff member of the *National Post*. His work has also appeared in the *Globe and Mail*, in *Maclean's* magazine, and on CBC Radio.

Jill Foran is a writer and editor specializing in children's and educational publishing. *Mr. Dressup* was her favourite childhood show.

Mike Ford is a Juno-nominated singer/songwriter known to many for his band Moxy Früvous, as well as for his solo albums featuring a growing repertoire of original Canadian history–based songs. He is also familiar for his Great Lakes Seaway project with colleague David Francey, his relentless itinerary of bilingual Canada Needs You high school and middle school concerts, and his folk festival appearances. He and his wife, Therese, live in Toronto.

Daniel Francis is the author of more than twenty-two books, principally about Canadian history. Titles include *The Imaginary Indian: The Image of the Indian in Canadian Culture* and *A Road for Canada:*

The Illustrated Story of the Trans-Canada Highway. He is Editorial Director of the online *Encyclopedia of British Columbia* and his book *L.D.: Mayor Louis Taylor and the Rise of Vancouver* won the City of Vancouver Book Award in 2004. His latest book is *Seeing Reds: The Red Scare of 1918–1919, Canada's First War on Terror.* He was born and raised in Vancouver.

James Gifford is Editorial Director for Non-Fiction and Collins Canada at HarperCollins Canada and the author of *Hurricane Hazel: Canada's Storm of the Century.* He made frequent national television and radio appearances during the fiftieth anniversary of Hurricane Hazel, spoke widely to local history societies, and attended memorial ceremonies for those lost during the storm. He lives in Toronto with his wife, Maria, and his children, Catherine and Jack.

J.L. Granatstein taught Canadian history for thirty years, is a Senior Research Fellow of the Canadian Defence and Foreign Affairs Institute, was Director and CEO of the Canadian War Museum, and writes on Canadian military history, foreign and defence policy, and public policy. Among his publications are *Canada 1957–1967: The Years of Uncertainty and Innovation*; *Canada's War: The Politics of the Mackenzie King Government, 1939–1945*; *The Generals: The Canadian Army's Senior Commanders in the Second World War*; *Canada's Army: Waging War and Keeping the Peace*; and *Who Killed Canadian History?*

Charlotte Gray (www.charlottegray.ca) chairs the board of Canada's History Society. The author of eight bestselling books of history and biography, including *Sisters in the Wilderness: The Lives of Susanna Moodie and Catharine Parr Traill* and *Gold Diggers: Striking It Rich in the Klondike*, she is one of Canada's best-known non-fiction writers. A Member of the Order of Canada and a winner of the Pierre Berton Award for popularizing Canadian history, she is an Adjunct Research Professor at Carleton University and frequent media commentator.

Lawrence Hill (www.lawrencehill.com) is the author of seven books, including the novel *The Book of Negroes*, which explores the story of the Black Loyalists of Nova Scotia and won the Commonwealth Writers' Prize, the Rogers Writers' Trust Fiction Prize, and Canada Reads. Hill is an honorary patron of Canadian Crossroads International, for which he volunteered as a young man in Niger, Cameroon, and Mali. He lives in Hamilton, Ontario.

Paul Jones is an independent business consultant, a speaker and an award-winning writer. During his thirty years in corporate life, he published leading business, financial, and news magazines and served as a director of many organizations. He holds the highest career honours conferred by leading associations in both the magazine and advertising industries and is a Director and Chair of the publications committee of Canada's History Society. By avocation, he is also a trained genealogist, a committed genealogical volunteer, and a regular Roots columnist for *Canada's History*.

Phil Koch writes, edits, and studies in Winnipeg, where he is the News and Reviews Editor of *Canada's History* magazine and an interdisciplinary graduate student at the University of Manitoba. He co-founded and co-edited the culture magazine *Tart*, was a copy editor for the Canwest News Service, and is the winner of the 2006 Canadian Association of University Teachers Award for Excellence in Education Journalism.

Jacques Lacoursière is a popular historian and broadcaster and the author of many books about Canadian history. A Director of Canada's History Society, he has been involved in history education and curriculum development in the province of Quebec. He is a recipient of the Pierre Berton Award, a Member of the Order of Canada, and a Knight of the National Order of Quebec.

Steven Loft, of Mohawk-Jewish heritage, is a 2010 Visiting Trudeau Fellow at the Trudeau Foundation. A curator, writer, and media artist, he has been Artistic Director of the Native Indian/Inuit Photographers Association (NIIPA), First Nations Curator at the Art Gallery of Hamilton, and Director of Urban Shaman Gallery in Winnipeg. In 2007 he was named Curator-in-Residence, Indigenous Art, at the National Gallery of Canada. Loft co-edited *Transference, Technology, Tradition: Aboriginal Media and New Media Art*, published by Banff Centre Press in 2005. His video works have been screened across Canada and internationally.

Tina Loo teaches environmental history at the University of British Columbia, where she holds a Canada Research Chair. She has written about wildlife conservation in Canada and is currently looking at the social and environmental impacts of hydroelectric development in British Columbia. As one of the presenters with Al Gore's Climate Project, she facilitates public discussions about global warming and solutions for it—in return for bus fare.

The Hon. Peter Lougheed, PC, CC, QC, served as Premier of Alberta from 1971 to 1985. He is currently counsel at the Calgary-based law firm of Bennett Jones LLP and serves as director of several public and private companies. He is the Canadian Co-Chair of the North American Forum and is Chancellor Emeritus of Queen's University. He is a Companion of the Order of Canada, holds eight honorary degrees from Canadian universities, and is the recipient of the Alumni Achievement Award from Harvard Business School. He and his wife, Jeanne, live in Calgary. They have four children.

Old Man Luedecke is a Nova Scotia–based singer/songwriter. He performs songs mostly with the rhythmically driving five-string banjo. He's a well-loved performer known for songs that blend a timeless sound with contemporary lyricism. Born and raised in Toronto, he has lived in Quebec, Yukon, and British Columbia, but has become quite settled (for a full-time travelling musician) in Chester, Nova Scotia, with his wife, clay artist Teresa Bergen. He has twice won Juno Awards in the category of Best Roots and Traditional Album: in 2009, for his third album, *Proof of Love*; and in 2011, for his latest release, *My Hands Are on Fire and Other Love Songs*.

Peter Mansbridge is the Chief Correspondent of CBC News. In more than forty years with the CBC, Mansbridge has provided coverage of the most significant stories in Canada and around the world. He has received twelve Geminis as well as eight honorary degrees from universities across the country, and has been recognized by leading universities in the United States and United Kingdom. In 2008 Mansbridge was made an Officer of the Order of Canada. In 2010 he was installed as Chancellor of Mount Allison

University in Sackville, New Brunswick. Born in London in 1948, he was educated in Ottawa and served in the Royal Canadian Navy in 1966 and 1967.

Don Martin was a journalist for thirty-two years, working for the *Calgary Herald* as a reporter and columnist before joining the *National Post* as its national affairs columnist. His current job is host of the CTV News Channel's *Power Play* broadcast, an hour-long public affairs program airing five times weekly. He is married with three daughters.

Joe Martin is Director of Canadian Business History at the Rotman School of Management, University of Toronto, and author of *Relentless Change: A Casebook for the Study of Canadian Business History*. He is also President Emeritus of Canada's History Society.

Rona Maynard (www.ronamaynard.com) is a speaker, author, memoir teacher, online community builder, and former long-time editor of *Chatelaine*.

Ken McGoogan has been called "the rightful successor to populist historian Pierre Berton." Besides the Pierre Berton Award for popularizing Canadian history, McGoogan has won the Drainie-Taylor Biography Prize, the UBC Medal for Canadian Biography, and the Canadian Authors Association Lela Common Award for Canadian History. His books include *Fatal Passage: The Untold Story of John Rae, the Arctic Adventurer Who Discovered the Fate of Franklin*; *Lady Franklin's Revenge: A True Story of Ambition, Obsession and the Remaking of Arctic History*; *Race to the Polar Sea: The Heroic Adventures of Elisha Kent Kane*; and *How the Scots Invented Canada*. Based in Toronto, he serves as Chair of the Public Lending Right Commission and sails with Adventure Canada.

Penni Mitchell is Managing Editor of *Herizons* magazine, a position she has held since the feminist magazine's inception in 1992. She is also an occasional newspaper columnist who writes about environmental and women's issues.

Christopher Moore (www.christophermoore.ca) is a long-time columnist for *Canada's History* magazine and a well-known writer whose work has ranged widely across many aspects of Canadian history. His books include *Louisbourg Portraits: Five Dramatic, True Tales of People Who Lived in an Eighteenth-Century Garrison Town* (winner of the Governor General's Award for Non-Fiction); *1867: How the Fathers Made a Deal*; and for young readers, *The Story of Canada* and, most recently, *From Then to Now: A Short History of the World*.

Deborah Morrison is President and CEO of Canada's History Society. She is also Publisher of *Canada's History* and *Kayak: Canada's History Magazine for Kids*, which she launched in 2004. Actively involved in the field of history education and the promotion of greater popular interest in Canadian history with Canada's History, Historica Foundation, and the CRB Foundation since 1991, she's living proof to young students of history that you can, indeed, have a fulfilling and rewarding career in Canadian history.

Desmond Morton was the 2010 recipient of the Pierre Berton Award. He has published forty books on Canada's military, political, and labour history, and has taught at the University of Toronto Mississauga and McGill University. A frequent contributor to *Canada's History* magazine, he retired in 2007 but continues to teach and write about history.

Don Newman, Chairman of Canada 2020, offers strategic advice to clients at Bluesky Strategy Group Inc. A respected journalist, he served as Senior Parliamentary Editor of CBC Television News and host of *Politics*. A Member of the Order of Canada and a life member of the Canadian Parliamentary Press Gallery, Newman has been awarded a Gemini for lifetime achievement in public affairs broadcasting, as well as the Charles Lynch Award and the Public Policy Forum's Hy Solomon Award. Educated in Winnipeg, Montreal, and England, he holds honorary degrees from Queen's University and the University of Winnipeg and is a board member of Canada's History Society.

Peter C. Newman has been writing about Canadian politics and business for nearly half a century. The author of twenty-four books that have together sold more than two million copies, Newman has won some of the country's most illustrious literary awards, both as an author and as a journalist. A former editor-in-chief of the *Toronto Star* and *Maclean's*, Newman has been recognized with seven honorary doctorates, a National Newspaper Award, and election to the Canadian News Hall of Fame. He has been called twice to the Order of Canada and has earned his title as Canada's "most cussed and discussed" commentator.

Nelle Oosterom is the Senior Editor of *Canada's History* magazine. She has had a long career as a journalist, covering major events as an employee of the Canadian Press, CBC Radio, Canwest News Service, and several newspapers. She was also a contributor to *100 Photos That Changed Canada* and *Native Leaders of Canada*. Her work has appeared in various magazines. She has lived and worked in Winnipeg, St. John's, Thunder Bay, and southern Ontario's Niagara region, and has travelled extensively throughout the world.

Lesley Parrott is a public speaker, a facilitator, a humanitarian, and a friend to many. Her beloved daughter, Alison, was murdered in 1986, and through learning to live with this tragedy, she has reached out with hope and healing to inspire and help others who confront adversity in their personal and professional lives. Parrott divides her time between her country home near Durham, Ontario, and her consulting practice in Toronto.

Jacques Poitras is the Provincial Affairs Reporter for CBC News in New Brunswick, where he covers the legislature and produces a political podcast called *Spin Reduxit*. He teaches journalism part time at St. Thomas University and is the author of three books, including the award-winning *Beaverbrook: A Shattered Legacy*, a national bestseller. His new book is on the history and culture of the international border between New Brunswick and Maine.

Richard W. Pound is a Montreal lawyer, partner with Stikeman Elliott LLP, Chancellor Emeritus of McGill University, a member of the International Olympic Committee, and Past President of the Canadian

Olympic Committee. He was the founding Chairman of the World Anti-Doping Agency and is the current Chairman of Partnership for a Drug Free Canada. A director of Canada's History Society, he has written several books and contributes regularly to professional and historical publications.

The Hon. Bob Rae is the Member of Parliament for Toronto Centre and the Interim Leader of the Liberal Party of Canada. Rae served as Ontario's twenty-first premier and has been elected ten times to federal and provincial parliaments. Rae has a BA and an LLB from the University of Toronto and was a Rhodes Scholar from Ontario in 1969. He obtained a BPhil degree from Oxford University in 1971. Rae was appointed to Her Majesty's Privy Council for Canada in 1998 and was appointed an Officer of the Order of Canada in 2000. Rae has written three books, including *Exporting Democracy: The Risks and Rewards of Pursuing a Good Idea.*

Joel Ralph is the Manager of Education and Outreach Programs for Canada's History Society and a graduate of the MA in Public History program at the University of Western Ontario. He continues to write for *Canada's History* magazine and blogs about history, education, and technology. Joel lives in Winnipeg with his wife, Jessie, and their son, Jack.

Mark Reid is Editor-in-Chief of *Canada's History* magazine. His first book, *100 Photos That Changed Canada*, was a national bestseller. He has worked as a reporter and editor for Canwest News Service, the *Calgary Herald*, and the New Brunswick *Telegraph-Journal*, and also as the Associate Director of Communications for the University of Calgary. He holds degrees in anthropology and journalism and lives in Winnipeg.

Nolan Reilly is Professor of Canadian History and Director of the H. Sanford Riley Centre for Canadian History at the University of Winnipeg. He also co-directs the Oral History Centre and is Co-editor of the *Oral History Forum d'histoire orale*. His research and publication interests are in labour, community, and oral history studies.

Sanford Riley is a Manitoban business executive who serves on a number of corporate and community boards. He is a former chancellor of the University of Winnipeg, and with his wife, Debbie, established the H. Sanford Riley Fellowship in Canadian History at the university to encourage study of the subject. He was a competitor in the 1976 Olympics as a sailor and, in 1999, chaired the highly successful Pan American Games. Among his many community awards, he was appointed a Member of the Order of Canada in 2003.

Beverley Tallon is Assistant Editor of *Canada's History* magazine and was a contributing writer for the national bestseller *100 Photos That Changed Canada*. She is a former editor of *@ltitude (Western Canada Aviation Museum)* and an award-winning artist with a penchant for history, gardening, and travel.

Elizabeth Waterston, Professor Emerita at the University of Guelph, is the author of *Magic Island: The Fictions of L. M. Montgomery*, and co-editor with Mary Rubio of the five-volume *Selected Journals of L. M. Montgomery* and of the *Norton Critical Edition of Anne of Green Gables*. Her other publications include *The Travellers—Canada to 1900: An Annotated Bibliography of Works Published in English from 1577* and *Rapt in Plaid: Canadian Literature and Scottish Tradition*. Since retiring from university teaching, she has written novels, including *Plaid Around the Mountain*. She was appointed to the Order of Ontario in 2011.

Margaret Wente, a columnist with the *Globe and Mail*, provokes heated debate with her views on social and political issues. She has twice won the National Newspaper Award for column writing. Wente has edited *Canadian Business* and *ROB Magazine*, as well as the *Globe's* business section, the *ROB*, and is a frequent commentator on radio and television. She holds a BA in English from the University of Michigan and an MA in English from the University of Toronto. Her latest book is *You Can't Say That in Canada*.

Brian Williams is a decorated sportscaster with more than forty years' experience and the dean of Olympic broadcasters. Vancouver 2010 was his thirteenth Olympic Games. Williams's respected broadcast style has endeared him to millions of Canadians from coast to coast. He has won praise from critics and numerous accolades, including eight Gemini Awards (the eighth for his work hosting the Vancouver Olympics) and two Foster Hewitt Awards. In 2010 he was inducted into the Canadian Football League's Reporters Hall of Fame. Born in Winnipeg, he has covered Canadian athletes both professional and amateur, not only in Canada but around the globe.

Garrett Wilson is a retired Regina lawyer turned author. A thirty-year association representing Regina police led to *Deny, Deny, Deny*, the bestselling account of the Colin Thatcher murder case. Next came *Diefenbaker for the Defence*, a well-reviewed biography of the controversial prime minister's legal career. Many years of involvement in Saskatchewan politics provoked *Guilty Addictions*, a political mystery short-listed for the Arthur Ellis Award. Garrett's long-held interest in early western history led to *Frontier Farewell*, the award-winning story of the 1870s on the Canadian plains. His current project is an account of the farm debt crisis of the 1930s.

Brian Young is Professor Emeritus at McGill University, where he taught history before retiring in 2010. He is perhaps best known for his biography of Father of Confederation George-Étienne Cartier and for his co-authored *A Short History of Quebec*. A native of Winnipeg and a board member of Canada's History Society since 2006, he has interests ranging from vegetable gardening to the history of elites and of Quebec museums.

PHOTO CREDITS

1	July 1, 1867	Rex Woods/Library and Archives Canada, C-148218. Reproduced with permission of Rogers Communications Inc.
2	November 19, 1869	Library and Archives Canada, C-033945
3	April 12, 1876	Saskatchewan Archives Board, R-A8223-1, R-A8223-2
4	September 22, 1877	Glenbow Archives, NA-4035-159
5	June 26, 1879	Richard Henry Trueman/Glenbow Archives, NA-250-15
6	November 16, 1885	A. J. Owen/Glenbow Archives, NA-504-3
7	July 24, 1886	Oliver B. Buell/Glenbow Archives, NA-4967-132 (original print at Canadian Railway Museum, St. Constant, QC)
8	June 23, 1887	McCord Museum, MP-0000.25.687
9	August 16, 1896	Leonard Delano/Alaska State Library, P44-03-015
10	June 22, 1897	RCMP Historical Collections Unit, 1961.44.1
11	November 29, 1899	Photo by Time Life Pictures/Mansell/Getty Images
12	December 12, 1901	Photo by Time Life Pictures/Getty Images
13	January 18, 1904	Toronto Star Archives/GetStock.com
14	March 16, 1907	Saskatchewan Archives Board, R-A23721
15	June 20, 1908	Sullivan Entertainment, Inc.
16	July 1, 1909	Library and Archives Canada, C-001198
17	December 4, 1909	Canada's Sports Hall of Fame (www.sportshall.ca), Smirle Lawson Collection, X981.632.1.7
18	September 2, 1912	Harry Befus, the Calgary Herald. Reproduced with permission of the Calgary Herald.
19	January 28, 1914	McDermid Studio, Edmonton/Glenbow Archives, NC-6-1746
20	April 1, 1918	Glenbow Archives, NA-1639-1
21	November 11, 1918	Toronto Star/The Canadian Press
22	June 21, 1919	Lewis Benjamin Foote/Archives of Manitoba, N12317
23	March 22, 1922	Library and Archives Canada, C-001350
24	March 22, 1923	Michael Burns. Courtesy of the Estate of Michael Burns.
25	October 29, 1929	Library and Archives Canada, PA-168131
26	September 12, 1930	© Lucien Aigner/Corbis
27	April 19, 1938	Lovat Dickson Collection/Library and Archives Canada, PA-147582
28	May 2, 1939	Ronny Jaques/National Film Board of Canada/Library and Archives Canada, PA-179108
29	June 9, 1939	United States Holocaust Memorial Museum
30	November 12, 1939	Toronto Star Archives/GetStock.com
31	July 2, 1941	Capt. Frank Royal/Canada. Dept. of National Defence/Library and Archives Canada, PA-037479
32	February 26, 1942	Library and Archives Canada, C-046355
33	June 6, 1944	Library and Archives Canada, PA-132651
34	June 15, 1944	Boris Spremo, Globe and Mail/The Canadian Press
35	November 22, 1944	Library and Archives Canada, PA-107910

36	May 8, 1945	John H. Boyd/City of Toronto Archives, Fonds 1266, Item 96241
37	July 1, 1945	Toronto Star Archives/GetStock.com
38	February 9, 1946	Arthur Cole/Canada. Dept. of National Defence/Library and Archives Canada, PA-175803
39	April 18, 1946	C. W. Greene/National Baseball Hall of Fame
40	May 14, 1947	The Province/Vancouver Public Library, Special Collections, VPL 41603
41	May 6, 1949	Louis Jaques, Montreal Standard/The Gazette (Montreal) © 1949
42	April 15, 1950	Archives of Manitoba, N19294
43	June 1, 1951	Ken Bell/Ken Bell fonds/Library and Archives Canada, PA-153947
44	October 15, 1954	York University Libraries, Clara Thomas Archives & Special Collections, Toronto Telegram fonds, ASC07085
45	November 7, 1956	© National Defence. Reproduced with the permission of the Minister of Public Works and Government Services Canada (2011). Canadian Forces Photographic Unit/National Defence Collection/Library and Archives Canada, e010900426
46	April 2, 1957	Leo Harrison/GetStock.com
47	February 20, 1959	Canada Aviation and Space Museum, CASM-4185
48	November 1, 1959	© Bettmann/Corbis
49	September 3, 1962	Contributor: Ralph Larson
50	January 16, 1964	Bob Brooks/Nova Scotia Archives and Records Management, Bob Brooks fonds, 1989-468 vol. 16, negative sheet 7, image 25
51	May 17, 1964	Hamilton Spectator
52	May 25, 1964	Yousuf Karsh
53	December 15, 1964	Ted Grant/National Gallery of Canada
54	August 6, 1965	Julian Hayashi/York University Libraries, Clara Thomas Archives & Special Collections, Toronto Telegram fonds, ASC01162
55	January 1, 1967	Roy Martin/CBC Still Photo Collection
56	February 13, 1967	Fred Phipps/CBC Still Photo Collection
57	April 27, 1967	© Government of Canada. Reproduced with the permission of the Minister of Public Works and Government Services Canada (2011). Canadian Corporation for the 1967 World Exhibition fonds/Library and Archives Canada, e000990971
58	September 9, 1967	Globe and Mail/The Canadian Press
59	September 30, 1967	Doug Griffin, Toronto Star/The Canadian Press
60	May 22, 1969	© Bruno Massenet/Library and Archives Canada, PA-153762
61	May 11, 1970	Peter Bregg/The Canadian Press
62	October 16, 1970	Peter Bregg/The Canadian Press
63	December 7, 1970	Reg Innell/GetStock.com
64	September 2, 1972	Fred Ross/GetStock.com
65	January 29, 1973	The Canadian Press
66	September 25, 1975	New Brunswick Museum, Saint John, N.B., NBM-F28-19
67	July 14, 1976	Barry Philp/GetStock.com
68	November 15, 1976	The Canadian Press
69	March 22, 1977	© Miroslav Brozek/Sygma/Corbis
70	May 7, 1977	Doug Ball/The Canadian Press
71	March 31, 1978	Frank Gunn/The Canadian Press
72	August 6, 1979	Drew Gragg/Ottawa Citizen
73	September 2, 1980	David Cooper, Toronto Star/The Canadian Press
74	October 28, 1980	The Canadian Press
75	November 2, 1981	Drew Gragg/The Canadian Press

76	February 15, 1982	Boris Spremo/GetStock.com
77	June 14, 1983	David Cooper/GetStock.com
78	July 25, 1984	Fred Chartrand/The Canadian Press
79	August 31, 1984	Tibor Kolley/The Globe and Mail
80	June 23, 1985	Julien Behal/PA Wire URN: 9071082 (Press Association via AP images) (100623012430)
81	December 6, 1989	Shaney Komulainen/The Canadian Press
82	March 7, 1990	Pat McGrath/Ottawa Citizen
83	June 23, 1990	Wayne Glowacki, Winnipeg Free Press/The Canadian Press
84	July 3, 1992	Bridget Besaw/GetStock.com
85	October 24, 1992	Rusty Kennedy, AP/The Canadian Press
86	September 16, 1993	Tom Hanson/The Canadian Press
87	November 2, 1994	Phill Snel, Maclean's/The Canadian Press
88	July 27, 1996	Doug Mills, AP/The Canadian Press
89	January 19, 1999	Mark Lennihan, AP/ The Canadian Press
90	April 1, 1999	Paul Chiasson/The Canadian Press
91	February 15, 2001	Mark Blinch/Reuters
92	September 11, 2001	Chao Soi Cheong, AP/The Canadian Press
93	March 17, 2003	Chhobi/Dreamstime.com/GetStock.com
94	April 13, 2003	Elise Amendola, AP/The Canadian Press
95	February 3, 2006	© Bill Grimshaw
96	December 4, 2008	Chris Wattie/The Canadian Press
97	January 22, 2010	Steve Russell/GetStock.com
98	February 28, 2010	Jeff McIntosh/The Canadian Press
99	June 27, 2010	Steve Russell/GetStock.com
100	November 16, 2010	Tom Hanson/The Canadian Press

Montage background photos reproduced courtesy of iStockphoto®, except p.112 (National Archives, U.K.)

INDEX